Problem-Solving Courts and the Criminal Justice System

Problem-Solving Courts and the Criminal Justice System

DAVID DEMATTEO, KIRK HEILBRUN,
ALICE THORNEWILL, AND SHELBY ARNOLD

OXFORD
UNIVERSITY PRESS

OXFORD
UNIVERSITY PRESS

Oxford University Press is a department of the University of Oxford. It furthers the University's objective of excellence in research, scholarship, and education by publishing worldwide. Oxford is a registered trade mark of Oxford University Press in the UK and certain other countries.

Published in the United States of America by Oxford University Press
198 Madison Avenue, New York, NY 10016, United States of America.

CIP data is on file at the Library of Congress
ISBN 978–0–19–084482–0

Contents

Problem-Solving Courts and the Criminal Justice System

1

Current Issues in the Criminal Justice System

Introduction to Problem-Solving Courts

Our society has an important interest in the outcomes that can result from the rehabilitative approaches to justice-involved individuals used in problem-solving courts. To provide the necessary context for this discussion, however, we must begin by describing the scope of the problems facing the criminal justice system, with a particular focus on behavioral health challenges (e.g., substance abuse, mental illness) among offenders and the increase in incarceration and recidivism rates over the past several decades. It is also important to consider the relatively recent shift toward rehabilitative justice. This first chapter will offer a description of this scope and the recent rehabilitative shift.

Scope of the Problem: Overrepresentation of Mental Illness and Substance Abuse Among Justice-Involved Individuals

It has been well established that individuals with behavioral health disorders—particularly substance use disorders and/or mental illness—are overrepresented in the criminal justice system (Casey & Rottman, 2005; Honegger, 2015; James & Glaze, 2006; Lamb & Weinberger, 1998). The reduction in available state hospital beds shifted the burden for providing appropriate treatment services onto communities, many of which were unprepared to provide it (Baillargeon, Binswanger, Penn, Williams, & Murray, 2009; Kinsler & Saxman, 2007; Palermo, 2010). The combination of fewer hospital beds and inadequate community treatment resources contributed to what has been called the "criminalization of the mentally ill" and accounts for the substantial number of justice-involved individuals with mental illness, substance use disorders, or both (Palermo, 2010; Rotter & Barber-Rioja, 2015).

It has been estimated that 25–40% of individuals with mental illness in the community will come into contact with the criminal justice system at some point during their lifetimes (Hasselbrack, 2001). However, the reported prevalence of individuals with mental illness in jails and prisons varies widely in the empirical literature and government reports, from as low as 15% (e.g., Lamb, Weinberger, Marsh, & Gross, 2007; Roskes, 1999) to as high as 50% (James & Glaze, 2006). In a large study of more than 20,000 adults entering five local jails, researchers documented serious mental illnesses (e.g., psychotic disorders or serious mood disorders) in 14.5% of men and 31% of women (Steadman, Osher, Robbins, Case, & Samuels, 2009). When these figures are combined, this makes up 16.9% percent of those studied, which is three to six times higher than the rate of mental illness in the general population (Steadman et al., 2009). One recent estimate suggests that approximately 1 million people with a major mental disorder are currently involved in the criminal justice system (Peterson, Skeem, Kennealy, Bray, & Zvonkovic, 2014).

Rates of substance use disorders among justice-involved populations are even higher than the rates of mental illness. More than 80% of criminal offenders were either arrested for a substance-related offense, under the influence of alcohol or drugs at the time of an offense, committed a crime to support their substance use, or have a history of substance abuse (DeMatteo, Filone, & Davis, 2015). Furthermore, approximately half of all substance-involved offenders meet criteria for a substance use disorder (DeMatteo et al., 2015). More than 60% of adult offenders tested positive for at least one illicit substance at the time of arrest (Office of National Drug Control Policy, 2012), and incarcerated individuals with mental health problems have higher rates of substance use than those without mental health problems (James & Glaze, 2006; Soderstrom, 2007).

The "Revolving Door": Increased Incarceration and Recidivism Rates

There is an important foundational question underlying the use of certain specialized interventions such as problem-solving courts: Does the "problem" addressed by such interventions actually increase the risk of criminal behavior? Are mental illness or substance abuse (or both, when they co-occur) associated with higher rates of criminal offending or probation failure? We review the relevant evidence in this section.

Mental Illness

Individuals with mental illness are overrepresented in the criminal justice system, and they are also disproportionately likely to fail under correctional supervision (Skeem, Manchak, & Peterson, 2011). In one large-scale study, individuals on parole with mental illness (nearly 45,000, which was approximately half of the sample) were two times more likely than parolees without mental illness to return to prison within 1 year of release (Eno Louden & Skeem, 2011).

Mental illness is also associated with a higher number of prior incarcerations (see Baillargeon et al., 2009). According to one survival analysis in Utah, individuals released from prison returned to incarceration nearly 1 year sooner if they were diagnosed with a mental illness relative to those without such a diagnosis (Cloyes, Wong, Latimer, & Abarca, 2010). Both the Baillargeon et al. (2009) and the Cloyes et al. (2010) studies controlled for demographic and offense characteristics in their analyses, making it somewhat more likely that mental illness is associated with increased risk of offending and supervision failure within a subgroup of justice-involved individuals.

But the relationship between mental illness and offending risk is neither straightforward nor strong. Major mental illness has been described as having a modest and indirect impact on criminal offending (Andrews, Bonta, & Wormith, 2006). Of note, it does not appear among the eight central criminogenic risk factors in the widely researched and adopted Risk-Need-Responsivity (RNR) model. Rather, mental illness appears to have an impact on other risk factors, such as antisocial cognition, antisocial personality pattern, and substance use. This is consistent with other evidence suggesting that mental illness by itself is weakly associated with criminal offending but can affect other RNR central risk factors (Bonta, Blais, & Wilson, 2014; Hall, Miraglia, Lee, Chard-Wierschem, & Sawyer, 2012). It may be, for example, that offenders who are mentally ill tend to recidivate at a higher rate than do justice-involved individuals without mental illness because they are disproportionately exposed to *other* risk factors that can increase reoffense risk, such as unstable housing, unemployment, substance abuse, criminal peers, and victimization (Skeem et al., 2011).

Another possible explanation for increased recidivism rates for justice-involved individuals with mental illness is nonadherence to treatment. According to one meta-analysis, offenders with severe mental illness (major psychotic disorders or mood disorders) were less likely to complete treatment programs and in turn more likely to reoffend (Olver, Stockdale, & Wormith, 2011). Even Forensic Assertive Community Treatment (FACT) models, which involve community-based treatment that includes crisis response, medication management, and therapeutic services, have shown mixed results in reducing rates of arrest or incarceration among those with mental health disorders (Marquant, Sabbe, Van Nuffel, & Goethals, 2016; Morrissey, Meyer, & Cuddeback, 2007).

Substance Abuse

Justice-involved individuals with substance abuse problems also have higher rates of recidivism than do individuals without substance abuse (DeMatteo et al., 2015). For individuals who seek or are referred to treatment, 50–55% fail to attend their initial intake appointments, 40–80% drop out of treatment within 3 months, and 80–90% discontinue treatment within 1 year (Marlowe, 2002). Without treatment, approximately 85% of substance-using offenders relapse within the first 6–12 months postrelease and 95% relapse within 3 years of release (see DeMatteo et al., 2015). One recidivism study suggested that, within 3 years of release, 68% of substance-using offenders are rearrested, 47% are reconvicted, and 25% are incarcerated for a new crime (Langan & Levin, 2002). Other evidence indicates that continued substance use is associated with a 200–400% increase in the likelihood of reoffending (Bennett, Holloway, & Farrington, 2008). Substance use is one of the "central eight" risk factors for criminal offending in the RNR model (Andrews & Bonta, 2010b; Andrews et al., 2006), reflecting a broader domain of evidence indicating that alcohol and drug abuse is a risk factor for criminal offending.

Co-occurring Disorders

Individuals with co-occurring substance use and mental health disorders are particularly at risk for criminal recidivism—a risk that is even higher than that of individuals with substance abuse but without mental illness (Baillargeon et al., 2009; Balyakina et al., 2014; Messina, Burdon, Hagopian, & Prendergast, 2006). There is also evidence that individuals with co-occurring disorders are more likely to violate the conditions of community supervision (Balyakina et al., 2014; DeMatteo, LaDuke, Locklair, & Heilbrun, 2013; Wilson, Draine, Hadley, Metraux, & Evans, 2011). The presence of a co-occurring disorder also may exacerbate other criminogenic risk factors, such as criminal attitudes and peers, unstable employment, educational deficits, and poor social support, and it is also likely to increase the risk of homelessness (Morgan, Fisher, Duan, Mandracchia, & Murray, 2010).

Principles Supporting Problem-Solving Justice: Therapeutic Jurisprudence

Therapeutic jurisprudence is a multidisciplinary approach to legal reform that seeks to improve the psychological and emotional health of those affected by the legal process (Wexler & Winick, 1991, 1996; Winick, 2000, 2005; Winick & Wexler, 2003). Many view the development and rapid growth of problem-solving courts as an application of therapeutic jurisprudence (King, 2008; Petrila, 2005; Redlich, Steadman, Monahan, Petrila, & Griffin, 2005; Winick, 2000, 2003; Winick & Wexler, 2003). Its emphasis on rehabilitation is substantial: therapeutic jurisprudence uses behavioral science to evaluate the therapeutic and countertherapeutic impact of the law, and it strives to reduce the former and decrease the latter without compromising due process and other legal priorities (Wexler & Winick, 1996; Winick, 2000). It is also important, under therapeutic jurisprudence, for legal actors to be mindful that decisions under the law have the potential for rehabilitation as contrasted with retribution (Casey & Rottman, 2005).

Therapeutic jurisprudence can be applied in a single case or used to provide structure for a larger court system. Several guidelines for the use of therapeutic jurisprudence have been offered (Casey & Rottman, 2005):

- Evaluate the therapeutic consequences of court procedures and decisions in the larger context of good court performance. For example, do not interfere with due process, violate the separation of powers doctrine, or introduce undue delay or backlogs in processing cases.
- Enact therapeutic jurisprudence in light of findings from empirical research and sound social science theory. Do not rely only on anecdotal or testimonial evidence. Assess the effectiveness of implemented strategies using empirical research.
- Avoid paternalism in the goals and implementation of therapeutic jurisprudence; this is not the intention in the development or implementation of therapeutic jurisprudence.
- Recognize the role played by judges in producing therapeutic (or nontherapeutic) results in each case.
- Systematically consider how problems arise and how they can be best addressed within the legal system.

Beyond its basis in therapeutic jurisprudence, there appear to be common aspects to the functioning of courts using problem-solving justice. Such common elements include the use of legal authority to address chronic societal problems in creative ways, the broadening of the focus of legal proceedings to include more situational influences that contribute to risk for criminal behavior, and the attempt to modify the criminal justice system by holding all relevant parties accountable (Berman & Feinblatt, 2005). Furthermore, problem-solving justice has been characterized as being guided by several primary principles (see Berman, 2009; Wolf, 2007), which are discussed next.

Enhanced Information

This principle involves gathering better information than is often available to courts and attorneys to make improved decisions regarding rehabilitative outcomes. Such information could be obtained in different ways. For example, it could be gathered directly from the defendants and victims involved in the cases before the problem-solving court, including through the administration of specific measures designed to yield information about criminogenic risk and needs. It could be obtained from the larger community through seeking information about treatment resources. It could be provided through formal research on similar courts and populations they serve. Greater and more specific training of court staff and rehabilitative providers could be sought, particularly training that focuses on influences that are often seen in problem-solving courts (e.g., trauma, domestic violence, substance abuse).

Community Engagement

The principle of community engagement involves seeking greater involvement of local citizens, interest groups, and neighborhood coalitions to assist in identifying, prioritizing, and solving challenges relevant to criminal justice. Often this involves promoting a greater orientation to improving public safety through rehabilitative interventions. By decreasing the perceived distance between the general public and justice-involved individuals, and between the systems that serve them, this principle promotes greater acceptance of the somewhat counterintuitive idea that certain kinds of criminal offending are better addressed when the community is more involved in local rehabilitation than when the courts and prisons incarcerate those who break the law.

Collaboration

This principle brings together justice partners from within the criminal justice system (e.g., judges, prosecutors, defense attorneys, probation officers, parole officers, police) and stakeholders from the community (e.g., service providers, victim groups, neighborhood coalitions, schools, hospital). It seeks to improve communication among these groups, thereby fostering creative responding to individuals involved with the problem-solving court and expanding diversion and alternative sentencing options. It takes advantage of the potential for partnerships between agencies and treatment providers through the setting of common goals that provide mutual benefits.

Several key elements of problem-solving courts include a team approach to judicial decision-making, incorporation of social services within and outside of the courts, judicial monitoring of the treatment process, direct contact between defendants and judges, community engagement, and a proactive role for judges within and outside of the courtroom (Farole, Puffett, Rempel, & Byrne, 2005).

A major component of problem-solving court collaboration involves the linkage between judges and lawyers to probation and parole officers, social workers, and other justice system partners to combine their efforts and increase internal motivation for lasting change within defendants (Winick, 2000), with the ultimate goal of reducing recidivism rates (Wiener, Winick, Georges, & Castro, 2010). Two consequences of this collaboration include a shift away from an adversarial approach and the encouragement of justice-involved individuals to take an active role in their rehabilitation.

Individualized Justice

The fourth principle relies on evidence-based risk–need assessment measures. Using such assessment approaches, court personnel can link the participant to specific and tailored services that address criminogenic needs such as substance abuse, job skill deficits, educational limitations, and family problems. Such an approach works toward the reduction of recidivism risk while treating the specific risk factors experienced by the justice-involved individuals. Individualizing services in this way enhances public confidence in the justice system and improves community safety.

Accountability

Careful monitoring combined with the use of clear consequences and sanctions for rule infractions help the justice system improve its accountability and the individual to improve his or her performance. Two kinds of accountability are particularly important in problem-solving courts: an individual's compliance with participation in specific services and the delivery of these services by justice providers. The key to making these services effective is the frequent and rapid communication of noncompliance so that any necessary response can be made.

Outcomes

The final problem-solving justice principle focuses on the active and ongoing collection and evaluation of data. Collecting and analyzing data allow all involved stakeholders and perhaps those responsible for funding to evaluate the effectiveness of interventions, which can increase evidence-based care and encourage future improvements. The data would ideally focus on outcomes such as relevant treatment goals and criminal offending. The characteristics of participants that are associated with success in problem-solving courts can help inform court personnel about how to modify their work in the interest of maximizing participant success; for example, by establishing eligibility criteria and better addressing participant needs (Berman, 2009; Wolf, 2007).

Moving from Punishment Toward Rehabilitation

A number of social and historical influences near the end of the twentieth century set the stage for the development of problem-solving courts, representing a shift under some circumstances from a predominantly justice-related orientation toward punishment to a stronger focus on rehabilitation (Berman & Feinblatt, 2001). One such shift involved the difficulty experienced by the criminal justice system in addressing the mental health and substance abuse problems of those on probation or parole. There was also a massive increase in jail and prison populations, largely the result of the War on Drugs, which stimulated an interest in reducing overcrowding. Improved technology allowed courts to better monitor participants and measure outcomes, making it less necessary to incarcerate individuals to protect public safety. Another development involved advances in evidence-based interventions aimed at addressing influences such as substance abuse and other criminogenic risk factors; these advances increased the justice system's trust in such programming as an alternative to incarceration. Changes in beliefs within our society, and associated changes in public policy, made it more palatable to citizens to allow the delivery of community-based services to justice-involved individuals. High caseloads and frustration with the "revolving door" effect, as well as breakdowns within traditional societal institutions (e.g., church, family) that have historically addressed problems that are now more frequently observed in the criminal justice system, are some of the remaining influences that affected the development of problem-solving courts (Berman & Feinblatt, 2001). As the number of justice-involved individuals with mental health and substance abuse problems grew, the criminal justice system began creating more community-based alternatives to better work with these problems (DeMatteo et al., 2013; Heilbrun et al., 2012).

The development of drug courts in the late 1980s spearheaded the movement toward problem-solving justice. Rather than punishing drug-involved individuals who became involved with the justice system, such individuals were placed in a specialty court designed to address the underlying causes of their offending through the use of mandated treatment, frequent monitoring, and the provision of social services (DeMatteo et al., 2013). The approach used by drug courts was expanded to include other special populations, such as those with mental health problems, veterans, and victims of human trafficking, among others.

The first drug court was established in 1989, in Dade County, Florida, in response to an increase in justice-involved individuals with drug-related charges or substance use disorders. Local authorities realized that standard prosecution and traditional punishment were contributing to the revolving door phenomenon and not working to decrease drug use and drug-related crime. Research suggested that community alternatives such as problem-solving courts could better target relevant criminogenic needs by providing community-based treatment because incarcerated individuals with substance abuse or mental health problems often did not receive proper treatment while confined (DeMatteo et al., 2013). This may be because community-based providers tend to use more evidence-based treatment protocols than do those in correctional facilities (Friedmann, Taxman, & Henderson, 2007).

As with many new initiatives that require changes in thinking and procedure, there were certain challenges to the growth of problem-solving justice. These included (1) an underlying need to change traditional attitudes and role orientations of relevant court personnel (e.g., judges, defense attorneys, prosecutors), (2) barriers to the implementation of problem-solving justice that primarily included constraints on funding and other resources, and (3) the importance of judicial support and leadership in expanding problem-solving justice (Farole et al., 2005). Despite these challenges, there are currently more than 3,000 problem-solving courts of various types in the United States, and this number is continuing to grow (Marlowe, Hardin, & Fox, 2016; National Drug Resource Center [NDCRC], 2014). As the number and types of problem-solving courts have grown, some of these courts have broadened their focus to include a broader range of offenders and targeted treatment needs, including veterans and cases of child abuse or neglect in which parents or other caregivers are drug-involved. Furthermore, some traditional trial courts also incorporate certain problem-solving dockets within their courts (Farole et al., 2005).

This Book: An Overview

This book has two primary goals: education and research improvement. We first strive to educate practitioners, researchers, trainees, students, administrators, and policymakers about the development of problem-solving courts and the role they currently play in the U.S. criminal justice system. Second, we hope to improve the quality of empirical research on problem-solving courts by discussing methodological considerations and highlighting existing research needs.

More specifically, we focus on five areas involving problem-solving courts in the United States: (1) their development, (2) the specific types of problem-solving courts (e.g., drug courts, mental health courts, veterans courts, community courts, domestic violence courts, DUI/DWI courts, family dependency courts, treatment courts), (3) the methodological challenges involved when conducting research on problem-solving courts, (4) the legal and ethical considerations inherent in alternative approaches to standard prosecution, and (5) the future directions relevant to research, practice, and policy. The end of most chapters features a section in which we discuss innovative or promising practices, research agendas, or programmatic expansion and its implications.

In Chapter 2, we introduce the Sequential Intercept Model (SIM), which provides a conceptual framework for problem-solving courts and other types of alternative approaches to working with offenders with certain identifiable needs. Focusing on alternatives to standard prosecution for special populations, the SIM contextualizes problem-solving courts by discussing their occurrence on one intercept in a sequence of several intercepts that are distinct from standard prosecution.

Chapter 3 offers a detailed overview of the assessments and interventions used in problem-solving courts. These include screening and assessment procedures, treatment approaches, and specialty tracks for subtypes of participants. Chapter 3 includes a discussion of the RNR model as a framework for assessing risk and identifying criminogenic risk factors and clinical needs.

In Chapters 4 and 5, we provide detailed discussions of drug courts and mental health courts, respectively, which are the two most prevalent types of problem-solving courts in the United States. As will be discussed, these problem-solving courts have received the most attention, and both courts have well-developed bodies of research.

Chapter 6 provides an overview of the other problem-solving courts in the United States. These include DUI/DWI courts, veterans courts, community courts, domestic violence courts, family dependency courts, and treatment courts. As will be discussed, only a few of these courts have been examined empirically, and an open question is whether there is a sufficient theoretical and empirical basis for the continued operation of these courts.

In Chapter 7, we offer a discussion of reentry programming and specialty courts designed to assist offenders who are reintegrating into society after being released from incarceration. Reentry courts are unique problem-solving courts because, rather than focusing on specific behavioral health needs (e.g., mental illness, substance use), they address criminogenic needs that are related to recidivism.

There are a number of methodological challenges faced by researchers attempting to study the operations and effectiveness of problem-solving courts. We talk about research challenges and limitations in each chapter that focuses on particular problem-solving courts, and Chapter 8 provides a more general discussion of the challenges faced by researchers and the ways in which those challenges can be overcome.

In Chapter 9, we provide an account of the legal and ethical considerations that are relevant to problem-solving courts. Problem-solving courts differ from traditional courts in several key respects, and those differences have legal and ethical implications. Chapter 9 focuses on the constitutional considerations relevant to problem-solving courts and how they impact pleadings, consent, and competency. It also focuses on the ethical issues associated with consent, confidentiality, and the roles of the key players in specialty courts.

Finally, the concluding discussion in Chapter 10 will be broad in focus. After summarizing the current status of problem-solving courts, we synthesize the information discussed in the first nine chapters into a series of recommendations for problem-solving courts. These recommendations are offered in the domain of establishing a problem-solving court; expanding and operating a problem-solving court; and the empirical, ethical, and legal considerations relevant to problem-solving courts. As part of this discussion, we also describe how problem-solving approaches can be incorporated into other aspects of the criminal justice system. Given its breadth, this final chapter will be a useful counterpart to Chapter 1.

2
Alternatives to Standard Prosecution
Problem-Solving Courts

The realization that individuals with behavioral health disorders, most notably mental health disorders and substance use disorders, are overrepresented among justice-involved populations led to dramatic changes in how these individuals are handled by the criminal justice system. The movement from a punishment-oriented response to a more treatment/rehabilitation-oriented approach was a paradigm shift in the criminal justice system's approach to offenders with certain identified needs. The development and proliferation of alternatives to standard prosecution, including problem-solving courts, provide the clearest evidence of the shifting paradigm for justice-involved individuals with behavioral health disorders.

In this chapter, we first describe the Sequential Intercept Model (SIM), which provides a useful conceptual framework for discussing a range of alternatives to standard prosecution. Next, we describe the historical development of alternatives to standard prosecution, with a particular focus on problem-solving courts. We then discuss some of the strengths and limitations of the problem-solving court model. Finally, because problem-solving courts require collaboration among multiple entities (e.g., judges, defense attorneys, prosecutors, probation/parole, treatment providers, social service agencies), many of which assume roles that are radically different from their counterparts in traditional criminal courts, we conclude this chapter with a discussion of the roles assumed by the key players in problem-solving courts.

The Sequential Intercept Model

The SIM is a theoretical framework used within the criminal justice system to identify several points at which community-based alternatives can be provided to individuals with mental illness in lieu of standard criminal justice processing (Munetz & Griffin, 2006; see SAMHSA's GAIN Center, 2013). Specifically, the SIM identifies five points or "intercepts" in the standard criminal justice process at which a treatment—or other rehabilitation-oriented intervention—could be delivered to offenders with identified behavioral health needs in lieu of standard prosecution. Using this model, individuals with mental illness and other behavioral health disorders, including substance use disorders, can be diverted to treatment or other programming that more adequately addresses their needs, with the dual goals of improving the functioning of offenders across multiple domains and reducing the likelihood that they will reoffend.

The five intercepts identified by the SIM are based on the flow of the criminal justice system, and they track the standard process of arrest, conviction, incarceration, and release to the community. Specifically, the SIM consists of the following five intercepts: (1) law enforcement and emergency services; (2) postarrest: initial detention or initial hearing and pretrial services; (3) post-initial hearings: jails/prisons, courts, forensic evaluations, and commitments; (4) reentry from jails, prisons, and forensic hospitalization; and (5) community corrections and community support (Munetz & Griffin, 2006; see Figure 2.1). The SIM is premised on the philosophy that although offenders should be held accountable for their criminal behavior, individuals with mental illness should not be arrested or incarcerated simply due to their mental illness or their lack of ready access to effective community-based treatment (Munetz & Griffin, 2006). Moreover, given the substantial evidence that standard criminal justice processing is not associated with positive outcomes for offenders with certain behavioral health disorders, the SIM can be used to focus efforts to develop alternatives to standard prosecution.

There are several reasons why community-based treatment alternatives for individuals with mental illness and/or substance use disorders are preferable to standard prosecution and correctional treatments. First, intervening at the SIM intercept points and implementing community-based treatments for justice-involved individuals with mental illness may reduce the disproportionate penetration of this population into the criminal justice system (Munetz & Griffin, 2006). Second, unlike the generalized treatments provided in many correctional settings, community-based treatments are more targeted and individualized, which means that they are more likely to effectively address the needs of individuals with mental illness and other treatment needs, thereby reducing recidivism (DeMatteo, LaDuke, Locklair, & Heilbrun, 2013; Heilbrun et al., 2012). Third, community-based treatments are much less financially costly than the standard treatment provided in correctional settings (Heilbrun et al., 2012). For example, research consistently suggests that drug courts produce significant cost savings over traditional criminal justice interventions for drug-involved offenders (e.g., Belenko, Patapis, & French, 2005; Bhati, Roman, & Chalfin, 2008). Finally, community-based treatments can be seen as serving a humanitarian value, particularly for individuals whose criminal behavior is the result of (or at least related to) mental illness, substance use, or other treatment needs. Indeed, if

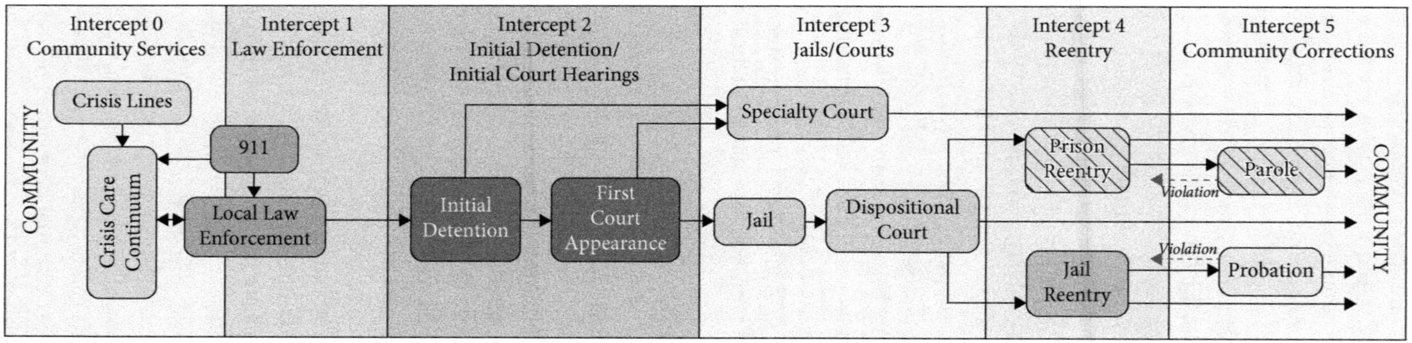

Figure 2.1 The Sequential Intercept Model.
Policy Research Associates, Inc., 2016.

offenders with mental illness and other behavioral health needs receive appropriately tailored treatment, the risk of reoffending can be substantially reduced. As such, from a humanitarian perspective, the best option for both the public and those individuals with behavioral health disorders is to provide access to community-based interventions (Heilbrun et al., 2012).

Specific elements characterize each of the five SIM intercepts at which individuals with mental health and substance use needs could be diverted to community-based treatments (Munetz & Griffin, 2006). The ultimate intercept is to prevent any penetration into the criminal justice system, although there are several points later in the process at which diversion or the use of alternatives to standard prosecution can be used.

Intercept 1 (Law Enforcement and Emergency Services)

This intercept encompasses an individual's initial contact with law enforcement officers or other emergency first responders. Interventions at this intercept seek to (a) prevent individuals from penetrating into the criminal justice system through implementation of alternatives to arrest and (b) reduce the likelihood that police officers will be physically harmed when dealing with individuals with mental health disorders or drug involvement. The interventions that can be provided at Intercept 1 typically consist of collaboration between law enforcement or emergency service personnel and community-based treatment providers (DeMatteo et al., 2013).

Police officers are often the first responders in situations involving an individual who is experiencing a mental health crisis or is under the influence of a substance. In their role as "gatekeepers" to the criminal justice system, police officers determine whether to take a person into custody, which would formally begin their involvement with the criminal justice system, or whether to link them with appropriate mental health services in lieu of justice involvement (Reuland & Yashuara, 2015, p. 40). Police offers can often encounter many challenges when responding to such calls because they may lack the tools and expertise that are necessary to handle mental health and drug-related crises. Although more law enforcement personnel are receiving specialized training, many police officers do not have the training or experience to de-escalate mental health crises, and they may be unaware of behavioral health resources in their communities that could provide a safe and effective alternative to arrest (Reuland & Yashuara, 2015).

To better prepare police officers to handle such encounters, various types of specialized policing responses (SPRs) have been developed. SPRs promote the safety of both police officers and the distressed individual, and they facilitate the linkage of the individual to appropriate behavioral health services (see

Steadman, Deane, Borum, & Morrissey, 2000). These programs encourage collaboration among police officers, behavioral health treatment providers, and individuals with treatment needs and their families. Where appropriate, this model prioritizes treatment over incarceration, thereby diverting individuals with treatment needs from the criminal justice system. There are three types of police-based programs that seek to divert individuals at Intercept 1: crisis intervention teams (CITs), co-responder teams, and follow-up teams.

CIT Training

CIT is one of the most widely implemented approaches to diversion. Through CIT training, first responders (typically law enforcement) are educated on mental illness and behavioral health issues, available community-based behavioral health services, and how to best engage in crisis intervention (Dupont, Cochran, & Pillsbury, 2007). Training is also provided to police dispatchers so they can better recognize crisis calls and assign CIT-trained police officers to handle crises involving individuals in distress. CIT training seeks to improve police response times, facilitate the provision of better care to individuals with mental illness, provide de-escalation techniques, and ensure the safety of the emergency personnel responding to psychiatric crises (Dupont et al., 2007; Strauss et al., 2005).

Of note, there is empirical support for the use of CIT training by police officers. Research suggests that CIT-trained police officers report feeling better able to manage crisis calls involving a psychiatric emergency (Borum, Deane, Steadman, & Morrissey, 1998; see Compton, Bahora, Watson, & Oliva, 2008), are less likely to use physical force and believe nonphysical responses to be more effective when dealing with psychotic individuals in crisis (Compton et al., 2011), are conservative in using physical force against individuals with mental illness who may be at risk of exhibiting violence (Skeem & Bibeau, 2008), and are likely to divert individuals with mental illness to community-based mental health facilities (Watson et al., 2010; see DeMatteo et al., 2013, for a summary of CIT outcome research). Since the implementation of CIT training, there has been an increase in the rate of individuals transferred to psychiatric treatment facilities by CIT-trained officers (Teller, Munetz, Gil, & Ritter, 2006), which reduces the burden on the criminal justice system and promotes the provision of more appropriate treatment to individuals with identified behavioral health needs. In summary, CIT training appears to be an effective way to respond more quickly to mental health crises, decrease rates of police injuries, and limit the financial costs that may be suffered by responses involving specialized police teams (Dupont & Cochran, 2000).

As with many new initiatives, the use of CIT training has faced some challenges, particularly in terms of implementation. For example, for CIT to be effective, there must be ongoing and collaborative relationships between the criminal justice system and community behavioral health systems (Dupont & Cochran, 2000). Unfortunately, for a variety of reasons, such collaborations may be difficult to form in certain jurisdictions. Furthermore, research suggests that some CIT-trained police officers harbor misperceptions, such as thinking that the CIT approach will be effective in all instances (Dupont & Cochran, 2000). Finally, research suggests that knowledge decreases considerably in the time period after the CIT training, particularly among less-experienced police officers (Compton & Chein, 2008), which could lessen the impact of CIT in the field.

Co-Responder Teams

Whereas the CIT approach relies on CIT-trained police officers to respond to emergency situations, co-responder teams involve the collaboration of police officers and mental health professionals in responding to a mental health crisis. Co-responder teams were developed in Los Angeles and San Diego based on the recognition that police officers encountered many people with mental illness who were not receiving adequate treatment and services (Reuland, Draper, & Norton, 2012). Since being developed in California, other jurisdictions have implemented similar teams. Co-responder teams seek to more effectively connect individuals with mental illness with community-based treatment services, transport the distressed individual to a crisis center if needed, promote the safety of the individual and any others involved, and engage in follow-up contact to address outstanding treatment and service needs (Reuland et al., 2012; Reuland & Yashuara, 2015). Research suggests that co-responder teams reduce the inappropriate use of jails to house individuals who are mentally ill (Steadman et al., 2000).

Follow-Up Teams

Follow-up teams are the third type of police-based programs that seek to divert individuals at Intercept 1. They are composed of specially trained police officers and mental health professionals, and they seek to identify repeat offenders who may need more specialized treatment. The follow-up teams then proactively attempt to ensure that the individual receives the interventions that are most likely to prevent future involvement with the criminal justice system. Although there is scant research, the available research suggests that these programs are effective in directing people with mental illness into mental health services when appropriate (Reuland, Schwarzfeld, & Draper, 2009).

Intercept 2 (Post-Arrest: Initial Detention or Initial Hearing and Pretrial Services)

This intercept occurs after an arrest has taken place but before an individual enters a plea or proceeds to trial (DeMatteo et al., 2013). Diversion at Intercept 2 generally involves an offender who is diverted during initial detention or pretrial hearings by those involved in the individual's detention (e.g., law enforcement officers, correctional staff) or those who participate in determining the individual's disposition (e.g., prosecutors, public defenders, probation staff, pretrial services, judges). Diversion at this stage is distinct from subsequent hearings that involve a specialty judge and problem-solving courts, which are found in Intercept 3 (DeMatteo et al., 2013). At this point, the individual has already penetrated into the criminal justice system, so interventions at Intercept 2 focus on diverting individuals from standard prosecution and preventing or limiting further penetration. Specifically, interventions at this stage seek to evaluate mental health needs and divert certain individuals to community-based alternatives to standard prosecution, such as specialized probation programs that involve targeted interventions (DeMatteo et al., 2013; Munetz & Griffin, 2006).

There are limited interventions at Intercept 2, and studies examining the effectiveness of the existing interventions are lacking. Logistical challenges may partially explain the underutilization of post-arrest diversion programs because individuals at this stage may be subject to mandatory sentencing systems, fast-paced criminal justice processing, and minimal collaboration with behavioral health systems. In addition, the nature of interventions at this stage vary widely with regard to the eligibility of offenders and the types of interventions that are offered (DeMatteo et al., 2013).

Given the limited interventions that exist, there are a relatively small number of empirical studies examining the effectiveness of diversion programs at Intercept 2, so the available research findings should be interpreted with caution. However, the research suggests that offenders diverted at this stage are more likely than nondiverted offenders to spend time in the community and engage in treatment activities on a regular and meaningful basis (Broner, Mayrl, & Landsberg, 2005; Hoff, Baranosky, Buchanan, Zonana, & Rosenheck, 1999; Lamberti et al., 2001; Steadman & Naples, 2005). In addition, some research suggests that diversion programs at Intercept 2 are associated with fewer arrests (Shafer, Arthur, & Franczak, 2004), shorter periods of incarceration (Broner, Lattimore, Cowell, & Schlenger, 2004; Broner et al., 2005; Steadman & Naples, 2005), and less homelessness (National GAINS Center, 2002) for diverted offenders when compared to offenders who went through standard criminal justice processing. Although the weight of the evidence suggests that these diversion programs result in improved outcomes, some studies have found inconsistent or neutral associations with criminal justice outcomes (Bertman-Pate et al., 2004) and clinical outcomes (Broner et al., 2004, 2005; Steadman & Naples, 2005). Research on the interventions offered at Intercept 2 is limited but growing, and, as more research is conducted, the effects of diversion at Intercept 2 should become clearer.

Intercept 3 (Post-Initial Hearings: Jails/Prisons, Courts, Forensic Evaluations, and Commitments)

The third intercept occurs after the initial hearing, and it encompasses an individual's contact with jails, prisons, courts, forensic mental health assessments, and commitments. Given that problem-solving courts are found at this intercept, Intercept 3 will be the primary focus of this book. Interventions as this stage typically involve diversion to problem-solving courts, such as drug courts, mental health courts, and other specialized courts that have been developed for specific offender populations (e.g., veterans courts, domestic violence courts, community courts, reentry courts, prostitute courts) (see DeMatteo et al., 2013; Heilbrun, DeMatteo, Strohmaier, & Galloway, 2015). In addition to problem-solving courts, other interventions found at Intercept 3 include commitment to treatment facilities (often in lieu of prosecution) and a number of jail- or prison-based programs that provide targeted treatment to offenders with identified needs.

Problem-solving courts are by far the most well-researched intervention provided at any intercept in the SIM (DeMatteo et al., 2013). A large and well-developed body of empirical research demonstrates the effectiveness of drug courts and, to a lesser extent, mental health courts in providing needed services, reducing drug use, and reducing recidivism (for a brief review of relevant research related to drug courts, see Huddleston & Marlowe, 2011; Marlowe, Hardin, & Fox, 2016; for a brief review of relevant research related to mental health courts, see Griffin & DeMatteo, 2009; Redlich, Liu, Steadman, Callahan, & Robbins, 2012). A later section in this chapter provides additional detail on Intercept 3, and later chapters in this volume provide detailed discussions of the research on drug courts (Chapter 4) and mental health courts (Chapter 5).

Intercept 4 (Reentry from Jails, Prisons, and Forensic Hospitalization)

The fourth intercept focuses on an individual's reentry into society from jails, prisons, and forensic hospitals after incarceration or commitment. Interventions at this point do not focus on diversion from the criminal justice system but instead use community-based treatment programs to facilitate an individual's transition back into society from an institutional setting (DeMatteo et al., 2013). Examples of such interventions include assertive community treatment and forensic assertive treatment programs, intensive case management programs, and correctional reentry programs (Heilbrun et al., 2012). The results are mixed regarding the effectiveness of these initiatives, but the weight of the evidence suggests that they are associated with positive short- and long-term criminal justice outcomes (e.g., reduced recidivism) and clinical outcomes (e.g., improved mental health functioning, utilization of treatment services, decreased substance use; see DeMatteo et al., 2013, for a summary of relevant research regarding Intercept 4 initiatives).

Intercept 5 (Community Corrections and Community Support)

The fifth intercept focuses on community corrections and community support as a means to support justice-involved individuals with mental illness and other behavioral health disorders who are living in the community. Examples of interventions provided at this intercept include specialty mental health programs and specialized probation and parole (Heilbrun et al., 2012). These programs seek to effectively meet the ongoing clinical and criminogenic needs of justice-involved individuals and to maintain and/or increase their engagement in treatment after their release from institutional settings (Munetz & Griffin, 2006). In earlier research, Skeem and Eno Louden (2006) found that specialty probation and parole programs are associated with improved clinical outcomes, including better integration into treatment services and enhanced participant well-being. There is, however, mixed evidence regarding whether these programs reduce the risk of reincarceration due to technical violations and arrests for new criminal offenses (see Perez, 2009).

Alternatives to Standard Prosecution

There are legitimate reasons to prosecute and convict individuals who violate social norms by engaging in prohibited behavior. Commonly cited justifications for punishing offenders include retribution (i.e., just deserts), specific deterrence (i.e., deterring the offender from engaging in future offending behavior), and general deterrence (i.e., deterring others from engaging in offending behavior). However, over the past several decades, it has become evident that standard criminal justice processing does not produce reliably favorable outcomes for certain subsets of offenders, including those with mental health disorders and/or drug involvement. Specifically, research has found that standard criminal justice processing has not produced significant and meaningful improvement in relapse to drug use, psychological functioning, and recidivism rates (Heilbrun et al., 2012).

In response to the dramatic overrepresentation of offenders with mental illness and drug involvement in the criminal justice system, combined with the realization that standard criminal justice processing is not effective for certain subsets of offenders, a variety of alternatives to standard prosecution have been developed over the past few decades. These alternatives to standard prosecution often consist of narrowly tailored and individualized interventions that identify and target the behavioral health needs and specific risk factors for certain types of offenders (DeMatteo et al., 2013; Heilbrun et al., 2012). The idea behind this approach is that effectively addressing an individual's criminogenic needs should reduce the likelihood that the individual will engage in future offending behavior (Andrews & Bonta, 2010a; Skeem & Monahan, 2011).

Underlying community-based alternatives is the premise that the most effective way to forestall further involvement with the criminal justice system is to address offenders' needs across various psychosocial domains. However, to ensure public safety and the safety of all inmates, correctional officers, and other staff within a correctional facility, correctional facilities must prioritize safety and order over the treatment and rehabilitation needs of individual inmates. This practice, although wholly justified, may prevent offenders with specific treatment needs (e.g. drug use, mental health disorders, learning disorders) from getting the type of help they need. Offenders with specific needs who are subject to standard criminal justice processing may not have the opportunity to receive the evidence-based interventions that have been shown to be effective at addressing their specific needs. By contrast, community-based alternatives involve interventions that target a narrow portion of offenders with specific criminogenic needs, and they focus on addressing those needs as a way to facilitate successful rehabilitation and prevent further involvement with the criminal justice system (DeMatteo et al., 2013; Heilbrun et al., 2012).

When offenders participate in community-based interventions prior to being tried in court for their offense or receiving a sentence, they have been "diverted" from the criminal justice system. Diversion is the process whereby an offender is removed from the standard criminal justice procedure and provided with a community-based alternative intervention prior to entering a plea or being sentenced. As such, diversion can only take place at Intercept 1 (when an offender has initial contact with law enforcement officers or other first responders) or Intercept 2 (post-arrest while an offender is detained and involved in preliminary court hearings) (DeMatteo et al., 2013).

Intercept 3

For the purposes of this book, a more in-depth examination of Intercept 3 is warranted given that interventions at this stage include a variety of problem-solving courts. Within the SIM, Intercept 3 is particularly important because it constitutes the final opportunity for intervention prior to a conviction and potential sentence of incarceration. Although diversion from standard prosecution is possible at Intercepts 1 and 2, a substantial number of individuals with mental illness, drug involvement, and other specific treatment needs end up in courts and, subsequently, in correctional facilities (Diamond, Wang, Holzer, Thomas, & Cruser, 2001; Heilbrun et al., 2012). Most research in this area has focused on individuals with severe mental illness (SMI). As noted in Chapter 1, prevalence estimates of those with mental illness in jails and prisons vary considerably. As also noted in Chapter 1, a widely cited source indicates that 14.5% of male inmates and 31% of female inmates have SMI (Steadman, Osher, Robbins, Case, & Samuels, 2009). In addition, inmates with SMI are more likely to be subject to longer periods of incarceration than those without SMI who were convicted of similar charges (McNeil, Binder, & Robinson, 2005). These statistics highlight the importance of providing community-based interventions at this stage to ensure that treatment needs are addressed and eligible individuals are diverted prior to incarceration.

The SIM provides a clear model for intervening at this stage and diverting individuals with SMI, drug involvement, and those who belong to certain populations that are at increased risk of justice involvement, such as veterans. By effectively targeting the needs of these individuals, interventions delivered at Intercept 3 can prevent the incarceration of individuals with SMI, drug involvement, or other specific treatment needs. As noted, the primary intervention at Intercept 3 is problem-solving courts. Using principles of therapeutic jurisprudence (noted in Chapter 1), these courts provide accountability and treatment to address the needs of specific populations (see Hora, Schma, & Rosenthal, 1999).

Several characteristics distinguish problem-solving courts from standard criminal courts. These include (1) a separate docket for offenders with specifically identified needs; (2) a dedicated and involved judge who oversees the primary hearing and subsequent monitoring sessions; (3) committed and involved counsel for the prosecution and defense; (4) a collaborative team-approach involving joint decision-making among the judge, attorneys, treatment providers, and other relevant actors; (5) offenders' voluntary participation and agreement to adhere to a treatment plan; (6) consistent judicial monitoring of offenders' progress and compliance; and (7) dismissal of charges or a reduced sentence for offenders who successfully complete the program (Moore & Hiday, 2006).

History and Development of Problem-Solving Courts

The idea of diversion from the justice system had its inception in the early nineteenth century when progressive reformers recognized the inhumanity of incarcerating individuals who were mentally ill. In 1830, several influential social reformers, including Dorthea Dix and Louis Dwight, fought against the incarceration of individuals with mental illness and successfully lobbied to establish treatment facilities for incarcerated offenders who had symptoms of a severe mental health disorder (Torrey, Kennard, Eslinger, Lamb, & Pavle, 2010). As a result, by 1880, the number of individuals with mental illness who were incarcerated had greatly decreased in the United States (Torrey et al., 2010). Although the release of individuals with mental illness from incarceration would seem to be—and indeed arguably is—a positive step, many of the released offenders were housed in substandard conditions in asylums and were deprived of the mental health treatment they needed (Wright, 1997). The development of the first juvenile court in 1899 is also viewed as a step toward developing specialized courts for offenders with specific needs (Casey, 2004; McCoy, 2003).

Several developments in the mid-twentieth century further paved the way for the advent of problem-solving courts. The National Mental Health Act, which was passed by the United States Congress in 1946, created community-based mental health treatment centers and set forth policy aimed at deinstitutionalizing individuals with mental illness (Rochefort, 1984). In the 1960s, several courts throughout the United States implemented programs to provide mental health counseling for offenders with mental health disorders. Although these programs were not able to successfully manage the large number of offenders who were experiencing mental health disorders, they served as an antecedent for modern-day mental health courts (Goldkamp & Irons-Guynn, 2000).

It is possible, however, that the push for deinstitutionalization unintentionally harmed individuals with mental illness. For example, many individuals with mental illness were placed in state hospitals, which often provided substandard medical and mental health care, and they often found themselves homeless upon release (Lamb, 1984). In addition, the War on Drugs, which began under President Nixon in the early 1970s and gained momentum in the 1980s, and enhanced (and increasingly mandatory) sentencing schemes implemented in the 1980s, may have led to the "criminalization" of individuals with mental illness (Goldkamp & Irons-Guynn, 2000; Palermo, 2010; Rotter & Barber-Rioja, 2015).

The incarceration rate in the United States has grown substantially over the past several decades, largely due to the harsher punishments for individuals charged with drug possession offenses as part of the War on Drugs. At year-end 2015, there were approximately 6.74 million people under the supervision of the U.S. adult correctional system; this figure includes individuals in jails, prisons, and under community supervision (e.g., probation, parole) (Kaeble & Glaze, 2016). A sizable portion of individuals under correctional supervision have behavioral health needs. Although reliable and recent statistics are lacking, it is estimated that 56% of state prisoners, 45% of federal prisoners, and 64% of jail inmates have a mental health problem (Glaze & James, 2006). These rates of mental illness are considerably higher than the rates of mental illness found in the general population.

Problem-solving courts were developed in response to the increasing number of offenders with behavioral health disorders and other treatment needs, and these courts have proliferated over the past several decades to provide alternatives to standard prosecution for offenders with mental health disorders, drug use disorders, and other specific needs. The first problem-solving court was established in Dade County (Miami), Florida, in 1989, in response to perpetual obstacles faced by criminal courts due to a constant inundation of drug-related cases and a "revolving door" of repeat drug offenders (Liu & Redlich, 2015, p. 82). Thus, the first drug court was developed. Drug courts are special criminal court dockets that provide judicially supervised treatment, mandatory periodic drug testing, community supervision, and the use of appropriate sanctions and other rehabilitation services in lieu of standard prosecution and incarceration for offenders charged with drug possession offenses. According to the National Association of Drug Court Professionals, which is a national nonprofit corporation founded in 1994 and consisting of more than 27,000 judges, prosecutors, defense attorneys, and clinical professionals, there are currently more than 3,000 drug courts operating in the United States that will serve more than 125,000 offenders in a given year (Marlowe et al., 2016). The drug court model has also been exported to more than 30 countries worldwide (Marlowe, 2014; Marlowe et al., 2016). Drug courts will be discussed in more detail in Chapter 4.

Based largely on the demonstrated success of drug courts in terms of reducing both relapse to drug use and criminal recidivism, a variety of other problem-solving courts have been developed over the past two decades (see Marlowe et al., 2016, for a description of different types of problem-solving courts). Other types of problem-solving courts include juvenile drug courts (see Chapter 4), mental health courts (see Chapter 5), veterans treatment courts, DUI/DWI courts, family dependency courts, co-occurring disorders courts, reentry courts (see Chapter 7), reentry drug courts, federal district drug courts, gambling courts, community courts, truancy courts, domestic violence courts, gun courts, homelessness courts, prostitution courts, tribal healing to wellness courts, and campus drug courts. Given the prevalence and volume of research, we include separate chapters for drug courts (Chapter 4), mental health courts (Chapter 5), and reentry courts (Chapter 7); many of the other types of problem-solving courts, for which there is considerably less research, are discussed in Chapter 6.

With more than 3,000 operational courts and several hundred more courts in advanced planning and development stages, drug courts are clearly the most common type of problem-solving court in the United States. However, several of the other types of problem-solving courts just noted are increasing in prevalence. For example, there are currently more than 400 mental health courts, 300 truancy courts, 200 domestic violence courts, and 20 community courts in the United States (Marlowe et al., 2016). However, some types of problem-solving courts are decreasing in prevalence, including gambling courts, gun courts, homelessness courts, and truancy courts (see Marlowe et al., 2016, for a summary of the growth and occasional decline of the various types of problem-solving courts). In terms of future growth, Marlowe et al. (2016) reported that mental health courts (for adults and juveniles) and reentry courts were the problem-solving courts (other than drug courts) that are most likely to see an increase in prevalence in the coming years.

Inclusion and Exclusion Criteria of Problem-Solving Courts

Because problem-solving courts provide for the noncustodial supervision of offenders, some of whom have been charged with serious criminal offenses, only certain types of offenders are eligible for these courts. Considerations related to public safety, for example, would preclude most types of problem-solving courts from accepting violent offenders or offenders who have committed certain types of offenses (e.g., sexual crimes against children or nonconsenting adults; arson). With the protection of the public being the top priority, problem-solving courts need to give close attention to the types of offenders who would be appropriate to include in these courts. Depending on the jurisdiction, referrals to problem-solving courts can be made by law enforcement, the prosecutor, defense attorneys, social workers, judges, or other professionals in the criminal justice system.

Eligibility criteria for problem-solving courts differ depending on the type of court and jurisdiction (see Belenko, Fabrikant, & Wolf, 2011; Orr et al., 2009). Formal eligibility criteria typically focus on the severity and nature of the index offense, and certain problem-solving courts only accept offenders who have committed specific types of offenses. For example, some problem-solving courts only accept offenders with misdemeanor charges, while others will accept offenders charged with specific types of felony offenses (see Hiday & Ray, 2010). Other formal eligibility criteria include an offender's criminal history and the degree to which the defendant's treatment needs align with the specialized objectives of the particular problem-solving court. Mental health courts, for example, may require that an offender have a formally diagnosed mental health disorder, although no uniform standard exists across mental health courts to determine whether an offender has a sufficient "mental illness" for purposes of gaining entry to mental health courts (see Wolff, Fabrikant, & Belenko, 2011). Some mental health courts refuse to admit offenders who have personality disorders or a history of substance use (DeMatteo et al., 2013). Drug courts typically require that an offender have a demonstrated history of substance use, although some drug courts will admit offenders based simply on a charge of drug possession or admitted drug involvement. Problem-solving courts also occasionally consider informal eligibility criteria, such as an offender's prior role in his or her community, guidance or insight provided by the referral source, and the apparent motivation of the offender for wanting to enter the problem-solving court. Unfortunately, and somewhat surprisingly, we were not able to find a resource that comprehensively examined eligibility criteria across the different types of problem-solving courts.

Problem-solving courts also have different requirements when it comes to an offender's plea status, with these courts coming in both pre-plea and post-plea models. Some courts require, for example, that an offender enter a guilty plea as a condition to being admitted into the problem-solving court. In those models, the guilty plea is typically held in abeyance (i.e., not formally entered or accepted by the court) as long as the offender complies with the problem-solving court's programmatic requirements. Other courts do not require any plea if the offender is being supervised. Eligible defendants who are accepted into problem-solving courts must agree to adhere to treatment requirements (e.g., group counseling, participation in self-help groups) and intensive supervision (e.g., drug monitoring, case management). Participation in a problem-solving court is voluntary, so an offender can choose to withdraw from the court at any time. However, withdrawing from a problem-solving court typically results in the resumption of standard criminal justice processing (see Chapter 9 for a detailed discussion of the legal and ethical considerations that are relevant to problem-solving courts). Given the voluntary nature of these courts, offenders in problem-solving courts are often referred to as "clients" or "participants" as opposed to "offenders" or "defendants" (Hiday, Moore, Lamoureaux, & Magistris, 2005).

Strengths and Limitations of Problem-Solving Courts

With the development of the first drug court in 1989, problem-solving courts have now been around for 30 years. As such, there has been sufficient time to assess the strengths and limitations of the problem-solving court model. Given the widespread buy-in and financial support for these types of courts, including a heavy push for the expansion of problem-solving courts by President Obama's administration (see Office of National Drug Control Policy, 2010, 2011) and widespread bipartisan support in Congress (Fruman, 2015; Maron, 2009), assessing the strengths and limitations of problem-solving courts has taken on increased importance. This section will focus broadly on the benefits and potential drawbacks of the general problem-solving court model, and in later chapters we discuss the strengths and limitations of specific types of problem-solving courts.

Strengths of Problem-Solving Courts

The most notable strength of problem-solving courts is the robust empirical support for the effectiveness of the model. As will be discussed in more detail in Chapter 4, drug courts are by far the most effective criminal justice intervention ever implemented for drug-involved criminal offenders in terms of reducing the likelihood of relapse to drug use and future offending behavior. Although there is much less research on mental health courts, the weight of the evidence (as will be discussed in Chapter 5) suggests that these courts improve access to treatment, improve overall functioning, and reduce recidivism. Research on several other types of problem-solving courts, such as veterans courts, is beginning to emerge, and the results look promising. Given that an important litmus test for a criminal justice intervention is reducing the likelihood of recidivism, the problem-solving court model appears to be on solid ground.

Two other strengths of the problem-solving court model are important to note. First, problem-solving courts have the potential to bring multiple benefits to the criminal justice system in the form of better-informed judges, increased offender accountability, enhanced accountability of treatment and service providers, and the introduction of community resources into the courtroom (Berman & Feinblatt, 2002). To function effectively, problem-solving courts require the collaboration of multiple entities, so these courts are forced to look outside of the courthouse to connect with government agencies, nonprofit organization and treatment providers, and surrounding communities. Second, research suggests that problem-solving courts have the potential to increase public confidence in the criminal justice system (Berman & Feinblatt, 2002).

Limitations and Criticisms of Problem-Solving Courts

There are, of course, several notable limitations to the problem-solving court approach. Although not a limitation of the problem-solving court model per se, it is important to note that problem-solving courts are serving a relatively modest proportion of justice-involved individuals with behavioral health disorders and other treatment and service needs. Despite the remarkable growth of problem-solving courts over the past few decades, nearly one-half of U.S. counties did not have an adult drug court as of year-end 2014, and more than 80% did not have a DUI court, juvenile drug court, family drug court, or veterans court (Marlowe et al., 2016). Drug courts serve a fraction—approximately 10%—of the large number of drug-involved individuals in the criminal justice system, and a significant proportion of justice-involved individuals with behavioral health needs do not have access to a problem-solving court in their jurisdictions. Furthermore, for jurisdictions with problem-solving courts, the often inconsistent or vague inclusion criteria, combined with exclusionary criteria for certain types of charges, are likely reducing the pool of offenders with behavioral health needs being served by problem-solving courts.

Several scholars have raised concerns relating to the constitutional rights of problem-solving court participants. For example, Liu and Redlich (2015) noted that problem-solving courts were created without any simultaneous discussion of legal policy issues, including due process rights and equal treatment in terms of referrals and acceptances into these types of courts. Similarly, Dorf and Fagan (2003) expressed concern that problem-solving courts may violate due process rights because these courts involved little to no adversarial interactions. In short, critics of the problem-solving court model question whether problem-solving courts can protect the individual rights of offenders. Although offenders voluntarily enter problem-solving courts, some scholars have raised concerns about the potential coercion of offenders into problem-solving courts; some courts may not have procedures in place to make it clear that participation is voluntary and to ensure that offenders provide freely given informed consent to participate (Berman & Feinblatt, 2001). Legal and ethical concerns relating to the problem-solving court model are discussed in more detail in Chapter 9.

Many problem-solving courts hold regularly scheduled meetings to ensure that all relevant stakeholders—judge, prosecutor, defense attorney, case manager, treatment providers, and others—remain informed about a participant's progress. This team approach, which is often cited as a strength of the model, has engendered some criticism. Whereas the judge, prosecutor, and defense attorney play different roles with distinct goals in conventional courtrooms, those three entities work as a team in problem-solving courts (along with case managers, treatment providers, social service agencies, probation and parole officers, and others). This blurring of the traditional roles is a stark departure from traditional legal practice, and it is seen by some as a deficiency of the problem-solving court model (Berman & Feinblatt, 2002).

Although research strongly suggests that the judge plays an integral role in the success of problem-solving courts (e.g., Marlowe, Festinger, & Lee, 2004), some scholars have expressed concerns regarding the role of the judge in these courts (Berman & Feinblatt, 2001, 2002). Given the collaborative and treatment-oriented approach of problem-solving courts, judges in these courts assume a much different role than traditional judges. For example, problem-solving courts include third parties in the judicial process, provide intensive judicial monitoring, and provide for the imposition of sanctions and rewards by the judges. Some scholars see this as judicial paternalism and question whether it is an appropriate use of judicial authority (see Berman & Feinblatt, 2001). Furthermore, although establishing relationships with outside entities (e.g., government agencies, treatment providers) is often described as a strength of the problem-solving court model, there is a concern regarding whether judges can remain independent and neutral arbiters and comply with the separation of powers doctrine (Berman & Feinblatt, 2002). Some have argued, for example, that judges are engaging in too much ex parte communication with researchers, treatment providers, and social scientists (Berman & Feinblatt, 2001). Finally, because judges in problem-solving courts are involved in more aspects of an offender's case (compared to a traditional judge), there is a concern that problem-solving courts represent unacceptable (and perhaps unconstitutional) overreaching by the judicial branch.

Another concern of the problem-solving court model relates to the role of attorneys. Berman and Feinblatt (2001) noted that defense attorneys in problem-solving courts may be less zealous advocates for their clients than attorneys in traditional courts. Given the collaborative nature of problem-solving courts and the team approach that is typically used, defense attorneys may feel less of a need to vigorously advocate on behalf of their clients. This, of course, raises concerns about the constitutional right to effective assistance of counsel provided by the 6th Amendment to the U.S. Constitution, which is made applicable to the states by the 14th Amendment. Constitutional considerations relevant to problem-solving courts are discussed in Chapter 9.

Finally, some have expressed concerns regarding the mental health of some offenders who are admitted to problem-solving courts. As noted by Liu and Redlich (2015): "An important research, policy, and practical question to pose and address . . . is whether problem-solving courts are being used in lieu of insanity defenses and as backdoors to override competence" (p. 90). They further state that it is important to consider "whether offenders eligible for problem-solving courts are the 'same' people who can claim legitimate consideration for insanity and incompetence" (Liu & Redlich, 2015, p. 90).

Stakeholders' Roles in Problem-Solving Courts

The creation and successful operation of problem-solving courts depends on the cooperation of many professionals serving in very different roles. Problem-solving courts require collaboration among various criminal justice professionals and community stakeholders. As such, judges, prosecutors, defense attorneys, probation/parole officers, and court managers must work with treatment providers, case managers, nonprofit organizations, and other nonjustice professionals. Because problem-solving courts use a team approach and are billed as being nonadversarial, the roles assumed by these entities—particularly the roles of the problem-solving court judge, prosecutor, and defense attorney—are much different from the roles assumed by these entities in traditional courts.

In traditional courts, judges typically focus on the specific circumstances of an offender's case without giving much, if any, consideration to the offender's past or what the offender might encounter upon leaving the courtroom. Generally, traditional judges impose a sentence according to law without measuring the results of the imposed sentence. Problem-solving court judges, by contrast, facilitate collaboration among various stakeholders in the criminal justice system and in the community in an effort to effectively address the needs of offenders (Wolf, 2007). This treatment/rehabilitation-oriented approach is a fairly radical departure from the more traditional punishment-oriented approach.

Defense attorneys representing participants in problem-solving courts are often expected to take a less active approach and not intervene while the judge and participant interact (Berman & Feinblatt, 2002). Some defenses attorneys do not support this "back seat" approach, suggesting that such an expectation could cause some defense attorneys to feel pressured by judges and prosecutors to keep objections to a minimum and always condone the proposed treatment requirements or sanctions for noncompliance (Quinn, 2000/2001). However, defense attorneys play a significant role leading up to an offender's decision to participate in a problem-solving court. Until that decision is made, defense attorneys strive to obtain the most desirable disposition for their clients. Defense attorneys also advocate for their clients in problem-solving courts regarding eligibility requirements, the intensity and duration of treatment mandates, and the type and setting of the required treatment program (Berman & Feinblatt, 2002).

Prosecutors also take on a unique role in problem-solving courts because they are asked to abandon the traditional adversarial approach, share work with defense attorneys, and work as part of a collaborative team (Faraci, 2004). In one focus group, a prosecutor observed that his definition of success would be sentencing a potentially dangerous defendant to a long period of incarceration, but acknowledged that someone else's definition of success may involve a treatment mandate (Porter, Rempel, & Mansky, 2010). However, in that focus group, both defense attorneys and prosecutors agreed that in problem-solving courts there needs to be buy-in from both sides regarding how to approach each participant's case (Porter et al., 2010).

Case managers also play an important role in the successful operation of problem-solving courts. Case managers often conduct an exhaustive intake interview to better understand the physical and mental health status of a participant. By conducting a thorough psychosocial assessment, a case manager will have knowledge of a participant's education, employment history, and physical and mental health concerns, among other things. All of this information can be used to develop tailored treatment plans for problem-solving court participants and help the judge make better-informed decisions about each participant (Wolf, 2007). Case managers also often have the role of monitoring implemented treatment plans and providing updates or communication between treatment programs and the court about the progress of problem-solving court participants.

Community service providers and community groups are integral to the success of many problem-solving courts. Many community service providers accept referrals from problem-solving courts, and in some jurisdictions community service providers are permitted to use space in the courthouse to make it easier for participants to get the services they need. Furthermore, because judges often lack knowledge about the community context of a particular crime or a particular offender, community groups play an important role in the operation of some problem-solving courts. For example, community groups can be a useful resource in terms of giving judges tours of local neighborhoods and providing advice about the conditions and concerns of those neighborhoods. Some problem-solving courts have developed advisory boards consisting of local community members and other interested stakeholders (Wolf, 2007).

Finally, research suggests that the general public supports problem-solving courts and tends to be more engaged in problem-solving court operations than in those of traditional criminal courts (Casey & Rottman, 2005). Support from the general public is an important consideration, particularly as public confidence in the court system is somewhat lacking. Moreover, because funding is an ongoing concern for problem-solving courts, public support can facilitate the appropriation of funds at national, regional, and local levels for the development and operation of problem-solving courts.

Conclusion

The past several decades have seen the development of a range of alternatives to standard prosecution for justice-involved individuals with behavioral health disorders and other treatment and service needs. These alternatives were developed out of necessity—the stark realization that individuals with mental health disorders and drug use disorders are overrepresented in the criminal justice system—and they represent a radical departure from standard criminal justice practice. There are various points in the standard criminal justice process at which offenders with particular treatment needs can be removed from standard criminal justice processing and provided with interventions to address their criminogenic and other needs. As described in this chapter, the SIM provides a useful conceptual framework for discussing these points of intervention.

The development of one particular alternative to standard prosecution—problem-solving courts—perhaps best illustrates the paradigm shift that has taken place in the criminal justice system when it comes justice-involved individuals with behavioral health disorders. Despite some limitations and criticisms, there is strong, albeit not universal, support for the problem-solving court model among criminal justice entities, community service providers, and other relevant stakeholders. In later chapters, we focus more specifically on the effectiveness of these courts in improving a range of criminal justice and mental health outcomes for justice-involved individuals with behavioral health needs.

3

Clinical Interventions in Problem-Solving Courts

At the heart of problem-solving courts is the idea that targeted treatment for specific clinical disorders or criminogenic risk factors will reduce recidivism, thereby decreasing the "revolving door" seen in the justice system for individuals with behavioral health concerns. Although there are varying models for how problem-solving courts operate, one aspect that recurs across all models is the use of treatment as an alternative to or follow-up from incarceration. Thus, it is important to examine the types of interventions commonly seen in problem-solving courts.

We begin this chapter with a discussion of the Risk-Needs-Responsivity (RNR) model as a framework for assessing risk and identifying criminogenic risk factors to target in treatment alongside clinical needs. With the community-based interventions used in problem-solving courts, risk assessment is particularly important to ensure public safety. We then discuss screening and assessment procedures used in problem-solving courts and then continue with an overview of different categories of evidence-based interventions commonly seen in problem-solving courts. We then discuss how problem-solving courts can serve as watchdogs for service provision. Finally, we explore future directions for the use of clinical tools and interventions in problem-solving courts.

Risk-Needs-Responsivity Model

The RNR model grew out of the treatment classification literature of the 1960s and 1970s by Sechrest, Palmer, and other scholars who suggested that treatment planning for people with mental health or substance abuse concerns should be individualized (Taxman & Marlowe, 2006). This model was formalized for criminal justice contexts in the 1990s (Andrews, Bonta, & Hoge, 1990) and is now widely supported in the empirical criminal justice literature.

The RNR model is comprised of three principles: *risk*, *needs*, and *responsivity*. The risk principle posits that individuals who are higher risk (e.g., those more likely to engage in a target behavior—in this case, reoffending) should receive a higher dose or level of intensity of treatment, and individuals who are lower risk are better served with minimal or limited intervention (Andrews et al., 1990). Further expansion of the risk principle indicates that higher risk offenders will show larger reductions in recidivism (e.g., experience greater treatment effect) than their lower risk counterparts (Prendergast, Pearson, Podus, Hamilton, & Greenwell, 2013).

The needs principle suggests that treatment should be targeted toward criminogenic risk factors as a way to reduce the likelihood of recidivism (Andrews et al., 1990). This principle led to the formalization of evidence-supported criminogenic risk factors and the identification of intervention targets. Table 3.1 presents the Central Eight risk factors (with the first four sometimes called the "Big Four" because they have the greatest impact on recidivism) and associated interventions. Although the Central Eight risk factors include some static risk factors, or risk factors that cannot be targeted by interventions (e.g., criminal history), most are dynamic in nature and thus can be addressed through interventions. Some controversy surrounds the inclusion of psychosis as a dynamic risk factor (see Douglas & Skeem, 2005), but it is not typically included in common conceptualizations of criminogenic risk. Although some research suggests that treating mental health symptoms results in reductions in recidivism

Table 3.1 "Big Eight" risk factors and corresponding interventions

Criminogenic risk factor	Intervention target
Criminal history	Notably, the only static risk factor included, and therefore does not have a specific treatment target
Antisocial personality pattern	Anger management, impulse-control training, problem-solving and decision-making skills
Antisocial cognitions	Cognitive-behavioral therapy to build prosocial attitudes, address criminal thinking
Criminal companions	Replace with prosocial companions
Substance abuse	Drug/alcohol treatment, motivational interviewing to enhance behavior change
Poor family/Marital relationships	Encourage reconnection to family, parenting skills classes
Poor educational/Vocational achievement	Connect to educational or job-training programs, encourage and help seek gainful employment
Lack of prosocial leisure activities	Encourage and connect to prosocial activities and hobbies

From Bonta & Andrews (2007).

(e.g., Han & Redlich, 2015; Van Dorn et al., 2011; Van Dorn, Desmarais, Petrila, Haynes, & Singh, 2013), other research suggests that individuals with mental health disorders share many of the same criminogenic needs as other justice-involved individuals, and thus criminogenic needs may be more applicable risk factors and more relevant intervention targets (e.g., Skeem, Winter, Kennealy, Louden, & Tatar, 2014). Ideally, both mental health and criminogenic needs are addressed in problem-solving courts, and problem-solving courts are most efficient when interventions target symptoms that are both mental health–related *and* criminogenic.

The responsivity principle relates to tailoring treatment style and modality to maximize effectiveness. This principle includes the concept of general responsivity, or the idea that offenders are most likely to see reductions in offending if they receive the most appropriate empirically supported treatment. Such research suggests that a cognitive social learning approach is the most effective for achieving behavior change among offenders (Andrews, Bonta, & Wormith, 2006). Interventions that fall into this category are described later in this chapter. The responsivity principle further encourages the individualization of treatment planning by incorporating specific responsivity, such as individual learning styles, into treatment design and implementation. Under this principle, it is also important to consider learning styles that tend not to be helpful for offenders, such as unstructured peer-support groups or client-centered support psychotherapy (Prendergast et al., 2013).

The RNR model has a large body of supporting research (e.g., Andrews & Dowden, 2006; Dowden & Andrews, 2000; Jolley & Kerbs, 2010; Lowenkamp, Latessa, & Holsinger, 2006; Ogloff & Davis, 2004; Thanner & Taxman, 2003). Research also supports the use of RNR with specific subtypes of offenders, including female offenders (Dowden & Andrews, 1999), violent offenders (Dowden & Andrews, 1999), and sex offenders (Hanson, Bourgon, Helmus, & Hodgson, 2009). As noted earlier, recent research suggests that the criminogenic risk factors outlined by the RNR model (seen in Table 3.1) are more predictive of recidivism than most mental health diagnoses alone (excluding antisocial personality disorder), and, as such, interventions targeting criminogenic risk factors hold significant promise for offenders with or without behavioral health concerns (Bonta, Blais, & Wilson, 2014; Skeem et al., 2014). However, recent research has found insufficient empirical support for the use of the RNR model among offenders with serious mental illness, including those offenders with psychotic symptoms (e.g., hallucinations, delusions) (Skeem, Steadman, & Manchak, 2015).

The RNR model provides a useful lens through which to frame treatment planning, particularly for many individuals involved in problem-solving courts. Not only does the RNR model reliably assess an individual's risk for reoffending, but it incorporates specific treatment domains to maximize the impact of the intervention and target the "whole picture." Unfortunately, empirical research examining the efficacy of the RNR model in problem-solving courts is quite limited. Later in this chapter, we discuss how the RNR model is perhaps underutilized in problem-solving courts despite the promise it has shown among criminal offenders generally.

Screening Procedures in Problem-Solving Courts

As discussed in more depth in later chapters, eligibility and screening criteria in problem-solving courts vary greatly by type of court and jurisdiction. As such, the procedures and instruments used for screening vary considerably. Screening involves the identification of potential participants for entry into a problem-solving court, and it consists of either record-based eligibility (i.e., based solely on records or arrest data) or a brief interview/assessment to ensure that a potential participant meets eligibility criteria. Surprisingly, we could not locate any empirical research regarding the use of specialized or evidence-based screening instruments in problem-solving courts, suggesting that many courts use "in-house" measures or simply consider certain factors about an individual's history rather than conducting a formal screening. This highlights an important area for research and development as problem-solving courts continue to proliferate. It is important, for example, to examine whether certain offender and offense-related characteristics that can be identified before an offender is accepted into a problem-solving court are associated with performance/success in the problem-solving court. Given the documented underrepresentation of minorities in problem-solving courts, another important question is whether screening procedures reflect unintentional implicit bias based on an offender's race.

Even when eligibility criteria are clearly defined, the process by which offenders are approved or selected to participate in a problem-solving court is generally specific to the court and relevant parties, and it is sometimes done on a case-by-case basis (Wolff, Fabrikant, & Belenko, 2011). The use of incentives or disincentives for participation further complicates the selection process because it can introduce selection bias (Redlich, Hoover, Summers, & Steadman, 2010) and raise legal and ethical concerns. Some research suggests that only approximately one-third of individuals eligible for a problem-solving court are admitted to the court due to exclusion criteria, such as the type of offense (Belenko, 2002b).

Despite the increasing prevalence of problem-solving courts, research on screening procedures is quite limited. One study reviewing drug court screening procedures identified two distinct processes—in diversion drug courts, the prosecution tends to act as the gatekeeper who ultimately determines which individuals are eligible to participate, while in post-plea diversion courts, court staff tend to take on the gatekeeper role (Belenko, Fabrikant, & Wolff, 2011). Research on mental health courts suggest there is more consistency across courts in terms of screening procedures, although the actual methods of identifying and screening eligible participants vary widely among courts (Wolff et al., 2011).

Assessments in Problem-Solving Courts

Similar to screening procedures in problem-solving courts, the use of formalized assessments varies greatly by jurisdiction. In general, specialized instruments have been used to assist courts or agencies in managing justice-involved populations and determining the proper dosage of treatment (e.g., level of care, frequency of contact; Chadwick, DeWolf, & Serin, 2015; Viglione, Rudes, & Taxman, 2015). Clinical assessments can serve two functions in the context of problem-solving courts: the first is to assess for specific eligibility criteria (e.g., diagnostic assessments), and the second is to evaluate risk and criminogenic needs so the court can plan interventions and determine if an individual's risk can be managed safely in community treatment. This section will focus on the latter of these functions.

Risk assessment is an important part of evaluating whether justice-involved individuals can be managed safely in the community (see Heilbrun, 2009). Although certain variables may categorically exclude some individuals from participating in community alternatives to incarceration (e.g., severity of charges, history of violence), specialized risk assessment measures serve an important function in problem-solving courts. Given the nature of problem-solving courts—and the buy-in needed from multiple parties to establish and run problem-solving courts—identifying and excluding individuals who present a serious risk of violence to the community is (or should be) a high priority.

Risk assessment is often viewed in terms of its generational development (for an overview, see Heilbrun, Yasuhara, & Shah, 2010). First-generation risk assessments involved unstructured professional judgment based on risk-relevant information gathered in an interview or through observation. Second-generation risk assessments utilize empirically supported instruments largely based on static risk factors alone, but provide little information relevant to rehabilitation needs (see Fass, Heilbrun, DeMatteo, & Fretz, 2008). Third-generation tools incorporate both static and dynamic risk factors and generate scores (or other outcomes) that can be evaluated as interventions target criminogenic needs. Fourth-generation risk assessment instruments are emerging as an extension of third-generation risk assessments; they are designed specifically to follow offenders from intake through case resolution (see Andrews et al., 2006).

Risk–needs measures were developed based on empirically identified and supported criminogenic needs (Andrews et al., 2006). See Table 3.1 for an outline of the main areas of risk–need. When discussing risk–needs, it is important to distinguish between evidence-based criminogenic risk factors (shown in Table 3.1) and other areas of need that have not been shown to have a strong relationship with increased criminality (e.g., mental illness, physical health problems; Andrews et al., 2006). These additional areas of need, such as mental illness, may serve as the basis for admission into a problem-solving court. It is important to evaluate and incorporate such areas of need into intervention planning but with the recognition that they may be less relevant in terms of reducing the likelihood of future offending.

Several empirically supported risk–needs instruments can be used to inform treatment planning. The Level of Service Inventory-Revised (LSI-R; Andrews & Bonta, 2001) is a third-generation risk assessment tool that measures particular characteristics of offenders and provides information relevant to treatment planning and level of care. The LSI-R relies on the Central Eight risk factors (see Table 3.1) and was developed to assist correctional professionals in determining the appropriate level of supervision for an offender (Kroner & Mills, 2001; Lowenkamp & Latessa, 2002). Similarly, the revised version of the LSI-R, the Level of Service/Case Management Inventory (LS/CMI; Andrews, Bonta, & Wormith, 2004), assesses risk for antisocial behavior and assists in treatment planning. The LS/CMI is also based on the Central Eight risk factors and has particular utility for case management because it identifies areas of need that relate to dynamic risk factors. The Inventory of Offender Risk, Needs, and Strengths (IORNS; Miller, 2006) assesses risk by examining both static and dynamic risk factors and by also considering protective factors, including personal and environmental resources.

Although these risk–needs measures have some empirical support, they are not without limitations. The LSI-R has demonstrated inconsistent validity when used with offenders of minority racial and ethnic backgrounds (see Fass et al., 2008). Also, some risk–needs tools have questionable reliability when used with special populations commonly seen in problem-solving courts, such as individuals with severe mental illness. For example, the LSI-R has been used with mentally ill offenders, but research shows it does not reliably predict recidivism for individuals with co-occurring mental illness and substance use disorders (Ferguson, Ogloff, & Thomson, 2009).

The Correctional Offender Management Profiling for Alternative Sanctions (COMPAS; Brennan & Oliver, 2000) is another tool that measures risk–needs in correctional populations and assists in decision-making related to community placements. The COMPAS calculates general risk scores and more specific risk scores related to failure under supervision, which may be of particular use in problem-solving courts. The COMPAS falls in a different category than the previously discussed measures; although it is widely used by courts across the country, it has not been subject to the same rigor of peer review as the other measures discussed because the algorithm that calculates risk scores was privately developed and not shared with the public. As such, the COMPAS has been subject to criticism within the field and even some litigation. In *Wisconsin v. Loomis* (2016), an individual who pled guilty to several criminal offenses was facing sentencing, and the presentence investigation report relied in part on a risk assessment based on the COMPAS. Among other things, the offender argued that use of the COMPAS violated his constitutional due process rights because the assessment's proprietary nature renders it immune from challenges to the accuracy of the resulting risk estimate. The Supreme Court of Wisconsin held that the use of the COMPAS did not violate the offender's due process rights because the risk estimate produced by the COMPAS was supported by other independent factors. However, the court also held that any risk assessments based on the COMPAS should be presented to the sentencing court along with recognition of several limitations, including the proprietary nature of the COMPAS. As such, although the COMPAS may be useful to problem-solving courts, it also has significant disadvantages and thus should be used and interpreted with caution.

Limited research has examined the utility of risk–needs measures in problem-solving courts. A small body of research has examined the use of such measures in mental health diversion programs. One study evaluated the use of the Short-Term Assessment of Risk and Treatability (START; Webster, Martin, Brink, Nicholls, & Middleton, 2004) in a jail diversion sample and found preliminary support for its reliability and validity (Desmarais, Van Dorn, Telford, Petrila, & Coffey, 2012). Another study supports the utility of the Level of Service family of measures for use with community-supervised offenders with mental illness (Canales, Campbell, Wei, & Totten, 2014). Notably, these studies involved small samples and the data came from one concentrated geographic area, so future research is needed to add to this initial empirical support. Overall, this domain is clearly an area requiring significantly more research. There is no shortage of risk–needs tools, so the next step is to empirically examine the utility of such measures in contexts in which they could be particularly useful, including in problem-solving courts.

Clinical Interventions in Problem-Solving Courts

This section will explore the variety of interventions commonly used in problem-solving courts. Although specific problem-solving courts offer treatment for particular participant needs (e.g., drug courts provide substance use treatment, mental health courts provide some combination of therapy and psychiatric care), this section discusses interventions that can be implemented across different types of problem-solving courts. As previously noted, many of these interventions involve the treatment of criminogenic needs based on the relationship between risk factors and recidivism. Additionally, many of the interventions discussed in this section can be implemented at various stages of involvement in the criminal justice system (e.g., upon initial arrest, while incarcerated, while on probation or parole). In this section, we discuss two broad categories of evidence-based interventions used with offenders: cognitive-behavioral interventions and problem-solving interventions (not to be confused with problem-solving courts more generally). We conclude with a discussion of specific behavioral health interventions used by various types of problem-solving courts.

Cognitive-Behavioral Interventions

Overview

Cognitive-behavioral interventions seek to identify and change faulty thinking patterns and modify beliefs that cause distressing emotions or problematic behaviors (Beck, 1976). Cognitive-behavioral therapy (CBT) is the most common intervention used in offender rehabilitation. In justice-related contexts, CBT interventions seek to identify irrational cognitions and criminal thinking styles, both of which are included in one of the Big Four risk factors identified in the RNR model. Examples of criminal thinking include self-justification of criminal behavior, displacement of blame, decreased moral reasoning, dominance or entitlement, misinterpretation of social cues, and overly optimistic views (see Lipsey, Landenberer, & Wilson, 2007). CBT in this context assumes that the distorted thoughts were learned and likely functioned in a way that reinforced their use. As such, CBT interventions seek to enhance awareness of such thought distortions that can potentially lead to criminal behavior (Lipsey et al., 2007).

CBT for justice-involved individuals can be delivered in a group or an individual context. Therapy initially involves helping offenders recognize and self-monitor automatic thoughts, and then to identify distorted, biased, or irrational thinking patterns. The therapist then helps offenders challenge and replace those faulty thoughts using cognitive restructuring (see Heilbrun, DeMatteo, King, Thornewill, & Phillips, 2016). Such cognitive restructuring can be accomplished in a variety of ways. The self-talk method can be used to restructure thoughts by reframing or replacing distorted thoughts with more positive ones (McMullin, 2000).

Cognitive-behavioral interventions in this context employ various evidence-based techniques, such as cognitive skills training, anger management, and relapse prevention, and they are often supplemented with social skills training and morality training (Lipsey et al., 2007). Cognitive skills training involves teaching strategies such as problem-solving skills, interpersonal skills, critical reasoning, consequence evaluation, long-term planning, and perspective-taking (Lipsey et al., 2007; Robinson, 1995). This training often involves role-plays with therapists and the evaluation of real-world events in offenders' lives (Heilbrun et al., 2016). Cognitive skills training aims to teach participants decision-making techniques that can slow down impulsive processes and help them generate alternative solutions or evaluate the consequences of various courses of action (Lipsey et al., 2007; Porporino, Fabiano, & Robinson, 1991).

Many cognitive-behavioral interventions for offenders focus particularly on anger management, which involves helping offenders learn to stop acting impulsively in situations that typically provoke anger reactions. Although this intervention is similar to CBT as described earlier, it focuses more on enhancing the awareness of anger cues and triggers for anger. An anamnestic approach to risk assessment that focuses on a detailed description of behavior involved in the individual's offense history and the consequent development of individualized risk factors may be particularly useful in this context (see Heilbrun, 2009). Additionally, anger management interventions can help offenders identify automatic thoughts that lead to anger, evaluate whether those thoughts are irrational, and replace irrational thoughts with more adaptive ones (Lipsey et al., 2007).

Relapse prevention involves teaching self-monitoring and self-management skills to control reactions that could lead to antisocial behavior (Milkman & Wanberg, 2007). Relapse prevention is taught in the later stages of an intervention to help offenders identify risky situations and use coping skills to avoid engaging in antisocial behavior (Little & Robinson, 1986). Relapse prevention can be particularly effective when implemented in conjunction with the interventions noted earlier.

Evidence-Based Interventions

The empirical literature generally supports cognitive-behavioral approaches to offender rehabilitation (Cullen & Gendreau, 1989; Gendreau & Ross, 1987; Husband & Platt, 1993; Landenberger & Lipsey, 2005; Wilson, Bouffard, &

Mackenzie, 2005). Some research suggests that cognitive-behavioral approaches are the most important and effective model of behavior change (Andrews et al., 1990; Gendreau & Andrews, 1990). Furthermore, several meta-analyses support the effectiveness of CBT interventions for both juvenile and adult offenders (e.g., Lipsey & Cullen, 2007). In one meta-analysis of group-based CBT programs (k = 20 studies), researchers found that CBT interventions, particularly those with a focus on cognitive restructuring and moral reasoning, were particularly effective in reducing recidivism (Wilson et al., 2005). Several other meta-analyses, including Landenberger and Lipsey (2005) (k = 58); Lipsey, Chapman, and Landenberger (2001) (k = 14); and Pearson, Lipton, Cleland, and Yee (2002) (k = 69), support the effectiveness of CBT-based programs in reducing recidivism.

Specific CBT Interventions

A variety of evidence-based CBT interventions are commonly used with offenders in criminal justice contexts. Although the research base is limited, there is some empirical evidence that these interventions can result in meaningful reductions in recidivism. One intervention, Thinking for a Change (T4C; Bush, Glick, & Taymans, 1997), was designed for small groups of individuals either in prison or during community supervision. T4C consists of 22 sessions that teach cognitive restructuring, problem-solving skills, and social skills, among other things. The sessions utilize a variety of techniques and strategies, including group exercises, role-plays, and homework, to reinforce the skills that are taught in group therapy (Bush et al., 1997). T4C has a limited evidence base, but the available research provides some empirical support for the reduction of recidivism for individuals who have participated in T4C (e.g., Golden, Gatchel, & Cahill, 2006; Lowenkamp, Hubbard, Makarios, & Latessa, 2008).

Reasoning and Rehabilitation (R&R; Ross, Fabiano, & Ross, 1986) was designed to help both youth and adults with a history of criminal or antisocial behavior. The program is delivered in a group therapy format, typically with 35 sessions of 2 hours in length each that include 6–12 individuals (Ross, Fabiano, & Ewles, 1988). R&R uses exercises that target impulsive, illogical, or rigid thought processes, and it seeks to replace them with more adaptive responses. In a review by Antonowicz (2005), 22 studies were identified that evaluated the effectiveness of R&R, with most studies lending support for its impact on recidivism reduction. In one meta-analysis (k = 16), R&R was shown to result in reduced recidivism (Tong & Farrington, 2006). Two meta-analyses of CBT interventions that included name-brand interventions as a moderator found that R&R's effectiveness was comparable to other name-brand and generic CBT programs (Landenberger & Lipsey, 2005; Lipsey et al., 2007).

Problem-Solving Interventions

Overview

Problem-solving interventions for offenders comprise two major categories: *training*, which comes from the correctional literature and is often based on interpersonal cognitive problem-solving models (e.g., Spivack, Platt, & Shure, 1976), and *therapy*, which is based on the social problem-solving model from clinical psychology (e.g., D'Zurilla & Goldfried, 1971). R&R (discussed earlier) includes components of the training model of problem-solving (e.g., a manualized intervention that uses cognitive-behavioral skills and role-plays to teach specific problem-solving skills), while interventions such as Problem-Solving Therapy for sex offenders (Nezu, D'Zurilla, & Nezu, 2005) and Stop & Think (McMurran, Fyffe, McCarthy, Duggan, & Latham, 2001) are examples of other social problem-solving models that seek to target more generally the way individuals approach real-world problems. The underlying premise of problem-solving interventions is that poor problem-solving skills are associated with adjustment problems and maladaptive behavior patterns. As such, these interventions seek to teach offenders how to adapt and engage in flexible thinking when faced with difficult situations, which in turn can reduce criminal behavior (Heilbrun et al., 2016). To teach such skills, problem-solving interventions often utilize cognitive-behavioral strategies including functional analysis, psychoeducation, practice and feedback, emotion regulation, and cognitive restructuring (McGuire, 2005).

Evidence Base

Research supports the premise that poor problem-solving skills are related to antisocial behavior. In a review of general problem-solving and adjustment, D'Zurilla and Nezu (2007) included information about offending behavior. They found that adolescents exhibit less effective problem-solving than their parents and that poorer social problem-solving skills are associated with behaviors such as drug use, truancy, running away from home, and risky sexual behaviors. Another study found that aggressive individuals with intellectual disability had greater problem-solving deficits than individuals with intellectual disability but no history of aggressive behavior (Basquill, Nezu, Nezu, & Klein, 2004). In adult offenders, research suggests that high levels of neuroticism are related to poor problem-solving for offenders with mental illness (McMurran, Egan, Blaire, & Richardson, 2001). Research has also found problem-solving deficits among inmates who experience poor adjustment to incarceration (Antonowicz & Ross, 2005), and one study also found that poor problem-solving often precedes recidivism in offenders with criminal histories (Zamble & Quinsey, 1997).

Of note, recent research has examined the use of a problem-solving measure among offender populations. Specifically, researchers have demonstrated the validity and reliability of the Social Problem-Solving Inventory-Revised (SPSI-R; D'Zurilla, Nezu, & Maydeu-Olivares, 2002) among sex offenders and offenders with intellectual disabilities (Lindsay et al., 2011; Wakeling, 2007). This measure has not yet been validated in general offender samples or for offenders with other behavioral health needs.

Specific Problem-Solving Interventions

This section reviews a selected group of well-known problem-solving interventions for offender populations. It is worth noting that R&R and T4C (both described earlier) also include problem-solving components; reviews of those programs and associated relevant research for R&R and T4C were described earlier.

Think First is a social problem-solving intervention that conceptualizes criminal behavior as a problem to be solved. This program was developed to be implemented in a correctional setting or in the community and seeks to teach effective problem-solving skills. We could not identify any randomized controlled trials on Think First, but earlier research indicates that participation in Think First is related to better scores on measures related to problem-solving, criminal thinking, and impulsivity (McGuire & Hatcher, 2001; Ong, Al-Attar, Roberts, & Harsent, 2003). A later study using a pre/post design found that program participants had lower levels of criminal thinking, external locus of control, and other negative problem-solving styles, although an unexplained increase in careless/impulsive problem-solving styles was observed (Burgoyne & Tyson, 2013).

Stop & Think is another social problem-solving intervention that shares some similarities with Think First. Pilot data for this program revealed improvement in social problem-solving abilities and decreased impulsivity among offenders with mental illness (McMurran, Egan, & Dugan, 2005). Later research found that participants who completed the program tended to have lower impulsivity than did program noncompleters (McMurran, Huband, & Duggan, 2008). Another study by Hayward and colleagues (2008) suggests that Stop & Think helps reduce emotional distress in prisoners with mental illness. No randomized controlled trials were identified, and we could find no research of any kind that has examined the impact of this program on criminal recidivism.

Despite some promising early results, subsequent research on various problem-solving interventions (e.g., R&R, Think First) demonstrates that participation is not associated with significant reductions in recidivism (Hollin et al., 2008; McGuire et al., 2008). However, in the study by McGuire and colleagues, when stratifying results by risk level, a small effect size was noted for moderate- and high-risk cases. Larger studies subsequently conducted suggest a treatment effect for very-high-risk individuals, but not for their lower risk counterparts (Palmer et al., 2008, 2009). Thus, the research on problem-solving interventions is mixed but generally suggests that a problem-solving component may have particular utility with offenders who are higher risk. Indeed, two meta-analyses examined effects by specific treatment component (e.g., cognitive restructuring, social skills, behavior modification) rather than by name-brand treatment, and they found that larger reductions in recidivism were only associated with programs that included a problem-solving or anger management component (Landenberger & Lipsey, 2005; Lipsey et al., 2007).

Specific Behavioral Health Interventions

In this section, we review common clinical interventions for specific behavioral health needs. Unlike the cognitive-behavioral and problem-solving interventions discussed earlier, which could be found in any type of problem-solving court, the interventions discussed in this section are specific to certain types of problem-solving courts that target various behavioral health needs. In this section, we provide an overview of these interventions, and more detail on these interventions will be provided in the chapters that focus on specific types of problem-solving courts.

Interventions for Substance Use

In drug court, a crucial component of intervention planning is treating underlying substance use issues that are related to an individual's charges and his or her risk for future criminal behavior. Given that substance use is a robust risk factor for offending behavior, targeting an offender's substance use should reduce the likelihood of recidivism. Treatment programs can consist of various levels of care, ranging from outpatient therapy to inpatient rehabilitation.

Therapeutic communities (TCs), which are commonly used in correctional facilities, are distinct units that provide a more treatment-focused environment than is commonly found in correctional facilities (Inciardi, Martin, & Butzin, 2004). TCs also exist in the community, and individuals participating in court-mandated treatment are commonly referred to such programs. TC programs are quite structured. They are often staffed by former substance users and rely on the support of other program members to create a treatment milieu. TCs incorporate intensive individual and group therapy to treat not only addiction but underlying mental health issues that may drive or trigger substance use. TCs utilize a step-down process by which treatment intensity and supervision is decreased progressively over time to maintain abstinence. TCs have a strong evidence base (see Mitchell, Wilson, & MacKenzie, 2012; Olson & Lurigio, 2014) and are frequently used for drug court participants as part of a treatment mandate or during an individual's incarceration. More recently, TCs have been incorporating cognitive-behavioral programming (Stohr et al., 2001).

Problem-solving courts may also recommend participation in a 12-step program (e.g., Alcoholics Anonymous or Narcotics Anonymous) as part of a treatment plan. This practice is controversial for several reasons. First, such programs are built on a foundation of anonymity, which makes it challenging to enforce participation. Second, some have criticized courts for requiring participation in a program initially founded in religious practices (Gallas, 2004). Third, 12-step programs have limited empirical support. As such, courts are more likely to require outpatient or inpatient substance abuse treatment, or participation in a TC, rather than a 12-step program. With that said, a 12-step program may be incorporated into a treatment plan for individuals interested in participating.

Interventions for Seriously Mentally Ill Offenders

Though not a specific criminogenic risk factor, research suggests that symptoms of serious mental illness can impact criminal behavior indirectly by changing other criminogenic risk factors, such as employment (see Bonta, Blais, & Wilson, 2014; Hall, Miraglia, Lee, Chard-Wierschem, & Sawyer, 2012). Thus, it is important that problem-solving courts, particularly mental health courts, treat underlying behavioral health concerns. A primary intervention for individuals with serious mental illness is to prescribe psychotropic medication. Research has shown that outpatient treatment and psychotropic medication can have a positive impact on symptom reduction and rearrest risk (Prins, Skeem, Mauro, & Link, 2015; Van Dorn et al., 2013). TCs with a specific focus on co-occurring disorders, which are referred to as *modified therapeutic communities*, are effective in reducing substance use and recidivism for individuals with mental health problems who require a higher intensity of care (e.g., Sacks, Sacks, McKendrick, Banks, & Stommel, 2004; Sacks, McKendrick, Sacks, & Cleland, 2010).

Forensic assertive community treatment (FACT) teams have also emerged as an intensive community-based treatment to reduce recidivism and monitor symptoms. Unlike general assertive community treatment, FACT teams utilize court sanctions to incentivize participation and include court staff and probation officers to help monitor individuals in the community (Lamberti, Weisman, & Faden, 2004). FACT teams show mixed results (see DeMatteo, LaDuke, Locklair, & Heilbrun, 2013), although some research suggests that they may be effective in reducing reincarceration rates and hospitalization rates (e.g., Cusack, Morrissey, Cuddeback, Prins, & Williams, 2010; Morrissey, Meyer, & Cuddeback, 2007).

Trauma-Informed Interventions

Given the high rates of trauma among incarcerated populations, it is important that interventions address any symptoms that may relate to trauma a person has experienced. Research suggests that between 4% and 21% of offenders meet criteria for posttraumatic stress disorder (PTSD), with women being disproportionally affected (Goff, Rose, Rose, & Purves, 2007). Trauma-informed treatment should incorporate a consideration of an individual's trauma history and seek to minimize triggers that may inflict future trauma or reactivate past trauma. Such interventions include specialized training for staff about trauma and its effects. We were unable to find empirical research specifically examining the use of trauma-informed care in problem-solving courts.

One specific cognitive-behavioral program used with justice-involved populations with a history of trauma is called Seeking Safety (Najavits, n.d.). The program involves psychoeducation, with a particular focus on the relationship between trauma and substance use. It also employs skills-training related to coping skills and improving interpersonal relationships. Early data showed support for Seeking Safety in reducing recidivism, substance use, and PTSD symptoms for female offenders (Lynch, Heath, Mathews, & Cepeda, 2012; Zlotnick, Johnson, & Najavitz, 2009; Zlotnick, Najavits, Rohsenow, & Johnson, 2003). More recent research also suggests promising results for male offenders (Barrett et al., 2015). As the intervention's research base grows, it should be considered for more frequent implementation in problem-solving courts if the results continue to be positive.

The Impact of Clinical Programs for Offenders on Communities

One of the foundational principles of problem-solving courts is the idea of community engagement and collaboration with community treatment providers. When offenders participate in community-based treatment under the supervision of the court (whether mandated as part of a diversion program or as a requirement of an individual's probation or parole), the court monitors the services that are provided. If an offender is mandated to engage in treatment and fails to make sufficient progress, the court may want to examine whether there is an issue with the quality of treatment provided. As such, problem-solving courts may scrutinize treatment providers to ensure they are delivering quality and evidence-based care that supports rehabilitation. This practice, however, may put problem-solving courts in a difficult position. On the one hand, such scrutiny could help to ensure that referred court participants receive high-quality care. On the other hand, treatment providers may be put off by the additional scrutiny and deny admittance to problem-solving court clients.

Next Steps

Research conducted over the past few decades has paved the way for the inclusion of evidence-based programming in the criminal justice system. An important next step is to determine how to incorporate such assessments and interventions into problem-solving courts. As the justice system continues to shift toward a rehabilitative model and diverts individuals into the community more frequently, utilizing a risk–needs framework becomes increasingly important.

Research supports the RNR model generally, but future research should examine this model as it applies to various subtypes of offenders or in special contexts. A common critique of the RNR model is that it is applied as a one-size-fits-all approach despite the emphasis on individualized programming. For example, a recent study suggests that general risk assessment tools and cognitive-behavioral interventions are effective for use with mentally ill offenders, but it did not find direct support for the applicability of the three RNR principles with populations of offenders with severe mental illness (Skeem et al., 2015). Thus, research should examine whether the RNR model works with different offender subtypes, or whether another model perhaps works better. Additionally, research supports the RNR model when it is implemented *well*. Although the RNR model is mentioned in many best practice guidelines for problem-solving courts, more specific guidelines for implementing the model on a community or court level would be useful and would streamline its implementation so that more research can be conducted.

The effective application of the RNR model to problem-solving courts requires focusing on screening and assessment. RNR-based screening and assessment measures should be developed, validated, and normed for use with specific offender subtypes *within* problem-solving courts. Although there are several evidence-based assessment measures that could be useful in a problem-solving court context, few reliable screening measures exist for use in this domain. This is a notable area for development within the field. Furthermore, research should examine the utility of evidence-based assessments (e.g., LS/CMI) in problem-solving courts. It is also important to strive for consistency in screening and assessment procedures within and across problem-solving courts. Increased consistency would likely improve court procedures and also make it easier to conduct research across courts.

Finally, further research on clinical programming for offenders in problem-solving courts should be conducted. When possible, researchers should seek to conduct randomized controlled trials or quasi-experimental studies to determine the effectiveness of specific cognitive-behavioral or problem-solving interventions. There are, of course, challenges to conducting rigorous research with justice-involved individuals (see Chapter 8). Treatment plans should seek to incorporate the RNR principles by delivering the appropriate interventions in the proper dose to appropriate problem-solving court participants.

Conclusion

Although there have been numerous advances made over the past several decades in evidence-based assessment and intervention with justice-involved individuals, specific application of these advances to problem-solving courts is still in its relatively early stages. Limited research identifies screening tools for use in problem-solving courts. Evidence-based assessments that incorporate risk assessment and criminogenic needs have been used with populations commonly seen in problem-solving courts, but there is not much research examining the specific utility of such instruments in problem-solving courts. Finally, there are several prototypical evidence-based treatments with proven effectiveness for justice-involved individuals with and without behavioral health concerns, but they are not widely used or researched in the context of problem-solving courts. With greater adherence to the RNR model, improved research and consistency in practice across problem-solving courts, and increased access to evidence-based care, the next several decades should continue to see significant further advances.

4
Drug Courts

The era of problem-solving courts in the United States began with the development of the first drug court in the late 1980s. The drug court model represents a paradigm shift in how the criminal justice system handles drug-involved offenders. Rather than simply punishing drug-involved offenders, which has failed to produce meaningful reductions in criminal recidivism or drug use, drug courts seek to target the underlying causes of offending behavior in a nonadversarial setting. Drug courts focus on reducing future criminal behavior and drug use by addressing the offender's drug problem, which is viewed by the court as the primary (albeit not the sole) cause of the participant's criminal behavior.

We begin this chapter by reviewing the relationship between substance use and criminal justice involvement. Next, we provide an overview of the history and development of drug courts, with a specific focus on their features, operations, and key components. We then review the extensive research on the effectiveness of drug courts, with a primary focus on the two outcomes that are of the most interest to the criminal justice system and policymakers: criminal recidivism and relapse to drug use. We also discuss the smaller, yet still impressive, body of research on other outcomes that are targeted by drug courts, such improved mental health functioning and the provision of social services. Given the large body of research on drug courts, there is a great deal of data on the correlates and predictors of success in drug courts, and we provide a summary of the key factors related to drug court success. As with all research, there are some methodological limitations in drug court research, and we provide a review of the primary limitations. We then discuss a newer drug court model—juvenile drug courts—with a focus on their key features and effectiveness. As we will discuss, the research on juvenile drug courts is lagging behind the research conducted on adult drugs court, but there is reason to be optimistic. Finally, after discussing best practices in the development and operation of drug courts in terms of reducing recidivism and containing costs, we focus on the future of drug courts.

Substance Use in the Criminal Justice System

As we noted in Chapter 1, the past several decades have seen a dramatic increase in the number of individuals with substance use disorders in the criminal justice system. Due to considerable increases in drug-related arrests and sentencing schemes that require mandatory minimums for certain drug convictions—both of which stem from the War on Drugs—correctional facilities in the United States have become overcrowded with offenders with substance use problems (see DeMatteo, Filone, & Davis, 2015, for a review of relevant statistics). The War on Drugs was a federal campaign involving the proliferation of stringent anti–drug use laws and increased enforcement efforts in response to drug offenses (Hora, Schma, & Rosenthal, 1999; National Association of Drug Court Professionals [NADCP], 1997). In the two decades between 1980 and 2000, arrests for drug offenses more than doubled in the United States (Bureau of Justice Statistics, 2002, 2005). Notably, in the 1990s, surveys revealed a general decline in drug use in the United States, but a steep increase in drug-related arrests and incarceration (Lurigio, 2008).

By the early 2000s, 21% of state inmates and 55% of federal inmates were incarcerated for a drug-related offense (Mumola & Karberg, 2006), and those figures have remained relatively steady since that time. Overall, jail and prison admissions more than quadrupled in the two decades following the start of the War on Drugs (Harrison & Karberg, 2004), with drug violations accounting for approximately 60% of the increase in the federal inmate population and more than 30% of the increase in the state inmate population (Belenko & Peugh, 2005; Harrison & Beck, 2003). A review of data from the Bureau of Justice Statistics is instructive. By 2004, drug offenders comprised roughly 55% of federal prison inmates and 20% of state prison inmates (Mumola & Karberg, 2006).

The degree of overlap between criminal offenders and drug users is extensive. When drug involvement is defined broadly to include being arrested for a substance-related offense, being under the influence of alcohol or drugs at the time of an offense, committing an offense to support a substance use problem, or having a history of substance use, more than 80% offenders can be considered drug-involved (see DeMatteo et al., 2015; Marlowe, 2002, 2014; National Center on Addiction & Substance Abuse, 2010). Furthermore, multisite studies reveal that large portions of adult arrestees—averaging more than 60% across studies—tested positive for at least one illicit drug at the time of arrest (Office of National Drug Control Policy, 2012).

A closer examination of the relationship between drug use and specific crimes reveals the extent of the overlap. Drug use is implicated in 50% of violent crimes (National Institute of Justice [NIJ], 2000), 50% of domestic violence crimes (Center for Substance Abuse Treatment, 2000), 60–80% of substantiated cases of child abuse and neglect (Child Welfare League of America, 1990), 50–75% of theft and property offenses (NIJ, 2000), and 75–99% of prostitution and drug dealing/manufacturing offenses (NIJ, 2000). Given the relationship between drug use and criminal offending, it is not surprising that substance use (including alcohol) is one of the Central Eight risk factors for criminal offending (Andrews & Bonta, 2010b; Andrews, Bonta, & Wormith, 2006).

A great deal of research conducted over the past several decades has also firmly established that incarceration by itself has little discernible impact on reducing criminal recidivism and substance use among drug-involved offenders (see DeMatteo et al., 2015, for a review). Compared to non–drug using offenders, drug-involved offenders released from incarceration have substantially higher rates of criminal recidivism and relapse to drug use. Without receiving treatment, approximately 85% of drug-using offenders relapse to drug use within the first 6–12 months after release from incarceration (Beck & Shipley, 1989; Hanlon, Nurco, Bateman, & O'Grady, 1998), and that figure increases to 95% within 3 years of release (Martin, Butzin, Saum, & Inciardi, 1999). The statistics are similarly discouraging when it comes to criminal recidivism. Within 3 years of release from incarceration, 68% of drug-using offenders are rearrested, 47% are reconvicted, and 25% are reincarcerated for a new crime (Langan & Levin, 2002).

Drug Courts: Development and Overview

The dramatic increase in the number of offenders charged with drug offenses throughout the 1980s placed a tremendous burden on the court system, which had difficulty managing the massive influx of drug-related cases. Standard criminal justice processing of drug-involved offenders required a tremendous amount of resources and yet was achieving little success in reducing the number of drug-related cases. As a result, several courts began looking for innovative ways to address the increasing numbers of drug cases that were overwhelming their dockets.

For several decades, drug policy in the United States vacillated between public health approaches and public safety approaches. The key difference between these approaches is how drug use is conceptualized because the conceptualization of drug use dictates the response. Under the public health approach, drug use is conceptualized as a medical disease, and the proper response to a disease is treatment rather than punishment. Unfortunately, as briefly noted in Chapter 1, the treatment of drug users has achieved limited success. For individuals who seek or are referred to substance use treatment, 50–55% fail to attend their initial intake appointments, 40–80% drop out of treatment within 3 months, and 80–90% discontinue treatment within 1 year (see Marlowe, 2002). Under the public safety approach, drug use is conceptualized as a crime, which calls for a punitive response. However, the public safety approach—a foundational premise of the

War on Drug—has not resulted in significant decreases in recidivism and drug use over the past several decades.

Instead of viewing drug use dichotomously as either a public safety problem or a public health problem, some courts began conceptualizing drug use as a combined public safety/public health problem that requires a coordinated response. This represented a dramatic shift in the criminal justice system's conceptualization of drug use, and it was this shift that led directly to the development of the nation's first drug court in Miami (Dade County), Florida, in 1989 (Liu & Redlich, 2015; Marlowe, 2002). Drug courts are separate criminal court dockets that refer certain offenders charged with drug possession offenses to substance abuse treatment programs, monitor their progress in treatment, and provide additional behavioral health and social services. The provision of judicially supervised treatment and a focus on offender accountability are two of the features that separate drug courts from other interventions that have been implemented with drug-involved offenders. The services provided by drug courts are provided in lieu of standard prosecution and incarceration, and participation in drug courts is typically limited to nonviolent offenders with a drug possession charge (as opposed to a drug distribution offense) (Marlowe, 2002).

The development and reported success of the first drug court in Miami, Florida, led to the rapid proliferation of drug courts throughout the United States. As courts in other jurisdictions began to hear about the Dade County Drug Court, they sought to develop similar courts to address the increasing number of drug cases seen in their jurisdictions. Within 10 years after the development of the first drug court, there were nearly 500 drug courts across the United States (National Drug Court Institute, 2007). The growth of drug courts has increased considerably over the past two decades. Since 2009, the number of drug courts increased in more than three-quarters (76%) of US states and territories (Marlowe, Hardin, & Fox, 2016). There are currently more than 3,000 operational drug courts in the United States, including a drug court in every state, and the drug court model has been exported to more than 30 countries (Marlowe, 2014; Marlowe et al., 2016; NIJ, 2015).

It is important to note that the philosophy underlying drug courts—that drug dependence is a disease that calls for more a treatment-oriented response as opposed to a punitive response—is not a new idea. Over the past 200 years, drug use has been variously viewed as a moral failing, bad habit, medical disease, mental health disorder, and criminal offense (see McKim & Hancock, 2013). A major step forward was taken in 1962, when the Supreme Court of the United States decided *Robinson v. California*, in which it recognized that drug dependence was an illness. After *Robinson*, treatment rather than punishment became a more acceptable response for individuals who are drug dependent, and that type of thinking led to the development of several nonpenal responses to drug dependence (e.g., Treatment Alternatives to Street Crimes [TASC]) and eventually to the development of drug courts (Tauber, 2011).

Features and Operations of Drug Courts

Drug courts operate under a variety of models. For example, some drug courts are true diversion programs that result in the dismissal of the offender's charges upon successful completion of the program. Other drug courts require a formal finding of guilt before the offender is admitted to the program, and yet other programs only include probation revocation cases that could result in the reduction of probation conditions. The primary models are summarized here.

In *pre-plea drug courts*, participants who successfully complete the program will not have the current case added to their criminal record because entry to the drug court takes place before a formal legal disposition is made on the charges, the current charges are dismissed if participants successfully complete the program, and participants are eligible to have their arrest record expunged in many jurisdictions (Marlowe et al., 2016). The benefit of expungement is that it permits the offender to respond truthfully on employment applications and other documents (e.g., applications for social services) that he or she has not been arrested or convicted (see Festinger, DeMatteo, Marlowe, & Lee, 2005). An additional benefit of this model is that the case is processed faster because preliminary hearings and discovery are typically not necessary (Hardin & Fox, 2011).

Another model is referred to as *diversion with stipulated facts*. In courts that use this model, the drug court participant signs a stipulation of facts upon entry to the drug court program. One benefit to this model is that the offender has essentially confessed to the offense, which would facilitate prosecution if the offender does not successfully complete the drug court program (Hardin & Fox, 2011).

In the *post-plea preadjudication model*, participants enter a formal guilty plea that is held in abeyance during their time in the program. If the participant completes the program, he or she may receive a lighter sentence (e.g., probation instead of jail), or the participant may be able to withdraw the guilty plea and seek a dismissal of the charges (Marlowe et al., 2016). Participants who do not successfully complete the program proceed to sentencing based on the guilty plea. This type of model often permits more serious offenders to participate in the drug court program (Hardin & Fox, 2011).

Participants in the *postadjudication probation model* of drug courts plead guilty and receive a sentence of probation that requires compliance with the drug court. This model is often seen as more attractive by prosecutors, particularly for serious offenders, because a final judgment of guilty has already been entered. Participants who successfully complete the program can have their probation reduced or terminated.

The *probation revocation model* of drug courts targets offenders who are already on probation and at risk of being found in violation of the terms of the probation due to their drug involvement (e.g., positive drug test, new drug charges). Instead of having their probation revoked, which could result in incarceration, these offenders are offered the opportunity to participate in the drug court program. Successful completion of this type of drug court results in the avoidance of incarceration or a reduction or possibly termination of probation (Hardin & Fox, 2011).

Researchers have considered which model is associated with the most favorable outcomes (see Hardin & Fox, 2011, for a useful summary of the research). First, research suggests that drug court outcomes are better when courts have leverage over the participants to keep them meaningfully engaged in the program (Goldkamp, White, & Robinson, 2001). For example, models in which participants must enter a guilty plea as a prerequisite to participation typically achieve somewhat better results than pre-plea models because participants who have pled guilty will be sentenced if they do not successfully complete the program. Second, the consistent use of one model is associated with better results (Shaffer, 2011), which suggests that drug courts should not switch between different models. Finally, there is no compelling empirical evidence that any single model is clearly better than any other model (Hardin & Fox, 2011).

There are several features that distinguish drug courts from standard criminal courts, including expedited case processing (particularly in pre-plea models), linkage to substance abuse treatment, the provision of wraparound services (case management, benefits, housing, vocational services, and the like), random drug testing, and regularly scheduled judicial hearings at which a participant's progress in the program is reviewed by the drug court judge. Drug courts utilize a behavior management approach in which the judge imposes sanctions and incentives to shape participants' behavior.

As with all problem-solving courts, participation in a drug court program is voluntary, and the local prosecutors typically serve as the gatekeepers to determine offender eligibility, which is usually based on the offender's criminal history and current criminal charges (Belenko, Fabrikant, & Wolff, 2011). In most jurisdictions, offenders with a history of violent offending are excluded (Mitchell, Wilson, Eggers, & MacKenzie, 2012), and only offenders charged with drug possession offenses are offered the opportunity to enter drug court. Participation in a drug court, which come in misdemeanor, felony, and combined courts, ranges in length from a few months to 2 years, with most drug court programs being 12–15 months (Rempel, Green, & Kralstein, 2012). There are also variations on drug courts, including family drug courts that handle abuse, neglect, and dependency cases in which parental or guardian drug use is a major contributing factor (see Chapter 6, for more information on family drug courts).

The Key Components of Drug Courts

In 1997, the Drugs Standards Committee of the National Association of Drug Court Professionals (NADCP) identified the 10 key components of drug courts (see Table 4.1). At the time these key components were identified, drug courts had been in existence for less than a decade, but there was already emerging empirical evidence that drug courts were effective in reducing drug use and recidivism. However, it was also evident that drug courts varied considerably by jurisdiction and that the differences in structure and operation could affect the drug court outcomes (Carey, Mackin, & Finigan, 2012; Rossman et al., 2011). The identification of the 10 key components was intended to provide guidance to jurisdictions that had or were planning to develop a drug court as way to promote uniformity in drug court structure and operation. Each of the 10 components also included performance benchmarks that could be used to assess the court's adherence to the component.

Table 4.1 Ten key components of drug courts

1. Drug courts integrate alcohol and other drug treatment services with justice system case processing.
2. Using a nonadversarial approach, prosecution and defense counsel promote public safety while protecting participants' due process rights.
3. Eligible participants are identified early and promptly placed in the drug court program.
4. Drug courts provide access to a continuum of alcohol, drug, and other related treatment and rehabilitation services.
5. Abstinence is monitored by frequent alcohol and other drug testing.
6. A coordinated strategy governs drug court responses to participant's compliance.
7. Ongoing judicial interaction with each drug court participant is essential.
8. Monitoring and evaluation measure the achievement of program goals and gauge effectiveness.
9. Continuing interdisciplinary education promotes effective drug court planning, implementation, and operations.
10. Forging partnerships among drug courts, public agencies, and community-based organizations generates local support and enhances drug court program effectiveness.

From National Association of Drug Court Professionals (1997).

Key Component 1: Integrate alcohol and other drug treatment services with justice system case processing. The first key component emphasizes the primary purpose of drug courts, which is to stop the abuse of drugs related to criminal activity. To achieve this goal, drug courts are advised to use a coordinated response involving the collaboration of judges, prosecutors, defense attorneys, probation officers, corrections personnel, law enforcement, pretrial services agencies, evaluators, local service providers, and the community in which the drug court operates. Organizations devoted to vocational training/rehabilitation, education, and housing should also be involved. Some have advocated for drug courts to use a multiphased treatment approach that is divided into a stabilization phase, intensive treatment phase, and transition phase (see Mitchell et al., 2012).

Key Component 2: Using a nonadversarial approach, prosecution and defense counsel promote public safety while protecting participants' due process rights. This second component focuses on the nonadversarial team approach that distinguishes drug courts from standard criminal courts. The prosecution and defense, under the judge's leadership and with the assistance of various coordinated agencies, work collaboratively to identify and implement the services that are needed to most effectively promote the participant's recovery. With that said, the prosecutor remains obligated to protect public safety by ensuring that potential participants are appropriate candidates for drug court and that current participants comply with all drug court requirements. At the same time, defense counsel should protect the participants' due process rights while encouraging the participant to engage fully with the drug court program (see Chapter 9 for a discussion of the constitutional and legal issues relevant to drug courts.)

Key Component 3: Eligible participants are identified early and promptly placed in the drug court program. One of the key features of drug courts and other problem-solving courts is the rapid identification of eligible participants and the prompt delivery of services. The time period immediately following an arrest provides a critical opportunity for "reaching" an offender who is drug-involved. Because they are experiencing a crisis, drug-involved offenders may be more willing to address their drug problem, so early identification of eligible offenders takes on increased importance. Moreover, the rapid identification and placement of an offender in a drug court could serve to increase public confidence in the criminal justice system.

Key Component 4: Drug courts provide access to a continuum of alcohol, drug, and other related treatment and rehabilitation services. This component recognizes that drug use is a complex phenomenon that requires a multipronged treatment approach. People begin and continue to use drugs for a variety of biological, social, psychological, cultural, and contextual reasons, so the provided treatment must address the various influences related to an individual participant's drug use. Drug court treatment is designed to be comprehensive;

some of the treatment takes places in the courtroom through the participant's interaction with the criminal justice and treatment professionals, while other treatment occurs in more traditional therapeutic settings (e.g., individual and group counseling, self-help groups, case management). This component encourages frequent communication among the many professionals involved in each participant's case as a way to effectively monitor a participant's progress in the program. Although drug courts are primarily focused on the participant's drug use, they should consider other problems that may be contributing to the participant's offending behavior, such as mental illness, medical problems, housing challenges, intellectual and educational deficits, unemployment, and family difficulties.

Key Component 5: Abstinence is monitored by frequent alcohol and other drug testing. Given the chronic nature of drug dependence and the tendency for some drug users to minimize or deny drug use, drug courts should rely on frequent, random, and objective drug testing protocols to promptly identify participant noncompliance. Monitoring a participant's use of prohibited substances provides a framework for accountability and an objective way to assess the participant's progress in the program. Drug courts typically take a zero-tolerance approach as opposed to a harm-reduction approach.

Key Component 6: A coordinated strategy governs drug court responses to participant's compliance. A primary goal of drug court is to prevent relapse to drug use by helping participants to develop skills that reduce the likelihood drug use will occur (e.g., identifying triggers for drug use, managing cravings, developing strategies for coping with high-risk situations). However, drug courts recognize that drug dependence is a chronic, relapsing condition, and a sizeable portion of drug court participants continue to use drugs in the early stages of the program (see DeMatteo, Marlowe, Festinger, & Arabia, 2009). As such, drug courts should have a coordinated plan for dealing with participant noncompliance. Consistent with established principles of behavior modification, the plan should involve both rewarding compliant behavior and swiftly responding to noncompliant behavior. Ideally, the responses should be uniform for all participants and appropriate in magnitude to the participant's compliance or lack thereof.

Key Component 7: Ongoing judicial interaction with each drug court participant is essential. Drug courts function most effectively when they have one dedicated judge who oversees the drug court team and establishes relationships with each of the participants. The consistency of the judge–participant relationship is thought to be one of the more important aspects of drug courts because it increases the likelihood that the participant will be compliant with program requirements. The ongoing supervision and attention from the judge also communicates to participants that someone in authority is invested in their well-being. The role of the drug court judge is unique and considerably different from the role judges assume in standard criminal court (see Meyer & Tauber, 2011). The judge may simultaneously need to reward compliant behavior and punish noncompliant behavior, and the judge must also have a working knowledge of effective treatment approaches.

Key Component 8: Monitoring and evaluation measure the achievement of program goals and gauge effectiveness. Drug court participation requires careful and coordinated monitoring of the program's operations and effectiveness. Effective drug courts have, among other things, clearly defined goals and rules, and there must be a way to objectively assess whether participants are satisfying the program benchmarks. Furthermore, drug courts should be designed to permit both process evaluations (i.e., operational and administrative functioning and goals) and outcome evaluations (i.e., overall program effectiveness in achieving the primary outcomes of reducing recidivism and relapse), which is particularly important when reporting to policymakers and funding agencies.

Key Component 9: Continuing interdisciplinary education promotes effective drug court planning, implementation, and operations. Given ongoing developments in substance use treatment, other services, and other aspects of a drug court's operation, it is important that those involved with the operation of the drug court—both directly and indirectly—participate in periodic education and training sessions. Continuing education/training helps to ensure that the drug court is remaining current with recent developments in numerous legal and clinical areas. This training should, of course, be a supplement to the training that the criminal justice and treatment staff received prior to the opening of the drug court. The interdisciplinary aspect of the training deserves special note. Criminal justice professionals may lack knowledge about the nature of substance use and the effectiveness of various treatment approaches, while treatment professionals may not have a working understanding of the criminal justice system and the legal complexities and operations of the drug court. As such, interdisciplinary training has the potential to ensure that all involved parties have a shared understanding of the relevant issues faced by drug courts.

Key Component 10: Forging partnerships among drug courts, public agencies, and community-based organizations generates local support and enhances drug court program effectiveness. For drug courts to function effectively, they must establish collaborative relationships with criminal justice agencies (e.g., probation, parole), private community-based organizations, and various treatment providers. Given the nature of drug courts, it is essential that collaborative agencies and organizations have sufficient "buy in." Among other things, establishing these collaborative relationships helps to ensure that participants have access to a continuum of services both during and after their time in the program.

The Effectiveness of Drug Courts

The overarching goal of drug courts is to reduce recidivism among a group of offenders—those with substance use involvement—who have been dramatically overrepresented in the criminal justice system over the past several decades. Reducing recidivism by deterring future criminal behavior is, of course, consistent with the broader goals of the criminal justice system. To achieve that goal, drug courts target several participant needs that are related to recidivism, with drug use being the primary need that is addressed. However, rather than focusing exclusively on a participant's drug use, drug courts also target other needs that may contribute to criminal offending, including other behavioral health disorders, medical disorders, mental health disorders, and social service needs (e.g., lack of benefits, unemployment, homelessness, child care).

Given the broad focus of drug courts, there are numerous process and outcome variables that can be examined to assess the effectiveness of these courts. After presenting some descriptive data on drug courts, we examine the two outcomes that have received the most attention from researchers and policymakers: recidivism and substance use. Then we examine a variety of other behaviors and outcomes that are often targeted by drug courts (e.g., rates and length of incarceration, provision of services, cost effectiveness). Next, we discuss the correlates and predictors of success in drug court, which includes an examination of both court-specific and participant-specific factors. Finally, we end this section with a discussion of methodological and research-based limitations in drug court research.

Drug courts are by far the most researched type of problem-solving court, and there is more research on drug courts than on virtually any other intervention for drug-involved offenders (see Marlowe et al., 2016; Marlowe & Meyer, 2011). Hundreds of studies on drug courts have been conducted over the past several decades, and the resulting body of empirical research is extensive and impressive. Given the volume of drug court research, we focus primarily on meta-analyses, systematic reviews, and large-scale studies, and only occasionally reference a single study.

The effectiveness of drug courts has been supported by controlled research, program evaluations, multisite studies, and meta-analyses (see, e.g., Belenko, 1998, 1999, 2001, 2002a; Belenko, DeMatteo, & Patapis, 2007; Government Accountability Office, 2011; Mitchell et al., 2012; Shaffer, 2011; Wilson, Mitchell, & Mackenzie, 2006). Taken as a whole, the research indicates that drug courts are the most effective intervention for reducing recidivism and drug use among drug-involved offenders. In fact, there is more research supporting the effectiveness of drug courts than there is research supporting the effectiveness of many US Food and Drug Administration (FDA)-approved medications. The standard for FDA approval is typically two concurrent controlled clinical trials, and there have been nine meta-analyses or national studies of drug courts involving more than 100 studies, including approximately one dozen randomized controlled trials (RCTs).

Descriptive Data on Drug Courts

In 2014, a national survey was conducted to better understand the characteristics of drug court participants and to gather data on general drug court outcomes (see Marlowe, Hardin, & Fox, 2016). The survey was conducted by the National Drug Court Institute (NDCI), which is a division of the NADCP. The NDCI was formed in 1997 and is responsible for training and technical assistance; it receives funding from the US Department of Justice, White House Office of National Drug Control Policy, and Substance Abuse and Mental Health Services Administration. The 2014 Painting the Current Picture (PCP) Survey was distributed to points of contact in all 50 states, the District of Columbia, Guam, Puerto Rico, and the Virgin Islands, and at least partial survey responses were received from 53 of the 54 jurisdictions. The results of the survey, which are summarized here, are reported by Marlowe et al. (2016).

At year-end 2014, there were 3,057 drug courts in the United States, which was a 24% increase in the number of drug courts over the previous 5 years. Approximately one-third (32%) of the drug courts were successful in diverting graduates from having a criminal record (using either a pre-plea or post-plea model), 27% of the drug courts handled cases as a condition of sentencing, and 41% combined diversion and postsentencing cases. Approximately half (48%) of the drug courts handled felony cases, 9% handled misdemeanor cases, and 43% handled both felony and misdemeanor cases.

Despite the proliferation of drug courts over the past several decades, the PCP Survey revealed that nearly half of US counties did not have an adult drug court. In total, drug courts were estimated to have served more than 125,000 participants in 2014, and nearly 90% of surveyed drug courts indicated that the drug court capacity in their jurisdiction needed to be expanded to accommodate the number of people who need services.

The PCP Survey found an average graduation rate of 59%, with most graduation rates ranging from 50% to 75%. The graduation rate among drug court participants has increased slightly over the past two decades. Early reviews of nearly 100 drug court evaluations found that an average of 60% of drug court clients completed at least 1 year of drug treatment and roughly 50% graduated from the program (Belenko, 1998, 1999, 2001). Of note, drug court graduation rates are approximately two-thirds higher than probation completion rates and twice as high as the probation completion rates for individuals with substance use disorders (see Marlowe et al., 2016).

In terms of demographic characteristics, 67% of the drug court participants were Caucasian and 17% were African American, with 10% reporting as Hispanic. The rates of Caucasian, African American, and Hispanic participants varied greatly across drug courts, largely based on the geographic location of the drug court. Of note, the representation of minority populations in drug courts was lower than the rates of minorities among arrestee, probation, and incarcerated populations. Furthermore, some of the survey data indicated that drug court participants from minority backgrounds graduated at substantially lower rates than Caucasian participants. Approximately one-third of drug court participants were female, and data from approximately 50% of US states and territories indicate that female participants graduated from some drug courts at rates that were substantially lower than those of male drug court participants. There has been some research evaluating if gender-specific programming may remediate this discrepancy, but the results are inconclusive (Marlowe et al., 2016; Messina, Calhoun, & Warda, 2012).

Drugs of choice varied substantially based on the geographic location of the courts. Among urban drug courts, the most common drugs of choice were alcohol (38%), marijuana (22%), and opiates (22%), followed by lower rates of methamphetamine (11%) and cocaine (3%). Suburban drug courts reported that the most common drugs of abuse were opiates (heroin and prescription opioids) (34%), alcohol (29%), methamphetamine (21%), and marijuana (8%). Rural drug courts reported that alcohol (38%), opiates (31%), methamphetamine (21%), and marijuana (10%) were the most common substances. Consistent with drug-use trends in the general population, the majority of drug courts reported an increase in the abuse of prescription medications.

Recidivism

Reducing criminal recidivism is an explicit goal of all problem-solving courts, so most of the drug court research has examined the ability of drug courts to prevent future offending. As will be discussed, the ability of drug courts to reduce criminal recidivism is supported by several systematic reviews, multisite studies, and meta-analyses, and even a few RCTs support the recidivism-reducing impacts of drug courts.

Systematic Reviews and Multisite Studies

In 2001, an early systematic review of drug courts that included 37 published and unpublished studies found that drug courts reduced recidivism considerably more than standard criminal justice interventions (Belenko, 2001). One year later, Belenko (2002a) found that in the majority of evaluation studies that included a suitable comparison group (15 of 21 studies), drug court clients had significantly greater reductions in criminal recidivism compared to offenders on probation.

The U.S. Government Accountability Office (GAO), which is the research arm of the U.S. Congress, has conducted several systematic reviews of drug courts. In an earlier review, the GAO (2005) systematically reviewed 117 evaluations of adult drug courts published between May 1997 and January 2004. Among the 27 evaluations of 39 drug courts that met the GAO criteria for high-quality research, program completion rates varied from 27% to 66%. However, the GAO (2005) concluded that drug courts reduce during-treatment criminal recidivism to a greater degree than do standard criminal justice interventions, such as probation. The GAO (2005) also concluded that drug courts reduce criminal recidivism up to 1 year post program completion, particularly for offenders who completed the drug court program.

The GAO conducted another systematic review of drug courts in 2011 that included 32 drug court programs that received funding from the Bureau of Justice Assistance prior to 2011. Using comparison groups composed of offenders in standard criminal justice processing, the GAO (2011) found significantly lower rates of recidivism among drug court participants in 18 of the 32 studies, with differences in recidivism ranging from 6% to 26%. Notably, reductions in recidivism were considerably higher—12% to 58%—when the GAO limited its analyses to participants who successfully completed the drug court programs (GAO, 2011).

A couple of multisite studies have also provided support for the drug court model in reducing recidivism. The Multisite Adult Drug Court Evaluation (MADCE), which is a large multisite quasi-experimental study (23 sites) conducted by the National Institute of Justice, found a recidivism rate of approximately 13%, which is considerably lower than the average recidivism rate for offenders on probation. Specifically, this study found that drug court participants had significantly lower rates of drug-related crime (e.g., sales, possession, and driving while intoxicated) and reduced property crime (Rempel et al., 2012; Rossman et al., 2011). Another large multisite study (69 sites) found that drug courts reduced recidivism by 32%, although analyses conducted in this study did not control for any variables that could have influenced the results, such as programmatic or population characteristics, which potentially explains why this study found a rate of recidivism reduction than is considerably higher than the rate reported in other studies (Carey, Mackin, & Finigan, 2012).

A recent national multisite study involving 2,295 drug court participants examined factors associated with relapse and recidivism (Wilson, Bandyopadhyay, Yang, Cerulli, & Morse, 2018). Several factors were found to be associated with reduced recidivism. Employed drug court participants were 23 times less likely to be arrested at a 6-month follow-up than unemployed drug court participants and those in community-based treatment (Wilson et al., 2018). Furthermore, for the drug court participants, older age was a protective factor against rearrests (Wilson et al., 2018).

Meta-Analyses

A handful of meta-analyses have examined the effectiveness of drug courts in reducing recidivism. There is a good deal of variability in the meta-analytic findings, but taken together they suggest that drug courts effectively reduce recidivism (see Marlowe et al., 2016). In 2005, the first meta-analysis included 22 studies and found that drug courts reduced recidivism by approximately 8%, although the reduction in recidivism was higher when the analyses were limited to high-risk, high-need participants (Lowenkamp, Holsinger, & Latessa), which is consistent with the Risk-Need-Responsivity (RNR) model.

A meta-analysis by Wilson et al. (2006) examined 50 published and unpublished studies representing 55 drug court programs that used experimental or quasi-experimental designs and involved a comparison group and a measure of criminal activity. Most of the studies reported reductions in reoffending among drug court clients relative to the comparison group, with a 26% reduction in offending across all studies. However, in two high-quality studies, the reduction was 14%. Based on these results, Wilson et al. (2006) concluded that drug court clients are less likely to reoffend than offenders in traditional criminal justice interventions, but they labeled their conclusions as "equivocal" due to the "weak" methodologies used in many of the studies (p. 479).

Another meta-analysis from 2006 included 66 unique drug court studies (Latimer, Morton-Bourgon, & Chrétien, 2006). Notably, this meta-analysis only included drug court evaluations that had either a control/comparison group or sufficient pre- and post-data. Although this meta-analysis was conducted in Canada, a large majority of the evaluations included in the study were from U.S. drug courts. Furthermore, only half of the studies included in the meta-analysis were published in peer-reviewed journals. Very few (13%) utilized an actual random control group, with most being simple or matched comparison groups. Of the control or comparison groups, more than half were comparable justice populations, with fewer studies using eligible nonparticipants or dropouts of drug courts. This meta-analysis also noted extremely high attrition rates in the studies it analyzed, with on average more than half of participants dropping out of the drug court program (ranging from 9% to 84%). The studies also included a large range in available follow-up data (3–18 months), and the studies with a longer follow-up period tended to have higher recidivism rates, likely due to the increased opportunity to reoffend. Overall, this study reported an average recidivism decrease of 9% among drug court participants (Latimer et al., 2006).[1]

A 2011 meta-analysis by Shaffer was unique in that it utilized existing study data and merged survey data to better assess factors that moderate drug court success. This meta-analysis evaluated 60 studies of 76 unique drug courts. Of the 60 studies, 18 were included in the Lowenkamp et al. (2005) meta-analysis and 30 were included in the Wilson et al. (2006) meta-analysis. Surveys of drug court personnel (via telephone interviews) were used to fill in missing data. Consistent with previous meta-analyses, Shaffer (2011) found an approximate recidivism reduction of 9%. It is perhaps not surprising that this study found results similar to previous meta-analyses because it only used resources (published and unpublished) from January 2006 and earlier.

A more recent meta-analysis on drug courts was conducted in 2012 by Mitchell and colleagues. This was by far the largest meta-analysis, with 92 drug court studies. Results revealed an average reduction in recidivism of 12%. These recidivism rates were lower for drug courts with higher graduation rates and for drug courts that accepted nonviolent and lower risk offenders (Mitchell et al., 2012).

Several studies, systematic reviews, and meta-analyses have also examined the long-term reductions in recidivism associated with drug court participation. For example, two RCTs (Gottfredson, Kearley, Najaka, & Rocha, 2005; Gottfredson, Najaka, Kearley, & Rocha, 2006) and one meta-analysis (Mitchell et al., 2012) found that reductions in recidivism lasted for 3 years following completion of the drug court program. One long-term quasi-experimental study of more than 11,000 individuals in an Oregon drug court found that reductions in recidivism lasted up to 14 years (Finigan, Carey, & Cox, 2007). Although limited, these studies suggest that the recidivism-reducing effects of drug courts can last for many years after program participation ends.

Randomized Controlled Trials

There have also been a few RCTs examining the effects of drugs courts on criminal recidivism. In the research design and methodology hierarchy, RCTs are

[1] A third meta-analysis published in 2006 examined 57 drug court studies and found an average recidivism reduction of 8% (Aos, Miller, & Drake, 2006). This meta-analysis was published as part of a larger government report and included a recidivism rate and cost-benefit analysis (discussed later) (see Marlowe et al., 2016). Additional information about the study results could not be located.

viewed as the gold standard (see Kazdin, 2017). By eliminating or minimizing confounding variables and competing hypotheses, RCTs permit the strongest and most defensible inferences of causality. Because RCTs require randomly assigning participants to treatment conditions, it is perhaps not surprising that there are so few RCTs of drugs courts or other types of problem-solving courts. There are financial and ethical considerations relating to the random assignment of offenders that limit the use of these types of research designs. We discuss the ethical considerations that are relevant to conducting research in problem-solving courts in Chapter 9.

The first RCT of a drug court program was conducted in 1995 in Maricopa County, Arizona, by Deschenes, Turner, and Greenwood. The Maricopa County Drug Court is a postadjudication program for individuals on probation for a first-time drug-related felony, and all treatment is provided on an outpatient basis. During 1992 and 1993, more than 600 offenders were randomly assigned to either drug court or standard probation (treatment as usual). During a 12-month monitoring period, there was no significant difference in rearrest rates between the two groups, although drug court participants had significantly fewer probation violations (Deschenes et al., 1995). However, this finding may be attributable to the way in which positive drug screens were categorized by the drug court. Specifically, the drug court classified technical violations, such as positive drug screens, as being a clinical issue rather than an actual program violation. There was, however, a long-term positive impact associated with participation in drug court, and drug court participants had a significantly lower rearrest rate within 3 years of discharge from drug court compared to offenders on probation (33% vs. 47%) (Deschenes et al., 1995). A follow-up study assessed the drug court participants' perceptions of the court's impact on their offending and drug use behavior, and the results revealed that participants believed the drug court helped them avoid criminal behavior but that it was less useful in helping them remain abstinent from drugs (Turner, Greenwood, Fain, & Deschenes, 1999). However, given that only 29 participants provided qualitative data, the results should be interpreted with caution.

A later RCT conducted in the Washington DC Superior Court's Drug Treatment Court included offenders with felony drug charges who were randomly assigned to one of three dockets: sanctions program (case management–assisted program with mandatory treatment sanctions for positive drug tests), intervention court (a drug treatment court model), and a standard docket (voluntary treatment along with general court supervision, which constituted "treatment as usual") (Harrell, Cavanagh, & Roman, 1998). Results revealed that self-reported criminal behavior was significantly lower in the 1 year following sentencing for both experimental dockets (sanctions docket and intervention docket) than it was for the standard docket (Harrell et al., 1998).

Finally, participants in the Baltimore Drug Treatment Court were randomly assigned to either drug treatment court or standard court processing (Gottfredson & Exum, 2002). At 1 year following admission, drug court participants (48%) were significantly less likely to have been rearrested than offenders who went through standard court processing (64%) (Gottfredson & Exum, 2002). The lower rates of rearrest for drug court participants held at 2 years post-admission, with rearrest rates of 66% for drug court participants and 81% for offenders who went through standard court processing (Gottfredson, Najaka, & Kearly, 2003). When limited to drug-related offenses, the rearrest rates were 41% for drug court clients and 54% of the comparison group (Gottfredson et al., 2003). A 3-year follow-up study found that the lower rates of recidivism were maintained for the drug court participants compared to offenders who went through standard court processing (Gottfredson et al., 2005, 2006).

Summary

Taken together, the results of the systematic reviews, multisite studies, meta-analyses, and limited RCTs suggest that drug courts reduce recidivism by 8% to 14% within 2 years of drug court involvement (see Marlowe et al., 2016). However, given the nature of systematic reviews and meta-analyses, which combine results from multiple studies, it is difficult to assess the variability among the individual studies. Individual drug courts have produced an exceedingly large range of success rates. Although the average recidivism reduction is between 8% and 14%, some drug courts have reported reductions in recidivism of 80% (see Carey et al., 2012). Moreover, not all studies support the recidivism-reducing effects of drug courts. As noted by Marlowe et al. (2016), research suggests that approximately 15% of adult drug courts have no significant impact on recidivism, and a small percentage of programs (6%) have been associated with increases in criminal behavior (Lowenkamp et al., 2005; Shaffer, 2011). Nevertheless, the weight of the empirical evidence overwhelmingly suggests that drug courts reduce recidivism more than standard criminal justice interventions.

Substance Use

Reducing criminal recidivism is the top priority of drug courts, as it is with all problem-solving courts. The primary means by which drug courts seek to reduce recidivism is through addressing participants' substance use problems. As previously discussed, the idea behind drug courts is that effectively treating an offender's substance use problem will in turn reduce the likelihood that the offender will engage in criminal behavior. This philosophy makes sense given the well-established relationship between substance use and crime.

Numerous studies and meta-analyses suggest that drug use is a robust risk factor for both criminal behavior and criminal recidivism (see DeMatteo et al., 2015, for a review of the relevant literature). For example, in their review of 30 studies, Bennett, Holloway, and Farrington (2008) concluded that individuals who reported drug use were 2.79 times more likely to engage in criminal behavior than individuals who did not report using drugs. In their meta-analysis examining the association between illegal drug use and criminal recidivism, Dowden and Brown (2002) reported a mean effect size of .19 for general recidivism and .14 for violent recidivism. Some research has suggested that continued substance use is associated with a 200–400% increase in the likelihood of recidivism (Bennett et al., 2008; Kopak, Hoffman, & Proctor, 2016; Walters, 2015).

The majority of the outcome research on drug courts has focused on its effectiveness in reducing recidivism, and there is surprisingly little research on the effects of drug courts in reducing relapse to drug use. Although some individual studies have looked at relapse to drug use, many of the meta-analyses and large-scale research studies reviewed in this chapter examined recidivism, but not relapse to drug use, as an outcome measure. In their large meta-analysis, Mitchell et al. (2012) commented on the noticeable lack of research on the impact of drug courts in reducing substance use. Of the 92 studies included in the Mitchell et al. (2012) analysis, only 9 incorporated a measure of drug court participants' substance use in follow-up data.

With these caveats in mind, we review the available research on the effects of drug courts in reducing relapse to drug use. In an early review, Belenko (2002a) found that in the majority of studies that included a suitable comparison group, drug court participants had a significantly greater reduction in drug use than offenders on standard probation or intensive supervised probation. The magnitude of the during-treatment effects ranged from 20 to 30 percentage points, while the magnitude of the posttreatment effects of drug courts on subsequent drug use ranged from 10 to 20 percentage points (Belenko, 2002a).

In its review of 117 evaluations of drug courts, the GAO (2005) concluded there was mixed evidence supporting the effectiveness of drug courts in reducing relapse to drug use. This conclusion was based on 27 evaluations of 39 drug courts that met GAO criteria for methodological soundness. Furthermore, the GAO (2005) noted that the majority of drug court evaluation studies used weak research designs (see Marlowe, DeMatteo, & Festinger, 2003, for a detailed discussion of this point). For example, some drug court evaluation studies used overly brief follow-up periods following graduation or termination, while other studies used questionable comparison samples, such as offenders who refused, were deemed ineligible for, or dropped out of the interventions. Other studies did not conduct intent-to-treat analyses and instead excluded participants who were terminated or absconded from the program. The GAO (2005) suggested that these methodological weaknesses may have led to an overestimation of positive outcomes, particularly when the analyses were restricted to the most successful cases in the drug courts.

In its 2011 review of 32 studies, the GAO summarized relapse data for 8 programs that compared the relapse data (either via drug tests or self-report) of drug court participants with a comparison group. The GAO (2011) concluded that drug court participants were less likely to use drugs than offenders in the comparison groups, but that the difference in relapse rates did not always achieve statistical significance. The GAO (2011) also noted that the results were the same for both within-program and postprogram measures. These results support the utility of drug courts in reducing relapse to drug use compared to standard criminal justice processing, but they raise questions regarding the magnitude of the reductions in relapse achieved by drug courts.

The previously discussed MADCE found that drug court participation was associated with significant reductions in relapse among drug court participants (Green & Rempel, 2012; Rossman et al., 2011). Results of the MADCE revealed that 29% of drug court participants tested positive for illicit drugs at 18 months postprogram completion, compared to 46% of the comparison group, and drug court participants also used drugs less frequently than offenders in the comparison group (Rempel et al., 2012). Importantly, drug court participation was not the sole factor that contributed to lower rates of relapse among drug court participants; the MADCE results revealed that less frequent drug use prior to arrest and the absence of mental health problems were also strong predictors of lower relapse rates (Rossman et al., 2011).

Finally, the RCT conducted in the Washington DC Superior Court's Drug Treatment Court looked at relapse to drug use in addition to recidivism (Harrell et al., 1998). As previously discussed, offenders with felony drug charges were randomly assigned to either a sanctions program (case management–assisted program with mandatory treatment sanctions for positive drug tests), intervention court (drug treatment court), or standard docket (Harrell et al., 1998). Results revealed that participation in both experimental dockets—sanctions program and intervention court—resulted in reductions in drug use during participants' time in the court, but there were no significant differences in self-reported drug use in the 1 year following sentencing (Harrell et al., 1998).

As the present review suggests, there is mixed evidence regarding the ability of drug courts to prevent relapse to drug use. When compared to the robust empirical literature regarding the effects of drug courts on reducing recidivism, the empirical literature on preventing relapse is clearly less well developed and more equivocal. With that said, the weight of the available evidence suggests that drug courts effectively reduce future drug use, even if many of the results were not statistically significant and some of the effect sizes were small in magnitude (see Mitchell et al., 2012).

Other Outcomes

Reducing recidivism and relapse to drug use are the main goals of drug courts, so most research has looked at the effects of drug courts on these outcomes. These outcomes have the most relevance to the goals of the broader criminal justice system, and the success of criminal justice interventions for drug-involved offenders is typically measured by examining the effects of the intervention on recidivism and relapse.

Some researchers have, however, examined other outcomes. For example, Sevigny, Fuleihan, and Ferdik (2013) conducted a meta-analysis ($k = 19$) to examine the impact of drug courts on rates and length of incarceration. They found that drug courts significantly reduced the *rates* of incarceration for the precipitating offense, but not the *length* of incarceration. Notably, this study also found that individuals who do not successfully complete drug court face lengthy jail or prison sentences and an increased period of intensive community supervision, which may ultimately be longer than the initial sentence would have been if the individual had declined to participate in drug court and instead proceeded with standard criminal justice processing (Sevigny et al., 2013).

One goal of drug courts is to provide a range of needed services to participants, and some research suggests that drug courts are achieving some success in this regard. Results of the MADCE revealed that drug courts improve access to treatment and educational/vocational services for offenders and that they have a positive impact on family relationships (Green & Rempel, 2012; Rossman et al., 2011). Additionally, drug court participants in the 23 courts included in the MADCE were more likely to be enrolled in educational training after 6 months, although this finding did not persist at later follow-up (Rossman et al., 2011). The MADCE also found that the positive impact on family relationships and other psychosocial factors can last for up to 18 months following completion of the drug court program (Rossman et al., 2011).

Research on the relationship between drug courts and outcomes such as housing, finances, and mental health, although limited, suggests that drug courts do not have a positive impact on these areas (Rossman et al., 2011). The MADCE found, for example, that participation in drug court does not reduce rates of homelessness. There were some differences between drug court participants and nonparticipants in their annual income, but the differences were modest and not statistically significant. Additionally, drug courts have not been shown to reduce mental health symptoms, and the MADCE concluded that drug courts may be less effective in promoting abstinence for individuals with co-occurring mental health concerns (Rossman et al., 2011).

There is mixed evidence regarding the cost effectiveness of drug courts. Earlier research found that drug courts produce significant cost savings over traditional criminal justice interventions (see Belenko, Patapis, & French, 2005, for a review). One of the earlier meta-analyses included a cost-benefit analysis and found that drug courts save crime victims approximately $5,000 per participant, save taxpayers approximately $4,300 per participant, and cost approximately $1,600 per participant, which yields a net benefit of $7,800 per participant (Aos et al., 2006). Later research also supported the cost effectiveness of drug courts. Bhati, Roman, and Chalfin (2008) found that for every $1 invested, drug courts produce $2.21 in benefits to the criminal justice system, and the rate of return was even higher when drug courts targeted higher risk offenders ($3.36 for every $1 invested). Although earlier research suggested that the net economic benefit to local communities ranged from $3,000 to $13,000 per drug court client (Logan et al., 2004), results from the GAO (2011) report were mixed. The GAO (2011), which reviewed 11 studies that provided cost-benefit data, concluded that the net benefit ranged from positive $47,852 to negative $7,108 for each drug court client, which suggests that some drug courts included in its analysis were not cost effective.

Success in Drug Court

As research supporting the effectiveness of drug courts has accumulated over the past few decades, researchers have begun taking a more nuanced look at the factors that are associated with participant success. Some research suggests that specific participant-level characteristics are associated with greater success in drug courts, while other research has examined certain features of the drug court model. Given that most of the available research is correlational, the factors associated with success in drug court should be viewed as correlates as opposed to predictors, although it is possible that some of these correlates are also functioning as predictors. There have also been several RCTs of drug courts that have identified predictors of drug court success.

Regardless of the drug court model, the use of incentives appears to be a key element that is associated with higher graduation rates (e.g., reduction or expungement of charges) (Wilson et al., 2006; Young & Belenko, 2002). The length of the drug court program is also an important factor. One study found that treatment length, which was dichotomized into under 1 year and over 1 year, was not related to success in the drug court program (Lowenkamp et al., 2005). However, Latimer and colleagues (2006) found that drug courts that provided services for

12–18 months were associated with lower recidivism rates than were shorter programs. With that said, the 95% confidence interval for shorter programs included zero, so the actual effect of shorter programs remains unclear.

A variety of factors relevant to drug court programs appear to be differentially associated with participant success. For example, Shaffer's (2011) meta-analysis of 60 studies of 76 drug courts revealed that court characteristics such as target population, program leverage, treatment intensity, and staff characteristics account for most of the variability in drug court effectiveness. The success of drug courts also appears to be moderated by the court's adherence to treatment objectives. One meta-analysis ($k = 38$) reported fairly strong correlations (*r*s ranging from .26 to .42) between program integrity and reductions in recidivism (Lowenkamp, Latessa, & Smith, 2006). Specifically, Lowenkamp, Latessa, and Smith (2006) found that program implementation, offender assessment, and evaluation are all related to the effectiveness of drug court programs. Finally, research suggests that the use of evidence-based practices in both assessment and intervention is associated with greater reductions in recidivism (Carey et al., 2012; Shaffer, 2011). Of note, several of these program-related characteristics are captured in the NADCP's (1997) 10 key components of drug courts.

An interesting line of research has examined the role of the judge in the success of drug court programs. The MADCE concluded that the judge is crucial to the success of drug courts, and participants who were surveyed after participation in drug court reported that positive perceptions of the judge were related to reduced recidivism and decreased substance use at an 18-month follow-up (Rempel et al., 2012). In a series of RCTs in misdemeanor and felony drug courts throughout the state of Delaware, a group of researchers led by one of the nation's foremost experts in drug courts (Dr. Douglas Marlowe) examined the effects of judicial status hearings, which is often viewed as the defining element of drug courts (Marlowe, Festinger, & Lee, 2003, 2004). Results revealed that high-risk drug courts participants, who were defined as those who met *Diagnostic and Statistical Manual of Mental Disorders* (DSM-IV; American Psychiatric Association, 1994) criteria for antisocial personality disorder (APD) or had a history of drug treatment achieved more drug abstinence and higher rates of graduation when they attended more frequent status hearings, whereas low-risk clients (i.e., no APD or prior drug treatment) performed equivalently or better when assigned to attend status hearings only in response to serious or repeated program infractions (Festinger et al., 2002; Marlowe, Festinger, et al., 2003, 2004). Subsequently, these results were replicated in a prospective study in which drug court clients were matched to an optimal level of status hearings based on their risk level and compared to clients who were randomly assigned to a standard hearing schedule (Marlowe, Festinger, Lee, Dugosh, & Benasutti, 2006). These results support the important role of the judge, but also highlight the importance of providing an appropriate dose of status hearings to participants.

Only a few studies have examined the relationship between participant-level characteristics and drug court success. Although young age is a risk factor for criminal offending, the results of two meta-analyses suggest that age is not significantly related to success in drug court (Latimer et al., 2006; Lowenkamp et al., 2005). One study showed that the risk level of participants had a significant impact on the effects of drug court intervention, with the effectiveness of drug courts nearly doubling when 50% or more of the participants in the court had a prior criminal record (Lowenkamp et al., 2005).

Methodological and Research-Based Limitations

As with most studies that are conducted in the context of real-world interventions, and particularly for studies that include justice-involved individuals, there are a variety of methodological limitations in drug court studies. One limitation is the differences in follow-up length in the studies included in the meta-analyses previously reviewed. In their 2006 meta-analysis, Latimer et al. found that studies with longer follow-up periods generally reported higher recidivism rates, likely because of the increased time at risk. With that said, the recidivism rates were still generally lower for drug court participants compared to the comparison groups over longer lengths of time (Latimer et al., 2006).

There are several specific aspects of the methodology used to study drug courts that may impact the study results. Latimer et al. (2006) noted that the studies in their meta-analysis involving random assignment generally reported less favorable effects for drug courts compared to studies that used quasi-experimental designs. The 95% confidence intervals for the RCTs in their meta-analysis included zero, so it unclear whether the effects of drug courts are maintained when random assignment is used. Furthermore, the choice of comparison group can obviously affect the results. Studies that used program noncompleters or those who dropped out of the program showed greater differences than studies that used eligible offenders who chose not to participate in drug court (Latimer et al., 2006). Another meta-analysis concluded that there was a greater recidivism reduction for drug courts that only accepted nonviolent offenders (Mitchell et al., 2012). Finally, research on drug courts may be compromised in some studies because drug courts (a) often select the most easily treatable offenders for admission to the program, (b) typically only retain 40–60% of eligible offenders, and (c) may lack significant long-term postintervention follow-up, particularly for those individuals who elect not to participate in the program or fail to complete the program (Fischer, 2003). A more detailed discussion of the methodological limitations involved in problem-solving court research is provided in Chapter 8.

Juvenile Drug Courts

Each year, nearly 250,000 teenagers are arrested for alcohol- or drug-related offenses (Puzzanchera, 2013). Notably, recidivism rates for youth in the juvenile justice system are high (approximately 70%) (Mulder, Brand, Bullens, & van Marle, 2011), and substance use tends to be a significant predictor of rearrest (Baglivio, 2009; D'Amico, Edelen, Miles, & Morral, 2008). Programming intended to reduce the high rates of recidivism and substance use among teenagers has often backfired. Research has shown, for example, that standard juvenile justice case processing, juvenile detention, and programs such as "Scared Straight" can actually increase recidivism by 6–8% (Aos et al., 2006; Drake, Aos, & Miller., 2009; Lipsey, 2009; Petrosino, Turpin-Petrosino, & Finckenauer, 2000; Petrosino, Turpin-Petrosino, Hollis-Peel, & Lavenberg, 2013).

A defining feature of traditionally used interventions with justice-involved youth is group treatment, but research suggests that it may be contraindicated in some contexts because it can paradoxically function as "deviancy training" (e.g., Dishion & Andrews, 1995). For example, several studies have found that aggregating adolescents who were high risk in group treatment led to increases in delinquency, drug use, and violence at 1-year and 3-year follow-ups (Dishion & Andrews, 1995; Poulin, Dishion, & Burraston, 2001). Other research has found that mixing adolescents who are high risk and adolescents who are low risk has a more pronounced negative effect on the offenders who are low risk (e.g., Petrosino et al., 2000). Some have hypothesized that these results are attributable to the socialization of adolescents who are low risk into an antisocial milieu in which they adopt the values and attitudes of deviant peers who have relatively greater influence in the group (see DeMatteo, Marlowe, & Festinger, 2006).

The increasing numbers of justice-involved adolescents with alcohol- or drug-related offenses, combined with the limited success of traditional juvenile justice interventions, led to the development of juvenile drug courts. Modeled after adult drug courts, the first juvenile drug court was opened in 1995 in Visalia, California. Like their adult counterparts, juvenile drug courts attempt to reduce recidivism by combining treatment and intensive judicial and clinical supervision. Juvenile drug courts have many of the same features as adult drug courts, including regularly scheduled status hearings, random and frequent drug testing, and the use of incentives and sanctions, and graduates can have their charges dropped or reduced or avoid detention (see Marlowe et al., 2016). Juvenile drug courts have 16 defining features/strategies (National Drug Court

Institute and National Council of Juvenile and Family Court Judges, 2003), which were adapted from the 10 key components of drug courts identified by the NADCP (1997).

Juvenile drug courts were designed to serve adolescents charged with delinquency offenses that were caused or influenced by substance use, and they also serve adolescents who have co-occurring mental health disorders. The 2014 PCP survey reported data on the substances most commonly seen in juvenile drug courts (Marlowe et al., 2016). Across juvenile drug courts, regardless of the setting (urban, suburban, or rural), marijuana was by far the primary drug of abuse, followed by lower rates of use of alcohol, pharmaceutical opiates, and other drugs. Furthermore, alcohol was the second most common drug of abuse across all drug courts, with rates of 33% in urban drug courts, 25% in suburban drug courts, and 30% in rural drug courts.

Unfortunately, the research on juvenile drug courts suggests that they are less successful than adult drug courts. Several early meta-analyses reported average reductions in recidivism of less than 5% (Aos et al., 2006; Latimer et al., 2006; Wilson et al., 2006), and more recent meta-analyses reported a slightly higher average reduction in recidivism of 8%, which is an obvious improvement but still a relatively small effect (Mitchell et al., 2012; Stein, Deberard, & Homan, 2015; see Stein, Deberard, & Homan, 2013). Although the reasons for the limited success of juvenile drug courts are not entirely clear, some researchers have speculated that juvenile drug courts achieve less success because they are targeting the wrong population of offenders (e.g., low-risk, low-need youth) and are less likely to use evidenced-based practices (see Marlowe et al., 2016). In their review of nine juvenile drug courts, Latessa, Sullivan, Blair, Sullivan, and Smith (2013) reported that 77% of the programs were not using evidence-based practices or adhering to the RNR model. Another study of 26 juvenile drug courts found that only approximately 25% of the courts were collecting participant outcome data (Yelderman, 2016), which has hampered the ability of courts and researchers to evaluate the effectiveness of these courts.

The limited success of the juvenile drug court model may explain why these courts have not experienced the same level of growth as adult drug courts. Less than 20% of the 3,201 surveyed counties in the PCP survey had a juvenile drug court (Marlowe et al., 2016), and the number of juvenile drug courts has been steadily declining in recent years. At year-end 2009, there were 476 juvenile drug courts in the United States, and that number declined to 420 by year-end 2014 (Marlowe et al., 2016). A 12% reduction in the number of juvenile drug courts over a 5-year period is quite substantial, and further examination regarding the reasons juvenile drug courts are becoming less common is needed to see if this trend can—and should—be reversed.

Best Practices in Drug Courts

Drug courts have been in existence for nearly 30 years, and, as previously noted, there is more research on the effectiveness of drug courts than on any other intervention for drug-involved offenders (see Marlowe et al., 2016). The identification of best practices for adult drug courts has been facilitated by the large body of empirical drug court research, which has highlighted the features of drug court programs that are most associated with and predictive of participant success. In recent years, the NADCP (2013, 2015, 2018a, 2018b) published 10 best practice standards to guide the development and operation of drug courts. NADCP's (2013, 2015, 2018a, 2018b) best practice standards were developed by consensus by a multidisciplinary committee of drug court experts and then reviewed by a large group of practitioners and researchers for clarity, justification, and feasibility.

Best Practice Standard 1—Target Population: Eligibility and exclusion criteria for the Drug Court are predicated on empirical evidence indicating which types of offenders can be treated safely and effectively in Drug Courts. Candidates are evaluated for admission to the Drug Court using evidence-based assessment tools and procedures. This standard emphasizes the importance of ensuring that drug courts are targeting the appropriate population of drug-involved offenders. Marlowe et al. (2016) noted that targeting the wrong population of offenders is a primary reason that some drug courts have achieved limited success. Ideally, drug courts use objective eligibility and exclusion criteria and validated eligibility assessments to identify offenders who are addicted to drugs or alcohol and at substantial risk for reoffending.

Best Practice Standard 2—Equity and Inclusion: Individuals who have historically experienced sustained discrimination or reduced social opportunities because of their race, ethnicity, gender, sexual orientation, sexual identity, physical or mental disability, religion, or socioeconomic status receive the same opportunities as other individuals to participate and succeed in the Drug Court. Because drug courts are courts of law, they must be guided by constitutional principles of due process and equal protection (see Meyer, 2011, and Chapter 9). Among other considerations, the eligibility criteria used by drug courts should be nondiscriminatory and aimed at promoting equal access to drug court services for all offenders, regardless of race, ethnicity, gender, sexual orientation or identity, physical or mental disability, religion, or socioeconomic status. Drug courts should also monitor retention rates to see if participants from minority backgrounds are disproportionately not completing the drug court program. Furthermore, drug courts should provide equivalent treatment, incentives, sanctions, and dispositions to all participants.

Best Practice Standard 3—Roles and Responsibilities of the Judge: The Drug Court judge stays abreast of current law and research on best practices in Drug Courts, participates regularly in team meetings, interacts frequently and respectfully with participants, and gives due consideration to the input of other team members. Drug court judges should have current knowledge of legal issues relevant to drug courts, judicial ethics, substance abuse and mental health treatment, behavior modification strategies, and community supervision. Also, to maintain consistency and facilitate the development of judge–participant relationships, it is recommended that drug court judges serve for at least 2 years. As the leader of the treatment team, the judge should attend pre-court staff meetings in which each participant's progress is reviewed by the team members. As a defining feature of drug courts, regular judicial status hearings should be held at least every 4 weeks, or more frequently if indicated for certain subsets of participants, and the judge should spend time during the hearings interacting with the participants. Furthermore, because drug courts use a nonadversarial approach, the judge should be supportive and encouraging while also imposing sanctions as needed in response to noncompliant behavior by participants (see Meyer & Tauber, 2011, for a detailed discussion of the varied roles of the judge in drug courts).

Best Practice Standard 4—Incentives, Sanctions, and Therapeutic Adjustments: Consequences for participants' behavior are predictable, fair, consistent, and administered in accordance with evidence-based principles of effective behavior modification. The imposition of incentives and sanctions should be preceded by advanced notice to all participants of the rules and policies of the court. The judge also provides participants with an opportunity to explain their views and behaviors before imposing incentives, sanctions, and therapeutic adjustments. Furthermore, the use of incentives and sanctions should be governed by established principles of behavioral modification (see Marlowe, 2011, for a discussion of the application of incentives and sanctions in drug courts).

Best Practice Standard 5—Substance Use Disorder Treatment: Participants receive substance use disorder treatment based on a standardized assessment of their treatment needs. Substance use disorder treatment is not provided to reward desired behaviors, punish infractions, or serve other nonclinically indicated goals. Treatment providers are trained and supervised to deliver a continuum of evidence-based interventions that are documented in treatment manuals. Among other services, drug courts should offer a range of treatments aimed at reducing substance abuse, including detoxification, residential treatment, day treatment programs, and intensive inpatient and outpatient services. Drug court participants should also receive an appropriate dose of evidence-based treatment over the course of their participation in the program, which is defined as approximately 200 hours of counseling over 9–12 months, provided through individual counseling, group interventions (if appropriate), and self-help groups. The use of prescribed medications, including psychotropic medications for mental health disorders and medications to address drug addiction (e.g., opioid antagonists), should be provided as needed by a physician with appropriate expertise. Finally, the drug court should facilitate the establishment of a continuing care plan focusing on relapse prevention for when the participant completes the program.

Best Practice Standard 6—Complementary Treatment and Social Services: Participants receive complementary treatment and social services for conditions that co-occur with substance use disorder and are likely to interfere with their compliance in Drug Court, increase criminal recidivism, or diminish treatment gains. As previously noted, although drug courts primarily target substance abuse, they also seek to address a range of other service needs that could decrease the likelihood of success in the program and afterward. Some of the services that should be considered include mental health treatment, treatment for those who have experienced trauma, interventions that target criminal thinking, educational/vocational counseling, and education to reduce risky health behaviors. By maintaining a broad scope of services, drug courts can effectively target responsivity needs, criminogenic needs, and maintenance needs.

Best Practice Standard 7—Drug and Alcohol Testing: Drug and alcohol testing provides an accurate, timely, and comprehensive assessment of unauthorized substance use throughout participants' enrollment in the Drug Court. The imposition of incentives and sanctions is based largely on participants' drug use behavior, so obtaining accurate, timely, and objective information on whether participants are abstinent from prohibited substances is essential to the successful operation of drug courts. Drug testing should be frequent, random, and consistent with best practices for detecting drug use (see Cary, 2011).

Best Practice Standard 8—Multidisciplinary Team: A dedicated multidisciplinary team of professionals manages the day-to-day operations of the Drug Court, including reviewing participant progress during pre-court staff meetings and status hearings, contributing observations and recommendations within team members' respective areas of expertise, and delivering or overseeing the delivery of legal, treatment and supervision services. The drug court team, which ideally include the judge, drug court coordinator, prosecutor, defense attorney, treatment provider representatives, community supervision officer representatives, and law enforcement representatives, should hold regularly scheduled pre-court meetings to review participant progress through the sharing of information from all team members. The treatment team should also be in attendance at regularly scheduled judicial status hearings at which each participant's progress is reviewed in open court. The multidisciplinary nature of the team helps to ensure that proper consideration is being given to the participant's needs and rights.

Best Practice Standard 9—Census and Caseloads: The Drug Court serves as many eligible individuals as practicable while maintaining continuous fidelity to best practice standards. Despite the proliferation of drug courts over the past several decades, it is estimated that they serve less than 10% of adults in the criminal justice system in need of their services (Bhati et al., 2008; Marlowe et al., 2016). Given the number of drug-involved offenders in the United States, drug courts should strive to treat all eligible offenders. With that said, drug courts with 125 or more active participants are encouraged to carefully monitor their operations to assess whether they are adhering to best-practice standards. The caseloads for community supervision officers (e.g., probation officers) and clinicians must be appropriate in size to permit sufficient attention to each participant. It is recommended that caseloads exceeding 30 participants for community supervision officers should trigger an examination of drug court resources and adherence to best practices. A similar examination of resources and fidelity to best practices should occur if clinician caseloads exceed 50 active participants for clinicians providing clinical case management, 40 active participants for clinicians providing individual therapy or counseling, and 30 active participants for clinicians providing both clinical case management and individual therapy or counseling.

Best Practice Standard 10—Monitoring and Evaluation: The Drug Court routinely monitors its adherence to best practice standards and employs scientifically valid and reliable procedures to evaluate its effectiveness. The continued success of drug courts depends in large part on the willingness of drug courts to be evaluated by independent researchers. Evaluations of drug courts should include both process and outcome variables, with a focus on adherence to best practices and the impact of drug courts on reducing recidivism and substance use, improving participants' mental health functioning, and addressing other areas of need that are common among drug court participants.

In addition to NADCP, several researchers have identified best practices for drug courts. Based on their review of 69 drug courts, Carey et al. (2012) identified the 10 best practices for reducing recidivism (in order from largest to smallest effect size):

1. Drug courts with a caseload of less than 125 had more than five times greater reductions in recidivism than programs with more participants.
2. Drug courts in which participants needed more than 90 days of drug-abstinence before graduation had 164% greater reductions in recidivism than programs that required less clean time.

3. Drug courts in which the judge spent an average of 3 or more minutes with each participant during status hearing had 153% greater reductions in recidivism than programs where the judge spent less time.
4. Drug courts in which treatment providers communicated with the court or treatment team via email had 119% greater reductions in recidivism.
5. Drug courts in which a treatment representative attended pre-court team meetings had 105% greater reductions in recidivism.
6. Drug courts in which internal reviews led to program modifications had 105% greater reductions in recidivism.
7. Drug courts in which a treatment representative attended status hearings had 100% greater reductions in recidivism.
8. Drug courts that admitted offenders with nondrug charges (e.g., theft, forgery) had 95% greater reductions in recidivism than drug courts that only accepted participants charged with drug offenses.
9. Drug courts with a law enforcement representative on the treatment team had 88% greater reductions in recidivism than programs that did not have such a representative.
10. drug courts that had evaluations conducted by independent evaluators and used them to make modifications in their operations had 85% greater reductions in recidivism than programs that did not use evaluation results to modify their programs.

Carey et al. (2012) also identified the 10 best practices related to cost savings. As can be seen, some of these best practices overlap with the best practices for reducing recidivism. In order from largest to smallest effect size, the 10 best practices are:

1. Drug courts that use internal reviews of data to modify their programs had 131% higher cost savings.
2. Drug courts that use evaluations conducted by independent evaluators to modify their operation had 100% greater cost savings.
3. Drug courts that imposed sanctions immediately after participant noncompliance had 100% greater cost savings.
4. Drug courts in which the defense attorney attended pre-court team meetings had 93% greater cost savings.
5. Drug courts in which participants must have a job or be enrolled in school as a prerequisite to graduation from the drug court program had 83% greater cost savings.
6. Drug courts in which a treatment representative attended status hearings had 81% greater cost savings.

7. Drug courts in which treatment team members are given a copy of the guidelines for sanctions had 72% greater cost savings.
8. Drug courts in which drug test results were available within 48 hours had 68% greater cost savings.
9. Drug courts in which drug tests were conducted at least twice per week during the first phase of the program had 68% greater cost savings.
10. Drug courts in which a law enforcement representative attended the regularly scheduled judicial status hearings had 64% greater cost savings.

Several other best practices for reducing recidivism are worth noting. The MADCE found that drug courts that most effectively reduced recidivism held judicial status hearings twice per month, held weekly clinical case management meetings, conducted drug testing on participants twice per week, provided at least 35 days of formal substance abuse treatment, and incorporated positive encouragement into judicial status hearings (Rossman et al., 2011). Another study found that multiweek jail sanctions for positive drug tests, nonindividualized treatment plans, and not providing appropriate medication had a negative impact on recidivism and other outcomes (Gutierrez & Bourgon, 2012).

Next Steps

Drug courts have proliferated quite extensively over the past several decades, and they have become a firmly entrenched intervention in the United States and elsewhere. The results of hundreds of individual research studies, along with program evaluations, multisite studies, and meta-analyses, provide strong support for the effectiveness of drug courts in reducing recidivism among drug-involved offenders. Although somewhat less robust, there is also considerable research supporting the effectiveness of drug courts in reducing relapse to drug use and effectively targeting other important outcomes (e.g., mental health functioning, rates of incarceration, access to treatment and other services).

Despite the proliferation and success of drug courts, there are several important future directions in both research and practice. A primary consideration is expanding the reach of drug courts. As noted, drug courts serve less than 10% of eligible offenders (Bhati et al., 2008; Marlowe et al., 2016), and the PCP survey revealed that nearly half (44%) of all counties in the United States did not have an adult drug court, and 87% of the survey respondents indicated that the drug court capacity in their jurisdiction needs to be expanded to meet their current need (Marlowe et al., 2016). As with many criminal justice initiatives, the primary barrier to the expansion of drug courts is lack of resources, particularly in terms of insufficient funding, treatment, and supervision (Marlowe et al., 2016). Hopefully, the bipartisan support that drug courts have received in Congress will translate into increased funding for drug courts and other problem-solving courts.

Although drug courts strive to be accessible to all eligible offenders, there is some evidence that the representation of minority populations in drug courts is lower than the rates of minorities among arrestee, probation, and incarcerated populations (see Marlowe et al., 2016). The reason for this discrepancy needs to be identified, and researchers are therefore encouraged to address this important issue. Several explanations are possible. For example, given that drug court eligibility is largely determined based on current charges, it is possible that biased charging practices in some jurisdictions are decreasing the number of offenders from minority backgrounds who are determined to be eligible for drug court. Another possibility is that the drug court gatekeepers—typically local prosecutors—are not offering admission to drug court to equivalent numbers of minority and nonminority offenders. There are likely a variety of factors that have led to the underrepresentation of offenders from minority backgrounds in drug courts, and additional research should help to identify those factors.

Furthermore, research suggests that graduation rates are lower for participants from minority backgrounds and for female participants (see Marlowe et al., 2016). Again, researchers are encouraged to examine these apparent discrepancies in graduation rates. Given that female offenders often present with different needs than male offenders (e.g., Anumba, DeMatteo, & Heilbrun, 2012; Covington & Bloom, 2006; Houck & Loper, 2002; James & Glaze, 2006), it is possible that the relatively uniform treatment provided in drug courts may not be sufficiently tailored to address the needs of female offenders. An examination of both process and outcome variables may be useful in identifying the factors that are associated with these lower graduation rates.

The incorporation of peer specialists in drug courts could be a promising practice for drug courts. The use of peer specialists in drug courts is not widespread, but there is growing evidence supporting the use of peers for individuals in recovery (see Reif et al., 2014). Within drug courts, peer specialists with lived experience in recovery and ideally in drug court can assist participants to attend treatment and engage in other services that promote continued recovery and stabilization (Taylor, 2014). One drug court has created a peer-run recovery community center with groups that can include drug court participants (Vermont Recovery Network, 2013). Peer specialists can also serve an important role once a participant has completed the drug court program by serving as a source of support, helping the participant to remain vigilant of potential relapses or other risk factors, and assisting the participant to obtain services if needed. Given the increased use of peer support specialists in other areas of the criminal justice system, it is likely that drug courts will make more use of these services in the coming years.

5
Mental Health Courts

The demonstrated success of drug courts led to the development of other problem-solving courts, including mental health courts. Although drug courts and mental health courts serve different (albeit overlapping) populations of offenders, they are based on the same underlying treatment-oriented philosophy. Like all problem-solving courts, mental health courts seek to address the causes of criminal behavior and focus more on rehabilitation than punishment. Specifically, mental health courts focus on mental health symptoms and disorders that may play a role in offending.

In this chapter, we first review the overrepresentation of individuals with mental illness in the criminal justice system, which was the impetus for the development of mental health courts. Next, we describe the history and current state of mental health courts in the United States. A substantial portion of this chapter is dedicated to summarizing the research on mental health courts. Although there is considerably less research on mental health courts than on drug courts, the available research is promising in some respects while lacking in others. Finally, we conclude the chapter with a discussion of innovative mental health court practices and the future of mental health courts.

Mental Health in the Criminal Justice System

As briefly described in Chapter 1, individuals with mental illness are significantly overrepresented in the criminal justice system. Although statistics vary widely, a conservative estimate is that nearly 25% of all individuals in the U.S. correctional system, which includes offenders in jails, prisons, and on community supervision (probation, parole), exhibit symptoms of mental illness (Baillargeon, Binswanger, Penn, Williams, & Murray, 2009; Diamond, Wang, Holzer III, Thomas, & Cruser, 2001; Ditton, 1999). When limited to incarcerated populations, more than 50% of all inmates in jails and state prisons have some form of mental illness (Kim, Becker-Cohen, & Serakos, 2015). A survey conducted by the Bureau of Justice Statistics indicated that, as of mid-2005, 65% of state prisoners, 45% of federal prisoners, and 64% of jail inmates reported experiencing mental health symptoms (James & Glaze, 2006). Furthermore, 49% of state inmates, 40% of federal inmates, and 60% of jail inmates reported symptoms of a mental health disorder included in the American Psychiatric Association's (1994) *Diagnostic and Statistical Manual of Mental Disorders* (DSM-IV), with some meeting criteria for personality and developmental disorders (James & Glaze, 2006).

With respect to specific mental health symptoms and disorders, the Bureau of Justice Statistics survey showed that approximately 20% of state and federal inmates had a depressive disorder, 12% exhibited symptoms of mania, 8% were diagnosed with an anxiety disorder, 7% had posttraumatic stress disorder, 6% were diagnosed with a personality disorder, and 5% had schizophrenia (James & Glaze, 2006). These rates of mental illness are considerably higher than the rates found in the general population. Furthermore, inmates suffering from mental illness are more likely to have co-occurring homelessness, previous incarceration, and drug involvement (Cloyes, Wong, Latimer, & Abarca, 2010).

Several large U.S. correctional facilities house more individuals with mental illness and substance use disorders than many inpatient psychiatric treatment centers (Ford, 2015; McCuan, Prins, & Wasarhaley, 2007; Torrey, Kennard, Eslinger, Lamb, & Pavle, 2010). In fact, the three largest providers of mental health services in the United States are Cook County Jail, Riker's Island, and the Los Angeles County Jail (Gavett, 2012). Unfortunately, most jails and prisons do not have sufficient resources or trained staff to address the needs of offenders who have mental health symptoms and disorders. Also, as the prevalence of mental illness tends to increase with the age of the correctional population, it is expected that the percentage of inmates with mental illness will increase as the U.S. correctional population grows older (Chiu, 2010; Sterns, Lax, Sed, Keohane, & Sterns, 2008). Furthermore, of the inmates with mental illness, only one-third of state prisoners and one-sixth of jail inmates reported receiving mental health treatment while incarcerated (James & Glaze, 2006). Indeed, only 15.1% of prisoners with a mental health problem were given a prescription for psychiatric medication, and only 12% received mental health counseling (James & Glaze, 2006).

These statistics highlight the prevalence of mental health problems within the U.S. correctional population, and they also demonstrate that the criminal justice system lacks adequate treatment and case management services for offenders with mental health problems. The concerns regarding mental illness among justice-involved populations are exacerbated by the recent prison overcrowding phenomenon. The United States incarcerates more people per capita than any other country in the world, and the U.S. correctional population quadrupled in size since the mid-1980s, with more than 2.3 million individuals currently incarcerated and several million more under correctional supervision in the community (Wagner & Rabuy, 2017; Wilper et al., 2009). Overcrowding has made it challenging for correctional facilities to provide even basic services, such as safety and security, and thus many correctional facilities are simply not sufficiently equipped to provide adequate mental health treatment (Kim et al., 2015).

Mental Health Courts: Development and Overview

Mental health courts were developed to better address the needs of the increasing number of offenders with mental illness who come into contact with the criminal justice system (Griffin & DeMatteo, 2009). In these courts, legal professionals (e.g., judges, attorneys, probation/parole officers) and community professionals (e.g., treatment providers, social services staff, case managers) work collaboratively to address offenders' needs. Mental health courts provide participants with community-based mental health treatment and other services aimed at reducing their symptoms of mental illness (Redlich, Steadman, Monahan, Robbins, & Petrila, 2006; Steadman, Davidson, & Brown, 2001). By addressing the needs that are most likely to lead to future offending, mental health courts seek to interrupt the cycle of arrest, conviction, incarceration, release, and rearrest that is often characteristic of offenders with mental illness (Castellano & Anderson, 2013).

The mental health court team also strives to help offenders with mental illness reintegrate into the community through intensive judicial monitoring and the provision of case management and other social services, including job training, employment, and housing support (Bazelon Center for Mental Health Law, 2003; Denckla & Berman, 2001; Steadman et al., 2001). Although the operations of mental health courts vary, underlying most mental health courts is the belief that facilitating access to mental health treatment and providing judicial monitoring will ameliorate clinical symptoms and improve functioning, which will ultimately reduce criminal recidivism (Farole, 2006; Griffin & DeMatteo, 2009). We return to a discussion of the underlying philosophy of mental health courts later in this chapter.

A precursor of the mental health court model was developed by Judge Evan Goodman in 1980 in Marion Country, Indiana (Coons & Bowman, 2010). Judge Goodman developed a program in which offenders with mental illness were diverted from jail to a nearby hospital for a psychiatric evaluation. A hospital recreation room was converted into a makeshift courtroom so that court proceedings could be held in the same building as the hospital's psychiatric unit. Prior to court proceedings, the offender would be assessed by a psychiatrist, and the court would then require eligible participants to complete outpatient treatment. A forensic team would monitor participants' treatment compliance and progress. This court was ultimately dismantled in the early 1990s, and such models were not used until several years later when significant events in Florida triggered the rapid development of mental health courts throughout the United States (Castellano & Anderson, 2013).

In 1997, the Florida legislature charged a special task force with investigating the relationship between mental illness and involvement in the criminal justice system. The task force found a growing incarceration rate for low-level offenses committed by offenders with mental illness, a dearth of psychiatric assessments for such offenders once they were taken into custody, and the inadequate provision of mental health treatment after release to the community. In response to this investigation, the Florida legislature allocated $1.5 million for the development of the country's first mental health court in Broward County (Castellano & Anderson, 2013; Orr et al., 2009).

The Broward County Mental Health Court, which is a division of the county criminal court, handles cases involving individuals who have been charged with nonviolent, misdemeanor offenses and identified as mentally ill or developmentally disabled. It is a voluntary preadjudication program that diverts offenders into treatment in lieu of a trial or other disposition. The court has several goals: (a) enhance communications and interactions between the criminal justice system and mental health system, (b) ensure that offenders with mental health involvement are not housed in jail, (c) balance the rights of offenders with public safety considerations, (d) divert offenders who are mentally ill and charged with minor offenses into community-based services, and (e) monitor the delivery of services and treatment.

By early 2005, less than 10 years after the development of the first mental health court, there were 90 functional adult mental health courts in the United States (Redlich et al., 2006), with several other courts in advanced stages of development. At that time, mental health courts could be found in 34 states, primarily in the western (37%) and southern (37%) regions of the United States (Council of State Governments, 2005). Although there were fewer mental health courts in the Midwest (15%) and northeast (11%) (Council of State Governments, 2005), Ohio had more mental health courts than any other state (Redlich et al., 2006). At that time, mental health courts were serving more than 7,500 offenders, with an average of 36 cases per court; there was a wide range of caseloads among mental health courts, with some courts handling as few as 3 cases and others as many as 852 cases (Redlich et al., 2006). Mental health courts varied in terms of the types of cases accepted, with 49% primarily managing misdemeanor cases, 14% primarily handling felony cases, and the remainder handling both misdemeanor and felony cases (Redlich et al., 2006).

By 2008, the number of mental health courts in the United States more than doubled to 182, with many others in advanced stages of development (Erickson, Campbell, & Lamberti, 2006; Griffin & DeMatteo, 2009; Thompson, Osher, & Tomasini-Joshi, 2007). This time period also saw the development of juvenile mental health courts (Cocozza & Shufelt, 2006; Thompson et al., 2007) and the adoption of the mental health court model by other countries, including Canada, the United Kingdom, and Australia (Griffin & DeMatteo, 2009). By 2011, there were an estimated 250 mental health courts in the United States (Council of State Governments Justice Center, 2011), and the National Drug Court Resource Center (2014) reported that there were 414 operational mental health courts in the United States by 2014. A recent publication from the National Drug Court Institute indicates that the number of mental health courts in the United States increased by 36% between 2009 and 2014, and mental health courts are projected to be the fasting growing type of problem-solving court over the next several years (Marlowe, Hardin, & Fox, 2016).

Goals and Philosophies of Mental Health Courts

Most mental health courts were developed in communities that had a preexisting drug court, and the mental health courts drew from the therapeutic jurisprudence philosophy that underlies drug courts (Griffin & DeMatteo, 2009). As such, mental health courts adhere to the premise that the criminal justice system can simultaneously protect public safety and provide needed mental health treatment and other services to offenders with specific needs (Odegaard, 2007; Rottman & Casey, 1999; Wexler, 2001). By providing mental health treatment services combined with intensive judicial supervision, mental health courts adhere to the therapeutic jurisprudence philosophy.

Although the specific operational protocols of mental health courts vary among jurisdictions (see Erickson et al., 2006), the basic goal/purpose of most mental health courts is the same: to divert offenders with mental health treatment needs into specialized criminal justice processing that involves the provision of judicially supervised community-based mental health treatment and other needed services (Boothroyd, Pothyress, McGaha, & Petrila, 2003; Moore & Hiday, 2006). By diverting offenders with mental health needs to treatment providers, mental health courts seek to ameliorate mental health symptoms that could contribute to criminal behavior and, as a result, minimize the "revolving door" pattern of the criminal justice system whereby the same offenders are frequently rearrested (Griffin & DeMatteo, 2009). Additional goals of many mental health courts include (1) reducing the criminalization of individuals with mental illness by preventing those offenders from being incarcerated inappropriately, (2) reducing the hospitalization rate of offenders with mental illness, (3) helping correctional facilities run more smoothly by diverting offenders with mental health needs from standard criminal justice processing that may lead to incarceration, and (4) saving money and resources for the criminal justice and mental health systems (Casey & Rottman, 2005; Griffin & DeMatteo, 2009).

Organization and Operation of Mental Health Courts

Mental health courts come in three models: preadjudication, postadjudication, and probation-based (Griffin & DeMatteo, 2009). Under the *preadjudication model*, an offender is not required to plead guilty prior to enrolling in a mental health court program. Rather, the court defers prosecution, and, in exchange, the offender agrees to comply with mandated mental health treatment (Almquist & Dodd, 2009). In the *postadjudication model*, a guilty plea or conviction is required prior to enrolling in a mental health court program, but the final disposition of the case is deferred until the offender completes the treatment program (Griffin & DeMatteo, 2009). Some mental health courts that follow this model allow for the expungement of an offender's criminal record upon successful completion of the mandated treatment program (Almquist & Dodd, 2009). Finally, under the *probation-based model*, an offender pleads guilty, is convicted, and receives a sentence of probation, and the mental health court imposes mandated treatment as a requirement of probation (Griffin & DeMatteo, 2009).

Several researchers have examined the prevalence of each of the three operational models of mental health courts. One study on early mental health courts found that of the eight courts that existed at the time, two operated under a preadjudication model, three operated under a probation-based model, and three operated under a postadjudication model (Griffin, Steadman, & Petrila, 2002). Even within these models there is considerable variability in how these courts operate. A 2003 national survey of 20 mental health courts found that half of the courts required a plea prior to participation in the program, and more than one-third provided for dismissal of criminal charges or record expungement upon successful completion of the program (Bazelon Center for Mental Health Law, 2003). A later study examining mental health courts found that of seven courts, six used the postadjudication model and one used the preadjudication model (Redlich, Steadman, Monahan, Petrila, & Griffin, 2005). In addition, a 2005 study of a mental health court in Clark County, Washington found that the court initially operated under the preadjudication model, but adopted the postadjudication model after receiving funding from the Substance Abuse and Mental Health Services Administration (Herinckx, Swart, Ama, Dolezal, & King, 2005).

Mental Health Court Staff

Mental health courts use a nonadversarial, multidisciplinary team approach to facilitate the effective supervision and treatment of participants. The team typically consists of some combination of the following: judge, defense attorney, prosecutor, probation officer, parole officer, case manager, and representatives from community-based treatment providers (Almquist & Dodd, 2009). The composition of the team varies by court. O'Keefe (2006) reported that a Santa Barbara, California, mental health court team consisted of judges, district attorneys, public defenders, probation officers, police officers, representatives from substance use and mental health treatment providers, a case manager, and an "intensive care team," which provided services to participants at their homes and focused on addressing participants' basic needs. Another study on a Washington mental health court found that the team consisted of a judge, attorneys for the defense and prosecution, probation officers and staff, case managers, and mental health providers (Herinckx et al., 2005). Two other Washington mental health courts (Seattle and King Country) had teams composed of judges, clinical social workers, prosecutors, probation advisors, defense attorneys who worked closely with social workers, and court coordinators (Trupin & Richards, 2003). In addition to attorneys, case managers, and a judge, a Brooklyn mental health court team included a project director, clinical director, forensic director, and resource coordinator, along with a psychiatrist and social workers (O'Keefe, 2006). A mental health court team in Pennsylvania (Allegheny County) consisted of a judge, assistant district attorney, public defender, clinical social workers, forensic case managers, and a liaison staff member to work with probation (Ridgely et al., 2007). Thus, despite some common components, the staffing in mental health courts can vary considerably by jurisdiction.

Several researchers have hypothesized that the quality of the relationships between mental health court participants and court staff plays a role in the participants' success, but there are very little data on this topic. In their meta-analysis, Sarteschi, Vaughn, and Kim (2011) concluded that positive relationships with mental health court staff are associated with greater participant success in mental health court programs, but we did not find any other empirical research on this important topic. The role of the judge and court staff in drug courts has received a good deal of attention (see Marlowe, Festinger, & Lee, 2004), and this area should be explored further in mental health courts, particularly because the relationships between mental health court staff and participants likely vary widely by court. Identifying the types of relationship that are associated with higher levels of participant success could help establish a gold standard for mental health courts moving forward.

Mental Health Court Referral Process

Referrals for mental health courts can be made by prosecutors, defense attorneys, judges, jail staff, and family members of offenders (Almquist & Dodd, 2009). A 2006 evaluation of a Brooklyn mental health court found that 44% of participant referrals came from defense attorneys, 30% from competency hearings, 10% from the district attorney's office, 10% from other judges, and 5% percent from other specialty courts (O'Keefe, 2006). An early study of four mental health courts found that most referrals came from county jail staff members (Goldkamp & Irons-Guynn, 2000).

The time between referral and enrollment in mental health court varies considerably among courts. Steadman and colleagues found that although 14% of participants were enrolled immediately, the average wait-time between referral and enrollment in the seven mental health courts ranged from 0 to 45 days (Steadman, Redlich, Griffin, Petrila, & Monahan, 2005). They also reported that, of the referrals received, 14% of offenders were accepted on the same day as the referral and 52% percent of all the referred offenders were accepted. The court rejected referrals for various reasons, including failure to meet mental health disorder criteria (30%), nature of the offender's criminal history (19%), lack of agreement from the prosecution (18%), and incompetence or instability of the offender (7%).

Some courts are quite efficient in enrolling referred participants. The mental health court in Broward County, Florida, frequently heard cases and was often able to admit participants on the same day they were referred (Petrila, Poythress, McGaha, & Boothroyd, 2001). However, a study examining a Brooklyn mental health court found the average postreferral wait-time was 2–3 months (O'Keefe, 2006). One study found that potential mental health court participants were typically not waiting for enrollment into the court from a jail cell because those charged with more minor crimes were usually released even without posting bail (Hiday, Moore, Lamoureaux, & de Magistris, 2005). Another study examined the length of time between initial arrest and either mental health court enrollment or criminal disposition for offenders with and without mental illness (Redlich, Liu, Steadman, Callahan, & Robbins, 2012). In that study, Redlich and colleagues found that the average length of time between arrest and mental health court enrollment was 70 days, the average length of time between arrest and disposition of offenders with mental illness going through standard criminal justice processing was 76 days, and the average length of time between arrest and disposition for offenders without mental illness was 37 days.

Linking Mental Health Court Participants to Treatment

Mental health courts also differ in how they connect participants with treatment services. Participants are typically linked with treatment providers by case managers who work within the mental health court. A national survey of 20 mental health courts found that courts tend to connect participants with treatment programs by reconnecting participants with previously or currently used treatment providers or directly referring participants to community treatment providers (Bazelon Center for Mental Health Law, 2003; see Almquist & Dodd, 2009). A small percentage of these courts simply provided participants with information about providers and encouraged participants to seek treatment, without any meaningful coordination of treatment (Bazelon Center for Mental Health Law, 2003). A Santa Barbara mental health court provided each participant with a case manager who connected the participant with treatment providers and also provided assistance with transportation, housing, job training, and substance use issues (Cosden, Ellens, Schnell, Yamini-Diouf, & Wolfe, 2003).

The specific treatments provided to participants vary by court and depend on participants' clinical needs and the availability and resources of the community treatment providers. Most mental health courts do not have in-house treatment providers or provide funding for external treatment services. As such, mental health courts often seek to develop positive relationships with treatment providers to ensure participants receive adequate treatment (Almquist & Dodd, 2009).

Encouraging Participant Engagement: Incentives, Rewards, and Sanctions

To encourage participants to engage in treatment, mental health courts typically use a behavioral modification scheme based on incentives/rewards and sanctions. Incentives and rewards are often used to motivate participants to comply with treatment requirements, and they typically include verbal recognition, gift certificates, reduction in the length or intensity of mandated treatment, and a reduction in the required number of judicial status hearings (Griffin & DeMatteo, 2009). For instance, a 2008 study evaluating a Utah mental health court found that compliant participants were rewarded with verbal praise and placed on a "Rocket Docket," which allowed them to be first in line at judicial status hearings so they could leave court early (Van Vleet, Hickert, Becker, & Kunz, 2008). Another study found that a mental health court in Arkansas used a wide array of incentives to encourage participant engagement with treatment, including verbal praise and applause, certificates of program completion, and fewer required court appearances (Ferguson, McAuley, Hornby, & Zeller, 2008). The provision of positive reinforcement in the form of incentives and rewards is intended to promote the continued compliance of mental health court participants.

When participants fail to comply with treatment requirements, mental health courts will often impose sanctions that could include verbal reprimands, an increase in the required number of status hearings, mandatory community service, jail time, and, in extreme cases, expulsion from the mental health court program (Goldkamp & Irons-Guynn, 2000; Griffin et al., 2002). In a 2003 survey of sanctions used by 20 mental health courts, 64% imposed jail time, 36% amended participants' treatment plans, 27% reprimanded noncompliant participants and increased the number of required court appearances, and 18% contemplated expelling participants who failed to comply (Bazelon Center for Mental Health Law, 2003). A Utah mental health court sanctions noncompliant participants by requiring them to perform community service (Van Vleet et al., 2008). The goal of punishing participant noncompliance is to shape participants' behavior to be more compliant with program requirements.

Early mental health court research by Griffin et al. (2002) found that mental health courts rarely used jail time and termination from the program as sanctions for noncompliance. A 2006 national survey evaluated the use of jail time sanctions by 90 mental health courts throughout the United States (Redlich et al., 2006). Although 92% of the courts reported a willingness to use incarceration as a sanction for program noncompliance, the majority of the courts reported using such sanctions very infrequently; only 2% of the courts used jail time as a sanction for more than 50% of their cases, 39% used jail time in 5–20% of their cases, and 33% used jail time in less than 5% of their cases (Redlich et al., 2006). Other investigators found that three of the four mental health courts they studied used jail as a sanction (Callahan, Steadman, Tillman, & Vesselinov, 2013). They also identified several factors that were associated with being sent to jail as a sanction, including being charged with a drug offense (as opposed to a crime against people), heavier drug involvement, a reputation of noncompliance, and frequency of in-custody hearings (Callahan et al., 2003).

Mental health court judges may be hesitant to use jail time as a sanction for participant noncompliance because incarceration can be detrimental to individuals with mental health disorders. Almquist and Dodd (2009) noted that incarceration could be highly stressful to such individuals and lead to further deterioration of their mental and emotional functioning, which could in turn lead to increased noncompliance. Indeed, research has shown that judges may be reluctant to impose jail time as a punishment when it appears that the offender's noncompliance was due to mental illness (Griffin et al., 2002). Moreover, incarcerating a mental health court client disrupts any progress the client is making in the program.

Nature of Mental Health Court Participation

As with other problem-solving courts, the decision to enter a mental health court must be made voluntarily by the offender. Although some mental health court participants do not perceive mental health programs to be coercive, some participants exhibit unawareness of the nature and purpose of the court. In a 2002 study of the Broward County, Florida, mental health court, participants reported experiencing minimal coercion when deciding whether to participate in the program (Poythress, Petrila, McGaha, & Boothroyd, 2002). However, a 2003 study of that same court found that only 28% of participants were given information about the goals and nature of the mental health court (Boothroyd et al., 2003). Boothroyd et al. (2003) also reported that 54% of participants reported understanding that participation was voluntary, but more than half of this group reported that the voluntary nature of the court was not explained to them prior to their initial hearing. Another investigator evaluated participants' perceptions in 10 mental health courts and found that most participants did not feel coerced into participation (Redlich, 2005). Notably, participants who knowingly and voluntarily enrolled in mental health court and who were made aware of the nature and goals of the program were more likely to succeed, whereas participants who felt coerced into the program were less likely to adhere to the program requirements (Redlich, 2005).

Mental Health Court Trends

Some studies have examined the difference between "first-generation" and "second-generation" mental health courts. The research conducted by Griffin and colleagues focused on eight early programs that constituted the first group of mental health courts in the United States (Griffin et al., 2002). These courts, which were established around the same time and shared common characteristics, including a focus on accepting defendants with misdemeanor charges, have been categorized as "first-generation" mental health courts (Redlich et al., 2005). Redlich et al. (2005) found that second-generation mental health courts are characterized by an increase in acceptance of offenders with felony charges, which in turn has led to an increase in the use of the postadjudication model. In addition, second-generation courts more frequently use jail as a sanction and provide increased supervision of participants.

Another study by Redlich and colleagues identified factors associated with the number of participants seen by mental health courts (Redlich et al., 2006). They found that the number of mental health court clients was associated with the length of time a court had been in existence (with more established courts having more participants), fewer initial status reviews, and more types of community supervision offered. These findings have important implications for mental health courts that are seeking to increase (or decrease) the number of participants they serve.

At least one study has examined mental health courts from a cost–benefit perspective. Ridgely et al. (2007) examined whether mental health courts are less expensive than their traditional court counterparts and found that an Allegheny County (Pennsylvania) mental health court exhibited a trend toward greater long-term net savings. Unfortunately, we were not able to find any large-scale studies evaluating the costs and benefits of mental health courts. Given the current economic climate, demonstrating that mental health courts are both effective and cost-effective should be a priority.

Mental Health Court Participants

Types of Crimes

There is significant variability among mental health courts in terms of the types of crimes that are deemed acceptable for admission into the court. Some courts only accept offenders with misdemeanor charges, others only accept offenders with felony charges, and some courts accept both misdemeanor and felony offenders (Almquist & Dodd, 2009). A national survey conducted in 2003 found that 10 of 20 existing mental health courts only accepted offenders charged with misdemeanors, while the other 10 courts accepted offenders charged with either misdemeanors or felonies (Bazelon Center for Mental Health Law, 2003). Of 87 mental health courts evaluated in a 2006 survey, 40% only accepted offenders charged with misdemeanors, 10% only accepted those charged with felonies, and 50% accepted offenders charged with misdemeanors or felonies (Redlich et al., 2006).

Whether a mental health court accepts offenders charged with misdemeanor or felony offenses is often contingent on the jurisdiction in which the court is situated. Some mental health courts, for example, function within a municipal court and therefore will primarily oversee offenders with misdemeanor charges, while other mental health courts operate within trial courts and can accept felony cases. Even without jurisdictional limitations, policy concerns may dictate the types of crimes that a mental health court is willing to oversee. Some funding entities, for example, have preferences regarding the acceptance of individuals with certain types of charges. There may also be preferences among the various stakeholders involved in mental health courts. The protection of public safety is a high priority, and it may lead some mental health courts to limit enrollment to offenders charged with misdemeanor offenses (Almquist & Dodd, 2009).

Early mental health courts tended to focus on offenders with misdemeanor charges, but an increasing number of courts are accepting individuals charged with felony offenses (Almquist & Dodd, 2009). Research on first-generation mental health courts found that seven out of eight early mental health courts primarily accepted individuals with misdemeanor charges, and many even imposed restrictions regarding the types of misdemeanors that would be accepted (Griffin et al., 2002). A 2003 study found that the first mental health court in the United States (Broward County, Florida) only accepted offenders with nonviolent misdemeanor charges, violation of an ordinance, or traffic offenses (Boothroyd et al., 2003). A later study found that, by 2005, several mental health courts that had initially only accepted offenders charged with misdemeanor offenses had begun accepting some offenders charged with felonies (Redlich et al., 2005). This study also found that several second-generation mental health courts accepted offenders charged with felonies, with some focusing exclusively on offenders with felony charges (Redlich et al., 2005).

Mental health courts are becoming increasingly more likely to accept individuals who have been charged with violent offenses. Accepting offenders charged with violent crimes is unusual among most types of problem-solving courts. However, a 2003 study found that of 20 mental health courts that were evaluated, only 4 utilized bright-line exclusions for offenders with a history of violence (Bazelon Center for Mental Health Law, 2003). Another 2003 study found that a mental health court in Santa Barbara, California, accepted individuals with a history of violence if the district attorney and mental health court staff determined that the individual was no longer a threat to the general public (Cosden et al., 2003). An evaluation of a Brooklyn mental health court that was developed in 2002 found that although the court initially only accepted individuals with nonviolent charges, the court later broadened its acceptance criteria and began enrolling individuals with violent felony charges on a discretionary basis; by mid-2004, 39% of the participants in the mental health court had been charged with a violent crime (O'Keefe, 2006). It is worth noting that some mental health courts require victim permission for an offender to participate in the program if the underlying offense was violent.

In a review of 20 studies, Honegger (2015) identified substantial variability in mental health court eligibility criteria. Of the mental health courts examined, some only accepted individuals with misdemeanor charges (Cosden, Ellens, Schnell, &Yamini-Diouf, 2005; Frailing, 2010; Hiday & Ray, 2010; Hoff, Baranosky, Buchanan, Zonana, & Rosenheck, 1999; Keator, Callahan, Steadman, & Vesselinov, 2013; Luskin, 2013; Moore & Hiday, 2006; Steadman, Redlich, Callahan, Robbins, & Vesselinov, 2011; Van Vleet et al., 2008), while others accepted individuals with both misdemeanor and felony charges (Boothroyd et al., 2003; Boothroyd, Mercado, Poythress, Christy, & Petrila, 2005; Christy, Poythress, Boothroyd, Petrila, & Mehra, 2005; Dirks-Linhorst & Linhorst, 2012; Hiday, Wales, & Ray, 2013; Trupin & Richards, 2003). A few of the courts included in Honegger's (2015) review only accepted certain types of felonies (Sneed, Koch, Estes, & Quinn, 2006; Steadman & Naples, 2005). The lack of uniform eligibility criteria across courts is one of the many reasons it is challenging for researchers to conduct empirical investigations comparing mental health courts.

Mental Health Diagnosis

Mental health courts also vary in terms of the procedures used to determine if an individual is an appropriate candidate (i.e., has the requisite mental health issues) for diversion into the court. Most mental health courts only accept individuals who exhibit signs of a serious mental illness (Almquist & Dodd, 2009).

However, some courts make acceptance contingent on an offender satisfying diagnostic criteria for a specific mental health diagnosis, while other courts accept participants by confirming a previous mental health diagnosis (Erickson et al, 2006; Griffin et al., 2002). The wide variability in eligibility criteria related to an offender's mental health function raises some concerns relating to equal protection (see Chapter 9, for more discussion on this issue), and it also contributes to the difficulties in empirically evaluating mental health courts.

A 2005 study examining the mental health diagnostic requirements of 90 mental health courts found that 37% only accepted individuals with a diagnosed DSM-IV Axis I disorder, 21% accepted individuals with a mental illness that was "serious and/or serious and persistent," and 16% indicated having some requirements regarding the types of mental illness required to be exhibited by participants; the remaining 26% had no specific requirements regarding mental health diagnoses (Criminal Justice/Mental Health Consensus Project, 2005). One study found that the most common diagnoses of participants from seven mental health courts were schizoaffective disorder, schizophrenia, bipolar disorder, depressive disorders, and other mood disorders (Steadman et al., 2005). The most prevalent diagnoses of participants in the Broward County, Florida, mental health court were depressive disorder (25%), bipolar disorder (24%), and schizophrenia (17%) (Boothroyd et al., 2005).

Mental health court participants often have co-occurring substance use and mental health disorders. Research on a mental health court in Santa Barbara, California, found that 83% of the participants had co-occurring substance use and mental health disorders (Cosden et al., 2003). Another study found that 59% of participants in a mental health court in Anchorage, Alaska, had co-occurring disorders (Ferguson et al., 2008). Finally, a 2007 study of a San Francisco behavioral health court (which is similar in structure and function to a mental health court) found that 56% of participants were diagnosed with both a severe mental health disorder and a substance use disorder (McNiel & Binder, 2007). Including participants with co-occurring disorders has implications for the types of community-based treatments and services that are needed to adequately address participants' needs.

In her comprehensive review of 20 mental health court studies, Honegger (2015) found substantial variability in terms of the nature and specificity of required mental health diagnoses for mental health court participants. One court excluded offenders with personality disorders or developmental disabilities (Herinckx et al., 2005), while other courts accepted offenders with developmental disorders, intellectual disability, and any other DSM-IV-TR Axis I disorders (Sneed et al., 2006). Some courts required that participants be diagnosed with major depressive disorder, bipolar disorder, or schizophrenia (Frailing, 2010; Luskin, 2013). Again, as with some of the other differences among mental health courts, differences relating to eligible mental health disorders make it challenging to compare mental health courts.

Demographic Characteristics

Some research suggests that there is an overrepresentation of female and Caucasian participants in mental health courts considering the proportion of those two groups within the broader criminal justice population. One study examined referrals made to seven mental health courts and found that referred individuals were more likely to be Caucasian, female, and older (Steadman et al., 2005). Another study found that female and Caucasian participants were slightly overrepresented in a Community Resource Court in North Carolina (Hiday et al., 2005). A more recent comprehensive review suggests that this trend may be changing. Specifically, a review of 18 mental health court studies by Sarteschi et al. (2011) found that most mental health court participants were Caucasian males in their mid-30s.

The Effectiveness of Mental Health Courts

As with most other interventions with justice-involved populations, participation in mental health courts results in a number of important outcomes. The shared goal of all problem-solving courts is to reduce recidivism among offenders who have historically been overrepresented and undertreated in the criminal justice system. However, each type of problem-solving court also has an interest in outcomes that are specific to the type of court. Whereas drug courts are primarily interested in the impact of the courts on criminal recidivism and relapse to drug use, mental health courts are primarily interested in how participation in the program affects recidivism and mental health.

The effectiveness of mental health courts can be measured by looking at a number of process and outcome variables. In terms of process, an important question is how quickly mental health court participants begin receiving services after they are enrolled in the court. In terms of outcome, there are important questions related to the effects of mental health courts on participants' mental health, connecting participants to behavioral health services, participants' quality of life, and criminal recidivism.

In the sections that follow, we examine the available research on mental health courts. As will be evident, the research on mental health courts is considerably less developed than the research on drug courts. Unlike the drug court research, there are very few meta-analyses, systematic reviews, and large-scale studies. With that said, mental health courts have received much more research attention than all of the other types of problem-solving courts (with the exception of drug courts). Taken as a whole, the body of research on mental health courts is promising in some respects, but it also highlights several areas in which much more research is needed.

Mental Health Outcomes

Some mental health court research has focused on the clinical outcomes related to participant treatment. Indeed, one philosophy underlying mental health courts is that recidivism rates can be reduced by ameliorating mental health symptoms (Honegger, 2015). Many studies have evaluated changes in mental health symptoms using various psychometric measures, including the Addiction Severity Index (ASI; McLellan, Luborsky, Woody, & O'Brien, 1980), the Behavior and Symptom Identification Scale (BASIS-32; Eisen, 1996), the Brief Psychiatric Rating Scale (BPRS; Overall & Gorham, 1962), the Colorado Symptom Index (CSI; Shern et al., 1994), and the Global Assessment of Functioning (GAF; Hall, 1995). Using well-established measures with acceptable psychometric properties, as opposed to locally developed measures with little validation research, improves the validity and reliability of the findings.

The available research on clinical outcomes among mental health court participants also reflects different methodological approaches. Honegger's (2015) review of 20 mental health court studies revealed that 8 of the 20 studies evaluated the impact of mental health courts on mental health functioning, with one study utilizing an experimental design, six studies using quasi-experimental designs, and one study using a pretest/posttest design. Given the importance of research methodology in terms of the types and strength of inferences that can be drawn, the methodologies commonly used to evaluate mental health courts will be discussed in more detail later in this chapter.

Early studies on mental health court outcomes produced mixed results. For example, Trupin and Richards (2003) found that mental health court participants exhibited improvement in scores on the GAF scale, which is a measure of psychological impairment. Cosden et al. (2003) compared outcomes of mental health participants with a control group and found that mental health court participants exhibited significant reductions in emotional distress and drug use issues, but that both groups exhibited improvements in alcohol problems, with no significant differences between the two groups in this area. A later study by Cosden et al. (2005) found that mental health court participants exhibited improvement on the GAF scale, but they also found no significant differences in GAF scores and BASIS-32 scores between mental health court participants and offenders involved in standard criminal court processing. Around that same time, Boothroyd et al. (2005) used a quasi-experimental design to compare mental health court participants to offenders going through standard criminal justice processing. They administered the BPRS to individuals from both groups during initial hearings and at 1, 4, and 8 months after the initial court appearance, and results revealed no significant between-group differences in BPRS scores across time points (Boothroyd et al., 2005). Finally, a more recent meta-analysis of eight studies that examined mental health outcomes was unable to calculate a valid effect size because there was insufficient homogeneity among the studies (Sarteschi et al., 2011).

Several researchers have focused on the use of emergency psychiatric services as a proxy for mental health court outcomes. The results of these studies were mixed. Steadman and Naples (2005) compared mental health court participants from six mental health courts (three pre-booking and three post-booking) with nondiverted offenders. In this study, the researchers tracked emergency room visits as a proxy for mental health symptoms and found that mental health court participants (31.3%) had significantly more emergency room visits than the nondiverted offenders (23.9%) over a 1-year period following diversion. This study also found that mental health court participants (31.7%) were hospitalized at a significantly higher rate than the nondiverted offenders (18.7%) over the same 1-year period (Steadman & Naples, 2005). Overall, mental health court participants were linked to community-based services at higher rates than the nondiverted offenders. However, Steadman and Naples (2005) suggested that one explanation for these results is that mental health court participants were better connected to mental health professionals who would encourage the use of emergency services when necessary.

Other studies, however, have not found differences between mental health court participants and offenders in standard criminal justice processing. For example, Luskin (2013) compared psychiatric hospitalization rates for mental health court participants and offenders in standard criminal justice processing after 6 months of enrollment. Results revealed that the rate of psychiatric hospitalizations decreased significantly from the first hearing to the 6-month follow-up, but there was no significant difference in hospitalization rates between mental health court participants and nondiverted offenders (Luskin, 2013). Another study found no significant differences in emergency room visits or contact with crisis services between mental health court participants and nondiverted offenders (Keator et al., 2013). However, when compared with the nondiverted offenders, Keator et al. (2013) found that mental health court participants were more likely to receive treatment from inpatient providers or drug detoxification facilities.

Finally, some research has looked at other clinical outcomes, such as substance use, among mental health participants. For example, in their 2005 study, Cosden et al. evaluated changes in substance use behaviors among mental health court participants using the ASI. Results revealed that both mental health court participants and nondiverted offenders exhibited significant improvements in ASI scores over time but that the mental health court participants exhibited greater improvements (Cosden et al., 2005).

When taken as a whole, it is apparent that the research evaluating the mental health outcomes of mental health court participants is still in its early stages. The relatively minimal extant literature provides conflicting evidence regarding the degree to which mental health courts improve the mental health functioning among participants. There is not enough evidence at this point to determine whether mental health courts are in fact superior to standard criminal justice processing in terms of improving mental health functioning. Consistent with Honegger's (2015) conclusion, we believe that additional data are needed to adequately evaluate the impact of mental health courts on participants' mental health functioning.

Connection to Behavioral Health Services

Underlying the development of mental health courts is the idea that they reduce criminal recidivism by increasing the connection to behavioral health services and ensuring participant adherence to treatment. As such, some research has evaluated the effectiveness of mental health courts using outcome variables operationalized under this theory, including the number of participant referrals to mental health providers, the number of participants receiving treatment, and the quantity of services provided. Rather than focusing on the outcome of participation in mental health courts, this research focuses on the ability of mental health courts to connect participants to needed services and the process they use to make such connections.

Some studies have examined the extent to which mental health courts provided improved access to psychiatric services (see Honegger, 2015, for a brief description of these types of studies). For example, Cosden et al. (2005) assessed mental health court participants and nondiverted offenders at baseline and 6, 12, 18, and 24 months after participation, and they found that mental health court participants utilized mental health services at significantly greater rates than did nondiverted offenders. A similar study found that mental health court participants exhibited a 17% increase in the utilization of behavioral health services and used mental health services at a scientifically higher rate than the nondiverted offenders (Boothroyd et al., 2003). In more recent research, Keator et al. (2013) evaluated the number of "therapeutic treatment episodes" (operationalized as individual therapy, group therapy, case management, and medication management) received by mental health court participants and nondiverted offenders, and they found that mental health court participants were more likely to receive treatment services. They also found that mental health court participants received treatment more quickly and received a greater number of treatment hours (Keator et al., 2013). Finally, in their study of 94 participants in a South Dakota mental health court, Sneed et al. (2006) found a 5% increase in the number of participants who reported receiving mental health services from the initial intake to the 12-month follow up.

Some studies have examined the ability of mental health courts to effectively connect participants to certain types of mental health services. For example, in early research, Steadman and Naples (2005) found that mental health court participants received treatment services significantly more than did nondiverted offenders. Specifically, the mental health group received significantly more medication than the nondiverted group (81.5% vs. 73.7%) and significantly more mental health counseling (62.2% vs. 56.8%) (Steadman & Naples, 2005). In another study, investigators compared the amount of services received 1 year before enrollment in mental health court with the amount of services received 1 year after enrollment in mental health court, and they found that participants received significantly more hours of case management and medication management and significantly more days of mental health treatment following enrollment in mental health court (Herinckx et al., 2005). In more recent research, Luskin (2013) evaluated outcomes from four mental health courts in Indiana and found no significant increase in the rate of general outpatient or individual counseling services at a 6-month follow-up (Luskin, 2013). However, when compared with a nondiverted sample, the mental health court participants received significantly more outpatient treatment and different types of treatment, including individual counseling, group counseling, and case management services (Luskin, 2013). Luskin (2013) explained that the differences observed between mental health court clients and nondiverted offenders at the 6-month follow-up resulted from improvements in treatment provision among the mental health court group *and* deterioration of treatment provision in the nondiverted group.

However, not all research supports the ability of mental health courts to effectively connect participants with needed services. For example, in their evaluation of two mental health courts in Washington (Seattle and King County), Trupin and Richards (2003) found no significant differences between mental health court participants and nondiverted offenders with respect to service utilization. Notable, though, is that King County participants received significantly more mental health treatment post-enrollment compared with the rates of service they received pre-enrollment (Trupin & Richards, 2003).

In related research, Cosden et al. (2005) examined the relationship between the quantity of treatment services provided and the psychosocial outcomes of mental health court participants. Although they did not find statistically significant results, they highlighted a trend whereby individuals with lower GAF scores (which indicates more severe psychological symptoms and impairment) received more hours of treatment services (Cosden et al., 2005). These results suggest that at least some mental health courts are providing higher doses of treatment services to participants who have greater mental health needs, which is consistent with the Risk-Need-Responsivity Model (Andrews & Bonta, 2010b).

Quality of Life

In addition to seeking to ameliorate mental health symptoms by connecting participants to needed treatment services, mental health courts also seek to improve participants' perceived quality of life. With that said, we could only identify one study that explicitly studied quality of life among mental health court participants. Cosden et al. (2005) evaluated participants' perceived quality of life using Lehman's Quality of Life-Short Form (QOL-SF), and they found significant increases in scores (indicating better quality of life) among both mental health court participants and nondiverted offenders. However, they also found that mental health court participants exhibited significantly greater improvements in life satisfaction scores over time when compared with the nondiverted offenders (Cosden et al., 2005). The results should be interpreted cautiously, however, because the mental health court group received more intensive treatment services than the comparison group, which creates a confound that could skew the results. As is evident, there is a notable lack of research on the impact of mental health courts on participants' quality of life, and additional research is needed before we can make firm conclusions about the effectiveness of mental health courts in this domain.

Recidivism

Because reducing criminal recidivism is an explicit goal of all problem-solving courts, it is not surprising that most mental health court research has examined recidivism rates. For the criminal justice system, reducing recidivism is a high priority, and demonstrating that mental health courts effectively reduce recidivism in a cost-effective way can provide considerable leverage with funding sources. Although mental health courts are also interested in other outcomes (e.g., mental health functioning, quality of life), recidivism is by far the most heavily emphasized goal.

Fifteen of the 20 studies reviewed by Honegger (2015) examined the relationship between mental health court participation and recidivism rates. In these studies, recidivism was variably operationalized as new arrests, new convictions, number of days in the community post reentry, or number of days incarcerated after mental health court participation. Thirteen studies that examined recidivism found a statistically significant relationship between mental health court participation and lower recidivism rates (see Dirks-Linhorst & Linhorst, 2012; Frailing, 2010; Herinckx et al., 2005; Hiday & Ray, 2010; Hiday et al., 2013; Hoff et al., 1999; McNiel & Binder, 2007; Moore & Hiday, 2006; Sarteschi et al., 2011; Steadman et al., 2011; Steadman & Naples, 2005; Trupin & Richards, 2003 [Note: Trupin and Richards (2003) consisted of two studies]). One of the studies reviewed by Honegger (2015) found that there was a statically significant relationship between mental health court participation and higher recidivism rates (see Cosden et al., 2005), and the final study found no significant difference in recidivism rates between a mental health court sample and a comparison sample (see Christy et al., 2005).

Sarteschi and colleagues (2011) conducted a meta-analysis focused on evaluating the degree to which mental health courts effectively reduce recidivism. After evaluating 18 peer-reviewed and non–peer-reviewed studies, they reported a medium effect size (–.054) for the relationship between mental health court participation and reduced recidivism (Sartechi et al., 2011). There were, however, some notable limitations in the meta-analysis. Most of the included studies consisted of nonrepresentative samples with disproportionate numbers of Caucasian males. Furthermore, the majority of the studies were quasi-experimental and did not control for differences between groups. It is important to note that many studies of mental health courts use quasi-experimental designs because mental health court stakeholders are likely reluctant to agree to random assignment of offenders to mental health court or standard criminal justice processing. Although quasi-experimental designs limit the nature and strength of the inferences that can be drawn, they can still provide valuable data.

Steadman et al. (2011) conducted one of the only multisite investigations of the effects of mental health courts on recidivism. They evaluated four mental health courts using a longitudinal design over 18 months with large sample sizes (447 mental health court participants and 600 nondiverted offenders), and they accounted for the differences between the two groups using propensity score matching. There was a significant difference between the two groups in recidivism rates during the 18-month period following reentry, with mental health court participants being significantly less likely to be rearrested than nondiverted offenders (49% vs. 58%). In addition, during this 18-month period, mental health court participants were incarcerated for significantly fewer days on average than the nondiverted offenders (82 days vs. 152 days) (Steadman et al., 2011).

In earlier research, investigators examined the frequency and nature of rearrests among mental health court participants and a comparison group of nondiverted offenders (McNiel & Binder, 2007). Results revealed that mental health court participants spent more time in the community prior to rearrest for nonviolent and violent charges, and they also exhibited a decrease in rearrest rates for nonviolent and violent offenses (26% lower and 55% lower than the comparison group, respectively). Also notable is that mental health courts seemed to produce a lasting impact, as the results remained consistent at an 18-month follow-up assessment (McNiel & Binder, 2007).

Several other quasi-experimental studies and pretest/posttest design studies have found a significant relationship between mental health courts and decreased recidivism rates. Specifically, studies have found decreased rearrest rates (Dirks-Linhorst & Linhorst, 2012; Herinckx et al., 2005; Hiday & Ray, 2010; Hiday et al., 2013; McNiel & Binder, 2007; Moore & Hiday, 2006), fewer new bookings (Trupin & Richards, 2003), fewer days of incarceration (Frailing, 2010; Hoff et al., 1999), a decrease in the commission of minor offenses (Moore & Hiday, 2006), and an increase in days spent in the community prior to rearrest (Steadman & Naples, 2005). In a randomized control trial, Cosden et al. (2013) randomly assigned 235 offenders to a mental health court or comparison group, and they found that mental health court participants had significantly fewer convictions than the comparison group (46% vs. 60%). However, they also found that mental health court participants were more likely to be convicted for violating probation requirements, while offenders in the comparison group were more likely to be convicted of a new crime (Cosden et al., 2013).

Research has also focused on identifying factors that may be associated with lower recidivism rates among mental health court participants. Studies have shown that successful graduation from a mental health court program is associated with lower recidivism rates (Burns, Hiday, & Ray, 2013; Dirks-Linhorst & Linhorst, 2012; Hiday & Ray, 2010; Kubiak, Tillander, Comartin, & Ray, 2012; Moore & Hiday, 2006; Snedeker, Beach, & Corcoran, 2017). Other research has shown that mental health court participants of Hispanic ethnicity were less likely to recidivate than Non-Hispanic participants (Burns et al., 2013) and that participants entering mental health court with more serious offenses are more likely to have lower recidivism rates (Hoff et al., 1999). One study found that lower recidivism rates were associated with fewer days of arrest and incarceration prior to mental health court enrollment, a lack of substance abuse issues, steady housing, and a diagnosis of bipolar disorder (as opposed to a diagnosis of schizophrenia or major depressive disorder) (Steadman et al., 2011). In a recent study, Snedeker et al. (2017) found that graduating from the program, having stable and consistent mental health treatment, and participating in a program that offered incentives are associated with lower odds of reoffending, increased time to new reoffense, and fewer criminal charges. Hiday and Ray (2010) compared recidivism rates of mental health court participants and an equally eligible group of offenders who went through standard criminal justice processing. Two years after completion, recidivism rates decreased in both groups, but the greatest reduction was exhibited by mental health court participants who completed the program (Hiday & Ray, 2010). Participants who completed the mental health court program had the lowest recidivism rate (25%) and the fewest arrests, while mental health court participants who did not complete the program had the highest recidivism rate (55%) (Hiday & Ray, 2010).

Other research has identified factors that are associated with more negative recidivism outcomes for mental health court participants. For example, participants who fail to complete a mental health court program are more likely to recidivate (Hiday et al., 2013), as are participants who have a substance abuse disorder (Hiday et al., 2013; Reich, Picard-Fritsche, Cerniglia, & Hahn, 2014) and those with higher rates of arrest (Reich et al., 2014) or more days in jail (Burns et al., 2013). Participants with a history of engaging in more serious criminal activities are also more likely to recidivate (Moore & Hiday, 2006), as are participants who are younger (Hiday et al., 2013; Reich et al., 2014; Trawver, 2013) and who are not Caucasian, have less education, and rely on disability benefits (Trawver, 2013). In other research using a pretest/posttest design, investigators found that mental health court participants who were arrested after enrollment had a significantly higher number of prior days in jail and more previous arrests (Case, Steadman, Dupuis, & Morris, 2009).

One study examined the relationship between the principles of therapeutic jurisprudence and recidivism rates within mental health courts (Redlich & Han, 2014). Specifically, the researchers examined whether certain therapeutic jurisprudence principles were present at enrollment, including procedural justice, knowledge of the nature of the mental health court, and perceived voluntariness of participation in the mental health court program. They found that higher levels of therapeutic jurisprudence principles were associated with higher rates of graduation from mental health court programs (Redlich & Han, 2014). Although this association became statistically nonsignificant when the researchers included mediating factors, Redlich and Han (2014) nonetheless concluded that an indirect relationship remained: the presence of therapeutic jurisprudence principles led to fewer rearrests, decreased incarceration times, and increased participant compliance, which subsequently increased the likelihood of successful completion of the mental health court program.

Overall, the available research suggests that mental health courts have promise in terms of reducing recidivism rates for offenders with mental illness. Although the research in this area is somewhat limited and some of the methodologies have notable shortcomings, the body of research is encouraging and growing. After discussing some of the more notable limitations in the research, we offer recommendations for researchers moving forward.

Methodological and Research-Based Limitations

It is important to note that many studies on mental health courts have significant methodological limitations. For example, much of the research on mental health courts is marked by high rates of participant attrition (e.g., Cosden et al., 2005), incomplete data regarding mental health (e.g., Herinckx et al., 2005), and non-representative samples that did not adequately represent the composition of the criminal justice population (e.g., Herinckx et al., 2005; Sneed et al., 2006; Trupin & Richards, 2003). As such, the research findings from these studies should be interpreted with caution.

Furthermore, as with research on other problem-solving courts and other criminal justice interventions, the majority of studies on mental health courts have not used experimental designs, which limits the nature and strength of the inferences that can be drawn. Rubin (2008) created a hierarchy of evidence that set systematic reviews and meta-analyses at the highest level, followed by large-scale replications of experimental studies, experimental studies, and quasi-experimental studies. Only two studies on mental health courts have used experimental designs (Cosden et al., 2003, 2005), with the majority of mental health court research studies using quasi-experimental designs or pretest/posttest designs. Of the quasi-experimental studies identified in Honegger's (2015) review, only four used techniques aimed to mitigate the influence of nonrandom assignment—two studies used propensity score matching (McNiel & Binder, 2007; Steadman et al., 2011) and two used covariates (Boothroyd et al., 2003, 2005). We only found one meta-analysis (Sarteschi et al., 2011) and two comprehensive literature reviews (Heilbrun et al., 2012; Honegger, 2015).

As may be gleaned from the available research, conducting methodologically rigorous research on mental health courts is quite challenging for several reasons. First, using experimental designs with mental health court participants raises several ethical and legal concerns. There are many reasons why judges, defense attorneys, prosecutors, and offenders would resist randomly assigning offenders to either a mental health court or standard criminal justice processing. However, without an experimental design, the ability to draw causal inferences regarding the effects of mental health courts is limited. Second, federal funding has allowed for the relatively rapid development of mental health courts throughout the United States, and this rapid growth has made it challenging for researchers to keep up (Wolff & Pogorzelski, 2005). As such, the development of mental health courts is continuing even though we still lack a firm understanding of their effects. Third, the majority of longitudinal mental health court research has been conducted over relatively short time periods. Because some serious mental health disorders are chronic, it is important to understand the long-term impacts of mental health courts on mental health and other outcomes. Finally, as with most research, some nonmeasured variables could impact the validity of mental health court research, including the experience and motivation of the mental health court staff, participant understanding of his or her own mental health disorder, and the personality and working styles of the judge and other court staff (Wolff, 2000).

The variability of mental health courts across jurisdictions is a major reason why it is difficult to draw broad conclusions about the effects of mental health courts. Mental health courts lack uniformity in structure and are idiosyncratic in operation (Erickson et al., 2006). As outlined earlier, variability is found in the following aspects of mental health courts: (1) mental health court eligibility criteria (misdemeanors only, felonies only, both), (2) psychiatric diagnosis criteria (e.g., Does the court require a DSM diagnosis? Does the court only accept participants with bipolar disorder, schizophrenia, or major depressive disorder? Does the court exclude personality disorders? Does the court accept individuals with co-occurring disorders?), (3) types and quality of services provided, and (4) measured outcomes (i.e., Is success measured by fewer days incarcerated? Fewer convictions? Improved mental health functioning? Increased use of mental health services?). The variability among mental health courts makes it difficult for researchers to effectively compare programs or make broad conclusions about mental health courts (Watson, Hanrahan, Luchins, & Luriggio, 2001).

Participant attrition and noncompliance also present challenges for researchers. Moore and Hiday (2006) reported that one-third of the mental health court participants failed to complete the program due to noncompliance or a decision to opt out. Many studies indicated that participants were "noncompliant" but did not operationalize the term. There are different types of noncompliance (e.g., failing to meet program requirements vs. a new arrest), so the lack of specificity regarding the nature of the noncompliance limits the conclusions that can be drawn.

The demographic characteristics of study samples are also a source of concern. Only 4 of the 20 studies included in Honegger's (2015) review evaluated mental health courts with samples that were representative of the demographic composition of a justice-involved population. Honegger (2015) speculated that this demographic disparity could be accounted for by the following factors: (1) studies were conducted in geographic areas with a largely Caucasian population, (2) there were higher opt-out rates among racial and ethnic minorities compared with Caucasian participants, and (3) racial and ethnic minorities exhibited disproportionate ineligibility factors that precluded mental health court enrollment. Some researchers have expressed concern that many mental health court studies evaluate samples of participants that are homogenous and fail to accurately represent the offender population that the courts were designed to target (Wolff & Pogorzelski, 2005). Conducting studies with representative samples is an important step toward understanding the potential impact of mental health courts and, in turn, justifying the development and implementation of these courts across the country.

The lack of representativeness among study samples is obviously a concern for researchers, but it also highlights a larger concern: mental health courts do not appear to be enrolling participants who are reflective of the larger correctional population. As previously noted, research suggests that mental health court participants are predominantly Caucasian males in their mid-30s (Sarteschi et al., 2011). Given the demographic makeup of the correctional population in the United States, this finding is concerning. Racial and ethnic minorities are overrepresented in the U.S. criminal justice system (Rosich, 2007; Sabol & Minton, 2008), yet they appear to be considerably underrepresented in mental health courts. This suggests that mental health courts are failing to enroll participants from the target offender population.

To evaluate behavioral health outcomes, much of the extant research focuses on the number of therapy hours or case management meetings provided to mental health court participants, with relatively little focus on the specific types of services provided. Research should consider whether the provided interventions are evidence-based and whether they were designed to target criminogenic risk factors (Keator et al., 2013). It is also important to examine whether mental health court participants received interventions designed to targeted problem-solving and criminal thinking (as opposed to general supportive therapy). Because behavioral health treatments are so varied, simply evaluating the number of treatment hours provided will inevitably leave many questions unanswered. To better understand the relationship among treatment, mental health outcomes, and recidivism rates, the nature and quality of the treatment must be considered.

Recommendations for Future Research

The research reviewed in this chapter provides reason to be cautiously optimistic about mental health courts. There is growing evidence that mental health courts reduce recidivism, but research on the ability of these courts to connect participants to needed treatment services and improve mental health outcomes is mixed. Given the number of mental health courts in the United States (400+), and the projection that mental health courts will be the fastest growing type of problem-solving court over the next several years (Marlowe et al., 2016), it is important that we have a clear understanding of the effects of these courts.

A key recommendation for researchers is to use rigorous methodology. As reviewed in Chapter 4, several researchers have conducted randomized controlled trials in drug courts, so there is precedent for conducting rigorous research in a problem-solving court. If an experimental design is not possible, researchers should use statistical methods to account for the differences between nonrandomized groups, such as propensity score matching or the inclusion of covariates. Furthermore, given concerns related to participant attrition, researchers should use intent-to-treat designs as the primary method of analysis, with protocol analyses being considered a secondary or parallel approach.

There are a number of other suggestions for future researchers. First, mental health courts should be compared to other diversion programs designed for offenders with mental health disorders (Wolff & Pogorzelski, 2005). Such research would provide an important comparative benchmark regarding the effects of mental health courts. Second, research should examine the relationship between the nature and quality of the provided services and various participant outcomes (e.g., mental health functioning, quality of life, recidivism). In their comprehensive quantitative review, Sarteschi et al. (2011) found that some studies suggested that there may be a relationship between the quality of the treatment services and the success of mental health court participants. Unfortunately, there is insufficient empirical evidence to support this claim at present. Examining the services provided to mental health court participants is complicated because mental health courts typically have limited control over the quality of the treatment provided to participants. As such, the court itself may not be responsible if a participant's mental health symptoms do not improve with the treatment. Third, more longitudinal and follow-up research is needed to examine the longer term effects of mental health courts. Fourth, research should examine the previously discussed demographic disparity in which mental health courts are primarily enrolling groups of participants who are not reflective of the correctional population. Fifth, research should examine whether mental health courts are cost-effective compared to standard criminal justice processing. Sixth, once more outcome research is conducted, researchers should conduct dismantling studies to examine which specific aspects of mental health courts are responsible for their effects.

Finally, more research is needed to examine the complex relationship among mental illness, criminogenic risk factors, and recidivism. Research suggests that offenders with and without mental illness share the same types of criminogenic risk factors (Andrews, Bonta, & Wormith, 2006; Bonta, Law, & Hanson, 1998). However, "Despite mounting evidence for a more complex understanding of recidivism among persons with mental illness, mental health court research has customarily assumed that clinical and psychosocial factors precipitate criminal behavior, and that improvement in symptomology reduces recidivism" (Honegger, 2015, p. 486). Indeed, Skeem, Manchak, and Peterson (2011) have asserted that providing treatment through mental health courts may not be the most effective way to reduce recidivism. As such, future research should consider using a more nuanced conceptual model that takes into account the relationship among mental health symptoms, criminogenic risk factors, and recidivism (see Skeem & Monahan, 2011).

Next Steps

Since the first mental health court was established in Florida more than 20 years ago, these courts have become a firmly established intervention in the criminal justice system. With more than 400 operational mental health courts and many more in advanced stages of development, it is safe to assume that mental health courts will continue to serve certain offenders with mental health involvement. Despite the proliferation of these courts, important questions remain about their utility, effectiveness, and how well they serve the intended population of offenders. As noted in previous sections of this chapter, we need a better understanding of the effects of these courts on recidivism and mental health functioning, among other things. There is also a need for cost–benefit research that examines whether mental health courts make fiscal sense compared to other interventions for offenders with mental illness.

In addition to further developing the research base, consideration should be given to how the mental health court model can be adapted or expanded. As with drug courts, mental health courts serve a fraction of the offenders with mental illness, so identifying ways to broaden the reach of mental health courts would allow them to serve more eligible offenders. One way to broaden the reach of mental health courts is to use less conservative eligibility criteria. As previously noted, some mental health courts require a formal psychiatric diagnosis for an offender to be eligible. Requiring a formal diagnosis as a prerequisite to eligibility may be too restrictive. There are likely many offenders with mental health symptoms that do not rise to the level of severity needed to satisfy diagnostic criteria, but who would nonetheless benefit from the services offered as part of mental health court. A loosening of the eligibility criteria, without compromising public safety, would be an effective way to expand the reach of mental health courts.

As mental health courts continue to be developed and refined, it will be important for these courts to address both criminogenic needs and behavioral health needs. For these courts to be effective, there cannot be a sharp distinction between behavioral health interventions and criminogenic interventions. Indeed, interventions for behavioral health needs and criminogenic needs often overlap, and eligible offenders may need help in the areas of mental health, substance use, family, housing, and jobs. There is a subgroup of offenders whose offending behavior is driven primarily by behavioral health symptoms, but the majority of offending behavior results from both behavioral health needs and criminogenic needs (Andrews et al., 2006; Bonta et al., 1998). Accordingly, mental health courts can be most effective by addressing both sets of needs.

Another possibility involves combining mental health courts with other types of problem-solving courts, an approach being considered in Delaware. Given the proliferation of problem-solving courts in Delaware over the past 20 years, Delaware Supreme Court Chief Justice Leo E. Strine, Jr. appointed the Criminal Justice Council of the Judiciary to review all of the problem-solving courts in Delaware to help determine how to increase their impact (Criminal Justice Council of the Judiciary, 2016). Delaware has a range of problem-solving courts, including truancy court, human trafficking court, gun court, reentry court, drug court, veterans treatment court, and mental health court. Among other things, this Council concluded that Delaware would benefit from creating a unified statewide treatment court that encompasses all of the other problem-solving courts, including mental health courts (Criminal Justice Council of the Judiciary, 2016). The Council asserted that the needs of offenders often span multiple problem-solving courts, and a single-source approach would enhance the likelihood that these multiple needs are addressed. Such an approach would also allow for the consolidation of treatment providers into a single unit, which would improve communication and the coordination of treatment services (Criminal Justice Council of the Judiciary, 2016). A statewide approach may be feasible in Delaware, which is a relatively small state geographically, and larger states could create several umbrella problem-solving courts spread out geographically throughout the state.

Finally, mental health courts may benefit from use of the restorative justice model. Restorative justice focuses on the rehabilitation of offenders through reconciliation with victims and the community. As mental health courts have become more willing over the years to accept offenders charged with violent offenses, victim involvement in mental health courts has increased. Restorative justice has been shown to have several benefits over standard criminal justice processing. In a meta-analysis, Latimer, Dowden, and Muise (2005) found that restorative justice programs were more effective than traditional nonrestorative approaches in terms of victim and offender satisfaction, restitution compliance, and recidivism. Adding in a restorative justice component may therefore boost the effectiveness of mental health courts in reducing criminal recidivism.

6
Other Specialty Courts

As drug courts and, to a lesser extent, mental health courts proliferated across the United States, several jurisdictions have begun developing other types of problem-solving courts. All of these other types of problem-solving courts are based on the same premise: addressing an offender's criminogenic and clinical needs will result in reduced recidivism and a better quality of life. The development of these other types of specialty courts, some of which target extremely narrow populations of offenders, has led to a discussion about whether such specialized courts are necessary and whether the types of offenders being targeted represent a distinct subset of offenders.

In this chapter, we begin by describing the various types of problem-solving courts—besides drug courts and mental health courts—that have been developed over the past few decades. Next, we review the empirical evidence for these courts. As will be discussed, only a few of these courts have any supportive research; most of these problem-solving courts have not yet received sufficient (or any) attention from researchers, so we lack an empirical basis for assessing the effectiveness of these courts. We conclude this chapter with an analysis of the utility of these specialty problem-solving courts, including a discussion of whether there is sufficient justification for their continued operation.

Other Problem-Solving Courts

As noted in Chapter 2, the success of drug courts in reducing relapse to drug use and criminal recidivism led to the development of a variety of other problem-solving courts over the past several decades (see Marlowe, Hardin, & Fox, 2016, for a detailed description of different types of problem-solving courts). These specialty problem-solving courts include:

- *Veterans treatment courts*: These courts, which serve military veterans and some active-duty personnel, promote sobriety, recovery, and stability through a collaboration among the criminal justice system, treatment providers, the Department of Veterans Affairs healthcare networks, the Veterans Benefits Administration, State Departments of Veterans Affairs, volunteer veteran mentors, and organizations that support veterans and veterans' families. Between 2009 and 2014, veterans courts increased 14-fold, and currently more than 350 problem-solving courts offer specialized services for military veterans and/or active-duty personnel (Marlowe et al., 2016).

- *DUI/DWI courts*: These courts serve individuals charged with instances of driving under the influence (DUI) or driving while intoxicated/impaired (DWI), and they occasionally serve first-time DUI offenders who have risk factors for future instances of impaired driving. These courts seek to protect public safety by addressing alcohol and drug abuse issues. DWI courts often provide enhanced monitoring through home visits, field visits, and advanced technology (e.g., ignition interlock devices, SCRAM transdermal alcohol detection device). There were 262 DUI/DWI courts as of year-end 2014, which represents a more than 50% increase in recent years (Marlowe et al., 2016).
- *Family dependency treatment courts (or family drug courts)*: Family dependency treatment courts consist of dockets for selected abuse, neglect, and dependency cases in which parental or guardian substance use is a major contributing factor. These courts involve a collaborative effort among judges, attorneys, child protection services, and treatment providers who seek to ensure safe homes for children while connecting parents to treatment services that will help them achieve and maintain sobriety.
- *Co-occurring disorders courts*: These courts serve individuals charged with juvenile or criminal offenses who have both a substance use disorder and a serious or persistent mental health disorder. There are relatively few of these courts, and it is important to note that may drug courts and mental health courts also serve co-occurring populations.
- *Gambling courts*: Based heavily on the drug court model, gambling courts target individuals with pending criminal charges or other legal actions (e.g., home foreclosure) who have a gambling disorder or exhibit problematic gambling behaviors. Individuals in these courts participate in judicially supervised recovery programs (e.g., Gamblers Anonymous) and can receive mental health services, debt counseling, and substance use treatment. To increase the likelihood of a successful outcome, these courts encourage participants' family members to be involved.
- *Community courts*: These courts, which were developed in Manhattan in 1993, focus on low-level, "quality of life" offenses, typically misdemeanors or summary offenses such as petty theft, public intoxication, vandalism, loitering, and turnstile jumping (see Hakuta, Soroushian, & Kralstein, 2008; Karafin, 2008; Malkin, 2003). Community courts hold offenders

accountable for their behavior while also providing treatment and other social services and encouraging/requiring participants to complete community service.

- *Truancy courts*: These courts seek to address the underlying causes of truancy (e.g., school phobia, bullying, learning disabilities, poor parental guidance) through the combined efforts of the court, school, treatment providers, families, and community. Students' attendance is closely monitored by the school, with regular (typically weekly) reports submitted to the court. As with other problem-solving courts, truancy courts consist of a separate court docket (they are not a separate court), so truancy court proceedings are often held at the school. Typically, regular school attendance results in the dismissal of the truancy petition.
- *Domestic violence courts*: These courts service individuals charged with domestic violence offenses and address problems typically associated with domestic violence, such as the low prevalence of reporting, withdrawn/dropped charges, threats to the victim, and high recidivism rates (see Ostrom, 2003). Domestic violence courts provide highly intense court oversight and require cooperation between the court and social service providers. Among other things, these courts ensure separation between the participant and the victim, and they help provide the victim with housing and job training to facilitate and encourage independence from the offender. The participant is closely monitored to ensure compliance with treatment requirements and protective orders. These courts exist at both felony and misdemeanor levels.
- *Gun courts*: These courts target adolescents and adults charged with firearm offenses that did not result in serious physical injury. The intervention provided by these courts typically involves educating offenders about gun safety.
- *Homelessness courts*: These courts target individuals charged with low-level summary or nuisance offenses (e.g., panhandling, vagrancy, loitering). Homelessness courts seek to help participants secure stable housing and necessary social services, including drug treatment, mental health treatment, life skills training, literacy classes, and job training.
- *Prostitution courts*: Philadelphia became the first jurisdiction in the United States to develop a problem-solving court designed specifically for women with repeat sex-work offenses. Participants often have significant trauma histories, drug involvement, and/or mental health problems, and they may have been the victim of human trafficking or other types of sexual exploitation. Philadelphia's court, known as Project Dawn Court, seeks to connect nonviolent repeat offenders with therapeutic and reentry services, reduce recidivism among prostitution offenders, and reduce the financial burden

that would result from housing these offenders in jail. Since the development of Project Dawn Court, several other jurisdictions across the United States have opened similar courts. There are fewer than 20 of these courts currently in operation (Marlowe et al., 2016).

- *Tribal healing to wellness court (or tribal wellness courts)*: These courts seek to meet the specific drug treatment needs of each tribal community, and they involve a collaboration among tribal judges, advocates, prosecutors, police officers, educators, treatment providers, tribal elders, and traditional healers.
- *Campus drug courts*: These courts apply the principles of drug courts to college students facing disciplinary action (suspension or expulsion) for drug- or alcohol-related behavior. These courts use existing college resources (e.g., health services and counseling) and involve collaborations among college administration, student development practitioners, treatment providers, and health professionals, along with their governmental, judicial, and treatment counterparts in the community.

The most prevalent types of problem-solving courts in the United States are drug courts and mental health courts. The most recent estimates indicate that, as of 2012, there were approximately 261 family courts, 244 youth specialty courts, 217 hybrid DWI/drug courts, 183 DWI courts, and 31 tribal wellness courts (see Strong, Rantala, & Kyckelhahn, 2016). Furthermore, Marlowe et al. (2016) noted that by year-end 2014, there were 18 prostitute courts (a 125% increase in the number of such courts over the previous 5 years) and 210 domestic violence courts. Also, by year-end 2015, there were an estimated 172 veterans treatment courts in the United States (Justice for Vets, 2015). These less common types of problem-solving courts are most likely to be established in counties with larger populations where there is more diversity in offending behavior and more resources to support the court's operation.

Identifying the number of problem-solving courts may be difficult, in part because these courts treat multiple offender populations, which impacts census counting. For example, although Justice for Vets (2015) indicates that there are 172 veterans treatment courts, Marlowe et al. (2016) noted that more than 350 problem-solving courts offer specialized services for military veterans or active-duty personnel, even if those courts are not technically classified as veterans treatment courts. Finally, in some states, there are restrictions on which courts can officially be called problem-solving courts, often stemming from questions regarding which entity is responsible for the costs of the program. However, some judges in these jurisdictions are essentially running a problem-solving court even though the court is not officially designated as such. Therefore, the figures just cited should be viewed as approximations—and likely deflated approximations—of the numbers of specialized courts and programs developed over recent decades.

Research on Other Problem-Solving Courts

The majority of problem-solving court research has focused on drug courts, and there is considerably less research focused on mental health courts. The research gap between mental health courts and the other types of specialty courts discussed in this chapter is substantial. As will be discussed, research on the other specialty problem-solving courts described earlier is much less developed, and we were unable to locate any research for several of these courts.

DUI/DWI Courts

Approximately 25% of individuals who are arrested for DUI are subsequently rearrested for another DUI offense (Warren-Kigenyi & Coleman, 2014). Furthermore, nearly half of all individuals arrested for DUIs have a diagnosable substance use and/or mental health disorder (Lapham, C'de Baca, McMillan, & Lapidus, 2006; Shaffer et al., 2007). These figures are alarming, and they have prompted the development of numerous interventions designed to reduce DUI and related offenses (e.g., DWI).

Unfortunately, research suggests that psychosocial interventions have no significant impact on reducing repeat DUIs. Similarly, ignition interlock devices—devices that prevent a car from starting until the driver passes a breathalyzer test—have low compliance rates and poor effectiveness in reducing rearrest once the device is no longer in the car (Miller, Curtis, Sonderlund, Day, & Droste, 2015). Some research, however, supports the effectiveness of certain substance abuse treatment services, probation/court supervision, and license restrictions (Lapham et al., 2006; Miller et al., 2015), although the effects of these interventions across studies are quite variable.

The limited success of most interventions for DUI offenders, combined with the demonstrated success of drug courts for drug-involved offenders, led to the development of DUI courts. The first DUI court was established in Doña Ana, New Mexico, in 1995 (Marlowe et al., 2016), and there are now nearly 200 across the country (Strong et al., 2016). DUI courts are modeled after drug courts and similarly require participants to take random drug tests, appear in court at regularly scheduled intervals for status hearings, and participate in various treatment options. The use of sanctions and rewards is also common (Marlowe et al., 2016). There is, however, a key distinction between DUI courts and drug courts.

DUI courts cannot drop or reduce charges in exchange for compliance, and thus lack the diversion element of some drug courts. DUI courts are generally postadjudication courts: some participants serve some jail time as part of the sentence and then are released early to participate in the DUI court, with the understanding that failure to comply with court requirements may result in a return to jail (Marlowe et al., 2016). Also, many DUI courts are hybrid courts that have a drug court program and a DUI court program; the same judge and staff participate in all cases, but separate dockets exist for each program. Similar to drug courts, DUI courts target high-risk/high-need offenders (Carey, Herrera Allen, Einspruch, Mackin, & Marlowe, 2015; NPC Research, 2014; Sloan, Chepke, Davis, Acquah, & Zold-Kilbourn, 2013). In terms of retention and completion rates, a Michigan evaluation of nine DUI courts found a retention and completion rate of 54–84% (Carey, Fuller, & Kissick, 2008), which is similar to the reported rates for drug courts.

The research on DUI/DWI courts consists of a mix of large-scale studies and program evaluations of individual courts. Although the research base on these courts is larger than the research base for the other types of problem-solving courts discussed in this chapter, there is noticeably less research on these courts than on mental health courts and drug courts. Also, as will be discussed, several methodological weaknesses limit the types and strength of conclusions that can be drawn.

Several large-scale studies of multiple DUI/DWI courts have examined these courts' ability to reduce recidivism (typically defined as a new DUI/DWI arrest). Although limited, several multisite studies have found that participation in DUI/DWI courts is associated with reduced recidivism. An early evaluation of three pilot DUI courts in Georgia provided some of the first data on the effectiveness of these courts (Fell, Tippetts, & Lanston, 2008). The retention rate of these three courts over a 4-year period was 79%. Individuals who graduated from the DUI courts had a recidivism rate of 9% compared to recidivism rates of 26% for individuals who were terminated from the DUI courts and 35% for matched individuals who would have been eligible for the DUI court had it existed at the time of their offenses (Fell et al., 2008). A study of nine Michigan DUI courts found significantly lower rearrest rates for DUI court participants compared to a historical sample of potential participants from the year prior to the creation of the DUI courts (Michigan Supreme Court State Court Administrative Office, 2008). Finally, a study of Idaho DUI courts revealed lower recidivism rates over a 4-year period among individuals who participated in DUI court compared to individuals who were eligible for DUI court but chose not to participate (Ronan, Collins, & Rosky, 2009). The overall recidivism rate, which was defined as reconvictions (not rearrests), for DUI court participants was 23% compared to 37% for the non–DUI court participants (Ronan et al., 2009). Finally, one meta-analysis of drug courts evaluated 28 studies that included hybrid drug/DUI courts (Mitchell, Wilson, Eggers, & MacKenzie, 2012). The majority of the studies (85%) found that DUI courts significantly reduce the risk of DUI recidivism and general criminal recidivism by an average rate of 12%.

Not all large-scale studies have yielded favorable findings for DUI/DWI courts. Cissner (2009) compared 90 participants from the Erie County and Niagara County DWI/Drug Courts in New York to 259 similar offenders from the same geographic area. Results revealed no significant differences in rearrest rates from the point of court entry between the two groups (Cissner, 2009).

A number of studies of individual DUI/DWI courts have also been conducted. In the first experimental study of these courts, DUI offenders classified as having an alcohol abuse disorder were randomly assigned to the treatment group (DUI court) or standard court processing (Breckenridge, Winfree, Maupin, & Clason, 2000). Results revealed that individuals who participated in DUI court had fewer reconvictions than those who went through standard court processing. Unfortunately, the results of this study must be interpreted with caution because the DUI court judge who originally agreed to random assignment left the bench for 9 months after the study began; the replacement judge did not agree to random assignment, which resulted in a small sample size (Breckenridge et al., 2000).

Several other studies of individual programs support the utility of DUI/DWI courts. A study of the Waukesha Alcohol Treatment Court evaluated outcomes for DWI offenders in Wisconsin (Hiller et al., 2009). The researchers compared DWI court participants to a wait-list comparison group using intent-to-treat statistical analyses, and results showed significantly lower recidivism rates for the DWI court participants (29%) compared to the wait list sample (45%) (Hiller et al., 2009). A study of a DUI court in San Joaquin County, California, found that individuals who completed DUI court were half as likely to be involved in any alcohol- or drug-related motor vehicle accident up to 18 months after participation (Carey, Allen, & Einspruch, 2012). An evaluation of the Kootenai County DUI Court in Idaho showed a 4% recidivism rate for DUI court participants compared to a 25% recidivism rate for individuals who were terminated from the program, which suggests that program completion is important for producing positive results (Crancer, 2003). However, this study was limited by its small sample size, with only 46 graduates and 20 terminated individuals (Crancer, 2003). Finally, the results of studies with longer follow-up time periods suggest that the benefits of DUI courts last up to 4 years (e.g., Kierkus & Johnson, 2015; Ronan et al., 2009).

Despite some supportive research, several studies have concluded that participation in DUI court is not associated with improved outcomes, and, in at least one study, participation was associated with worse outcomes. In an early research study, Bouffard and Richardson (2007) found that participation in a hybrid drug court/DUI court was not associated with a significant reduction in recidivism. Subsequent research (Bouffard, Richardson, & Franklin, 2010) resulted in similar findings, with results showing that participation in a hybrid drug/DUI court was not associated with reduced recidivism among chronic DUI offenders. In fact, participants from the DUI court had *increased* rates of recidivism (Bouffard et al., 2010). A randomized controlled trial on the Rio Hondo DUI court in Los Angeles involved the random assignment of 284 participants to either DUI court or traditional court, with interviews conducted at a 2-year follow-up (MacDonald, Morral, Raymond, & Eibner, 2007). Unlike other studies, this study did not focus on recidivism rates, but rather on the court's therapeutic impact. The researchers noted few significant differences on any outcomes between DUI court participants and standard court participants, which led them to conclude that DUI courts have minimal therapeutic and public safety benefits (MacDonald et al., 2007). Notably, this DUI court was discontinued after this study was published (Marlowe et al., 2009). Finally, a study of a DUI court in Texas found no significant differences in rearrest rates for DUI court participants and nonparticipants at 6-month and 12-month follow-up points (Cavanaugh & Franklin, 2012).

A small body of research has examined predictors of success in DUI/DWI courts. An evaluation of the Bernalillo County Metropolitan DWI/Drug Court looked at characteristics of successful and unsuccessful participants, and the factors associated with program success included having fewer dependents, being employed, having a longer history of substance use, being older, participation in prior inpatient treatment, successful completion of early phases of the court program, participation in acupuncture sessions, participation in at least one outpatient counseling session, and involvement with victim impact panels (Guerin & Pitts, 2002). These investigators also identified several factors associated with reduced program success, including having at least one failed drug screen and participating in intensive outpatient treatment. Of note, sex, ethnicity, marital status, years of education, and criminal history were not associated with either success or failure in the program (Guerin & Pitts, 2002). The Michigan evaluation of nine DUI courts found that participants were more likely to fail if they had illegal drugs in their system at the time of arrest, spent more days in jail prior to beginning DUI court, and had more positive alcohol screens and a higher number of sanctions imposed during the program (Carey et al., 2008).

Limited data exist on the cost-effectiveness of DUI/DWI courts. Although some studies have concluded that these courts are less expensive for communities than standard probation (e.g., Guerin & Pitts, 2002; Solop et al., 2003), a more nuanced study of the Rio Hondo DUI Court in Los Angeles found that costs of the DUI court exceeded the expenditures of traditional courts for second-time offenders but produced cost-savings for third-time offenders (Eibner, Morral, Pacula, & MacDonald, 2006). Findings from the latter study suggest that cost-savings associated with these courts may be greatest for repeat offenders.

The DUI court research base has significant methodological limitations, which restricts the nature and strength of conclusions that can be drawn (Marlowe et al., 2009). Some of the limitations are related to the research studies (e.g., no randomization, inappropriate comparison group), while other limitations are related to the courts themselves. For example, some researchers have noted that some courts cannot be studied due to the failure to maintain sufficient documentation and records (e.g., Belenko, 2002b; Guerin & Watkins, 2009). In terms of limitations of extant research studies, Miller et al. (2015) were unable to conduct a meta-analysis on DUI courts because many existing studies were nonexperimental and/or used poor methodology, which restricted the ability to calculate effect sizes. Other limitations include only reporting outcomes for program graduates, failing to account for attrition within the program, and evaluating programs too soon after development.

Taken together, the research on DUI/DWI courts is mixed, with some studies showing reduced recidivism and others showing no meaningful effects on recidivism. Some evidence suggests that standalone courts are more reliably associated with recidivism reduction, whereas hybrid DWI/drug courts seem to result in less meaningful reductions in recidivism. However, given the limited amount of DUI court research, including the small number of rigorous studies, it is premature to draw firm conclusions regarding the effectiveness of these courts. As the research base continues to grow, researchers can take a more detailed look at the different types of treatments provided across these courts; such heterogeneity in court operation makes it difficult to conduct large-scale studies and reach broad conclusions.

Veterans Treatment Courts

Veterans treatment courts were established to address the high rates of criminal justice involvement and the unique treatment needs of military veterans and active-duty military personnel (Marlowe et al., 2016). Although several courts attempted to create separate dockets for justice-involved veterans (Berenson, 2010), including a court in Anchorage, Alaska, in 2004 (Holbrook & Anderson, 2011), the first official veterans treatment court did not become operational until 2008 in Buffalo, New York (Marlowe et al., 2016). As previously noted, there are currently approximately 172 veterans treatment courts in the United States (Justice for Vets, 2015), although many more courts provide services to military veterans or active-duty personnel (Marlowe et al., 2016).

As with most problem-solving courts, veterans treatment courts are modeled after drug courts and mental health courts, so they include similar components, such as provision or referrals to substance abuse and mental health treatment, collaborative and nonadversarial approaches to case processing, drug testing and treatment adherence monitoring by the court, the use of sanctions and rewards, and frequent court hearings (Clark, McGuire, & Blue-Howells, 2010; Marlowe et al., 2016). Similar to other problem-solving courts, involvement in veterans treatment courts can begin at different time points during case processing. For pre-plea or diversion courts, successful completion can result in the charges being reduced or dismissed; for postsentencing programs, individuals can reduce their time on probation (Smee et al., 2013). Veterans treatment courts often consist of a separate docket nested within a different type of problem-solving court, typically either a drug court or mental health court (Douds, Ahlin, Howard, & Stigerwalt, 2017). Finally, 38% of veterans treatment courts do not accept individuals with a history of violent crime (Strong et al., 2016).

There are several distinct features of veterans treatment courts. A notable difference between these courts and other problem-solving courts is that veterans treatment courts rely on the use of VA services and seek to establish community partnerships between the court and local VAs (Baldwin, 2014, 2015). Moreover, some courts allow veterans who are ineligible for VA services to participate in their courts (McGuire, Clark, Blue-Howells, & Coe, 2013). Case management in veterans treatment courts is also generally outsourced to VA providers or VA-employed community agencies (Blonigen et al., 2016). Some veterans courts use representatives of the VA known as *veteran justice outreach* (VJO) coordinators as specially trained case managers for justice-involved veterans (Blue-Howells, Clark, van den Berk-Clark, & McGuire, 2013). Another key feature of veterans treatment courts is peer mentorship, whereby participants receive advice and support from other veterans. The use of peer mentors is becoming popular with other problem-solving courts, but it originated in veterans treatment courts (Vaughan, Holleran, & Brooks, 2019).

Very little research exists on veterans treatment courts. An early survey study of 14 veterans treatment courts revealed a recidivism rate of less than 2% (Holbrook & Anderson, 2011), but the small number of graduates across all 14 veterans treatment courts ($N = 59$) prevents any conclusions from being drawn. An early outcome study of the first veterans treatment court in Buffalo reported a 0% recidivism rate 1 year into the court's operation (Russell, 2009), although the short outcome period likely accounts for the unusually low recidivism rate. A pre/post evaluation of the Rochester Veterans Treatment Court in New York reported a 59% reduction in arrests after participants entered the program (Commaroto, Jewell, & Wilder, 2011), but the lack of a comparison group is a notable limitation. Based on their evaluation of a Substance Abuse and Mental Health Services Administration (SAMHSA)-funded veterans treatment court in Colorado, other investigators (Slattery, Dugger, Lamb, & Williams, 2013) reported reduced symptoms of substance abuse and posttraumatic stress disorder (PTSD) for veterans treatment court participants at both 6- and 12-month follow-ups. A more recent study examined the impact of veterans treatment courts for trauma-affected veterans (Knudsen & Wingenfield, 2015). This study concluded that veterans treatment court participation led to more positive recovery outcomes (e.g., mental health, trauma, substance use) and improved quality of life at both 6- and 12-month follow-ups. Finally, a study conducted on the Bexar County Veterans Treatment Court in Texas found significantly lower rearrest rates for court participants than for veterans who declined to enter the court (Frantzen, 2015).

Two studies examined factors associated with success/failure in veterans treatment courts. Using telephone survey data from numerous veterans treatment courts, Johnson et al. (2016) identified program elements that were associated with higher rates of termination from the court, including phase progression with measurable goals, frequent drug and alcohol testing, and sanctions for failing intermediate goals (e.g., sobriety) as relevant factors. Factors that were associated with lower rates of termination included programs in which later phases allowed for less stringent monitoring, the use of behavior contracts, and brief incarceration as a sanction for noncompliance (Johnson et al., 2016). Using a large VA database (N = 1,224), Johnson et al. (2017) evaluated variables related to incarceration for participants in veterans treatment courts. They found that parole violations, longer stays in the veterans treatment court program, and seeking necessary mental health treatment were associated with higher incarceration rates due to noncompletion with the requirements of the veterans treatment court program, whereas variables associated with lower incarceration rates included stable housing and participation in a veteran-specific substance abuse treatment program (Johnson et al., 2017).

Despite the existence of veterans courts for more than a decade, relatively little research has been conducted on these courts, and the extant research consists of only surveys, program evaluations, and single-court studies. Furthermore, many studies have significant methodological limitations, including anecdotal reports and either no comparison groups or biased comparison groups (see Christy, Clark, Frei, & Rynearson-Moody, 2012; Marlowe et al., 2016). Given that veterans treatment courts are likely to be expanded in the next few years (Marlowe et al., 2016), the research base will likely expand accordingly.

Community Courts

Community courts were developed to expedite case processing and provide service linkage for individuals charged with low-level, nonviolent crimes. These courts provide social service assessments, individualized treatment, and case management services to low-level offenders who commit "quality of life" crimes—that is, crimes that reduce property values, community cohesion, and public health status for the offender and the community (e.g., prostitution, drug dealing/possession, theft). Community courts are typically located in large cities and other areas or neighborhoods where these types of misdemeanors and summary offenses are common (Lang, 2011). The first community court was established in Manhattan in 1993 (Sviridoff, Rottman, Ostrom, & Curtis, 2000). There are relatively few community courts across the United States, with a recent estimate of 40–50 such courts (Grommon, Hipple, & Ray, 2017).

Although problem-solving courts typically target justice-involved individuals with particular needs (e.g., mental health, substance use) or a specific population (e.g., veterans), community courts are unique in that they tailor their services to the needs of the surrounding community (Lang, 2011). Community courts function as a convenient point of entry through which disadvantaged and severely impaired individuals can gain access to a wide variety of treatment services. Although there is variation, community courts maintain several of the same components as other problem-solving courts, including nonadversarial case processing, collaborative relationships between court personnel and community agencies, the involvement of case managers or clinicians in providing or linking individuals to services, and the use of sanctions and rewards. However, a unique feature of community courts is that both victims and local community members are encouraged to collaborate with the court, and judges have more discretion in how cases are resolved (Sviridoff et al., 2000, 2002). Community courts emphasize restitution and improving the quality of surrounding communities (Lang, 2011; Lee et al., 2013). Successful completion of a community court program can result in the dismissal of charges and expungement of the individual's arrest record.

As with several other types of problem-solving courts, research on community courts is lacking and we could not locate any large-scale studies. Community courts are intended to be responsive to the needs of the community, so in this sense community courts are expected to differ quite considerably. Given the wide variation of community court operation, multisite studies would be challenging to conduct and would perhaps yield limited useful data.

The available research on community courts is limited to program evaluations and single-court studies. In the first study of a community court, the National

Center for State Courts found that participants in the Midtown (New York) Community Court had considerably reduced arrests for low-level crimes, such as prostitution (63% decrease) and illegal vending (24% decrease), and increased compliance rates in community treatment by 50% (Sviridoff et al., 2000). Participation in the Red Hook Community Court (Brooklyn, New York) was associated with a significantly reduced likelihood of rearrest at a 2-year follow-up—approximately 10% for adults and 12% for juveniles (Lee et al., 2013). The San Francisco Community Justice Center has shown a positive impact on recidivism, with lower rearrest rates for individuals within the Center's catchment area (Kilmer & Sussell, 2014). At a community level, community courts are associated with a reduction in petty theft, burglary, and motor vehicle theft (Lee at al., 2013; Sviridoff et al., 2002).

Some research, however, suggests that participation in community courts is not associated with reduced recidivism. Using a retrospective quasi-experimental design, the Indianapolis Community Court found no significant differences between court participants and nonparticipants in terms of recidivism rates (Grommon et al., 2017). Furthermore, the Seattle Community Court saw no significant differences in recidivism at an 18-month follow-up, with 80% recidivism rates for both the community court group and non–community court group (Nugent-Borakove, 2009).

Several studies have examined the ability of these courts to improve outcomes other than recidivism. For example, research suggests that participants in the Midtown Community Court experienced shorter case processing time, increased rates of community service completion, significantly reduced use of jail sentences, and enhanced support from local communities (Hakuta et al., 2008; Sviridoff et al., 2000, 2002). The Hennepin County Community Court in Minneapolis saw significant reduction in the number of days between case filing and disposition, increased community service compliance, and increased community awareness and support (Eckberg, 2001; Weidner & Davis, 2000). The Seattle Community Court found increased rates of community service, and successful completers of the court had higher rates of service linkage than did noncompleters (Mahoney & Carlson, 2007). Bronx Community Solutions used records to compare sentences of defendants before and after implementation of the community court, and results showed that the court increased the use of alternative sanctions and decreased the use of jail as a punishment for noncompliance (Katz, 2009). The Philadelphia Community Court saw increased compliance with community service, and participant ratings indicated decreased criminal and other negative behavior (e.g., drinking, prostitution) (Durkin et al., 2009). An evaluation of the Red Hook Community Court in Brooklyn found that the court improved the timeliness of case processing, increased community service completion, and reduced the use of time-served sentences (Lee et al.,

2013). Finally, although the research is limited, studies have shown that community courts increase justice-involved individuals' perceptions of procedural fairness, which is correlated with better long-term outcomes (Frazer, 2006; Lee et al., 2013).

Community courts are expected to increase in number over the next several years, and the expansion of community courts has outpaced the research. As discussed earlier, the available research is limited. The absence of large-scale studies is a notable limitation in the literature base, and the heterogeneity of community courts makes it challenging to conduct multisite studies and meta-analyses. Research has produced mixed findings; community courts appear to have beneficial effects in terms of case processing, service linkage, and perceptions of fairness, but it is difficult to draw firm conclusions regarding the ability of these courts to reduce future arrests.

Domestic Violence Courts

Domestic violence courts were created to provide a specialized docket for managing cases related to intimate partner violence. As with other problem-solving courts, domestic violence courts are based on therapeutic jurisprudence principles, and they seek to increase coordination between social services agencies and the justice system, hold defendants accountable, and address the needs of victims (Gover, MacDonald, & Alpert, 2003). Many of these courts also focus on treating substance use, which frequently occurs in cases of intimate partner violence (Riger, Bennett, & Sigurvinsdottir, 2014). The first domestic violence courts were established in the early to mid-1990s (mostly as separate dockets as opposed to formal problem-solving courts), and Marlowe et al. (2016) reported that the first felony domestic violence court opened in Brooklyn, New York, in 1996. There are currently approximately 210 domestic violence courts in the United States (Marlowe et al., 2016). A unique feature of these courts is that they integrate survivor support services and treatment agencies into the judicial process, with the goal of holding perpetrators accountable and referring them to treatment for rehabilitative services (Tutty et al., 2008).

The literature on domestic violence courts is quite thin. An early study on a domestic violence program established in 1993 in Miami found that treatment needs for perpetrators of intimate partner violence included substance use and anger management, and the results revealed that program participants reoffended against the same victims at a lower rate (6%) compared to control offenders (14%) who did not participate in the program (Goldkamp, Weiland, Collins, & White, 1996). An evaluation of a domestic violence court in Lexington, South Carolina, revealed significantly lower rearrest rates among defendants processed through the domestic violence court compared to a sample of offenders who went through standard court processing prior to the establishment of the domestic violence court (Gover et al., 2003). A subsequent study on the same court evaluated procedural justice, and participants, court personnel, and victims reported satisfaction with their case processing, felt that they were treated fairly and with respect, and felt some sense of agency throughout the process (Gover, Brank, & MacDonald, 2007). Finally, a retrospective study of a domestic violence court in California, which mandated a 52-week counseling program for perpetrators of domestic violence, showed recidivism rates (measured as domestic violence arrests) over 4 years of 15% for court participants and 25% for non–court participants (Petrucci, 2010). Although the available research is limited, the preliminary evidence provides reason to be optimistic about the utility of domestic violence courts.

Tribal Healing to Wellness Courts

The first tribal healing to wellness court opened in Fort Hall, Idaho, in 1997 (Marlowe et al., 2016). As a component of the tribal justice system, these courts use the wellness model to treat substance abuse issues in Native American tribal communities (Marlowe et al., 2016). Tribal healing to wellness courts are modeled after more traditional problem-solving courts in that they use collaborative teams, intense supervision, a range of treatment services, sanctions and rewards, and community support (Marlowe et al., 2016). The main distinction is that these courts rely on the strengths and history of specific tribes and the existing resources and treatment mechanisms within those tribes (Tribal Law & Policy Institute, 2014a). These courts focus on individual and community healing, legal processes that promote tribal sovereignty, and holistic treatment services that incorporate culture and tradition (Tribal Law & Policy Institute, 2014b). These courts tend to be established in geographic areas where Native American tribes are more common.

There is little research on any aspect of tribal healing to wellness courts. A large-scale study funded by the Bureau of Justice Assistance evaluated the first four tribal healing to wellness courts that were developed under the Tribal Drug Court Initiative (Gottlieb, 2005). The study did not find any significant differences between program graduates and nongraduates, and participants in the court generally showed fairly high recidivism rates of 50–64% in adult courts and 90% in juvenile courts (Gottlieb, 2005). A positive finding was that the time to reoffending was longer for program graduates compared to nongraduates (Gottlieb, 2005). Notably, three of the four courts examined in this study discontinued their operation once the federal funding ended.

Family Drug Courts

Family drug courts, which are occasionally referred to as *family treatment drug courts* or *dependency drug courts*, were created to improve adherence to substance abuse treatment and improve outcomes in child abuse or neglect cases for parents with substance use disorders. The first family drug court was established in Reno, Nevada, in 1995. Although there were 322 family drug courts in the United States at year-end 2009, the number of family drug courts fell to 305 by year-end 2014 (Marlowe et al., 2016). With that said, family drug courts are expected to increase in number over the next few years.

As with most other problem-solving courts, family drug courts were modeled after drug courts and include similar elements, including a nonadversarial approach, a collaborative treatment team, substance abuse treatment referrals, frequent status hearings in court, drug and alcohol testing, and the use of sanctions/rewards (Marlowe et al., 2016). Court appearances in family drug courts are often more frequent, including weekly appearances in some courts (Harrell & Goodman, 1999). A key difference between a standard drug court and a family drug court is that family drug courts coordinate treatment and supervision with family court and child protective service agencies, and the proceedings in family drug court are also generally civil rather than criminal. Rather than a decrease in sentence or a reduction or dismissal of criminal charges, the incentive to participate in family drug courts is family reunification.

Relatively speaking, a good deal of research has been conducted on family drug courts, including some large-scale studies. The first large-scale outcome study on family drug courts compared 301 families from three different family drug courts to a matched sample of families with parental substance abuse who received traditional child welfare services (Worcel, Furrer, Green, Burrus, & Finigan, 2008). Using propensity score matching, results revealed that family drug court mothers had more positive treatment outcomes, were more likely to enter and adhere to substance use treatment, and were more likely to be reunited with their children than mothers receiving traditional child welfare services (Worcel et al., 2008).

A retrospective study of four family drug courts from across the United States found that parents involved in family drug courts were more likely to enter treatment, stay in treatment, and complete treatment, and to be reunited with their children (Green, Furrer, Worcel, Burrus, & Finigan, 2007). This study had a relatively small sample size (50 families from each site), and comparison groups were created using a retrospective "pre–family drug court" sampling process, so the observed differences could be the result of changes over time rather than the family drug court intervention. The same researchers continued this line of research with larger samples from each court and comparison groups that more closely matched the participants in family drug courts. They found that parents in family drug courts were more likely to be reunified with their children and that children spent more time with their parents (vs. out-of-home placements) compared to children from the comparison groups (Green, Furrer, Worcel, Burrus, & Finigan, 2009).

Several single-court studies have examined the effects of family drug courts. Given the varied goals of these courts, researchers often focus on outcomes other than recidivism. An early study of family drug courts in Pima County, Arizona, compared family drug court participants (n = 33) to a treatment-refusal group (n = 42) and a treatment-as-usual group (n = 45) (Ashford, 2004). Results showed that family drug court participants had higher rates of treatment engagement (97%) than either the treatment-refusal group (69%) or treatment-as-usual group (67%) (Ashford, 2004). Moreover, families who participated in family drug courts had higher rates of treatment completion (48%) than the other two comparison groups, and they were also substantially more likely to be reunified with children (52%) than either the treatment-refusal group (39%) or the treatment-as-usual group (30%) (Ashford, 2004). Separate studies published in 2012 found that participants in family drug court had higher rates of family reunification, and that participants' children ended involvement with the child welfare system sooner and were less likely to reenter the child welfare system (Bruns, Pullmann, Weathers, Wirschem, & Murphy, 2012; Chuang, Moore, Barrett, & Young, 2012). A later study in North Carolina also found reduced lengths of stays in foster care for children of parents in family drug courts (Gifford, Eldred, Vernerey, & Sloan, 2014). An evaluation of the Sacramento Dependency Drug Court found that parents who participated in the program had more admissions to treatment but spent less time in treatment and were no more likely to complete treatment than the control group (Boles, Young, Moore, & DiPirro-Beard, 2007). They found, however, that families in the program were more likely to be reunited than were families who did not participate in the program (42% vs. 27%, respectively) (Boles et al., 2007). A later study on the same court found that predictors of successful family reunification included attending support group meetings and negative drug tests (Child & McIntyre, 2015).

Two studies by Carey and colleagues (2010a, 2010b) examined recidivism outcomes for parents in family drug courts, and both studies showed promising results. Over 2 years, graduates of the family drug court were significantly less likely to be rearrested than the comparison group (21% vs. 67%) (Carey et al., 2010a). The other Carey et al. (2010b) study, which took place over 4 years, revealed that graduates of the family drug court were significantly less likely to be rearrested than the comparison group (20% vs. 63%) (Carey et al., 2010b). In both Carey et al. (2010a, 2010b) studies, the comparison groups consisted of individuals who were eligible for family drug court but did not participate, either because the program was full or because their petitions occurred before the program was implemented. The family drug court participants and comparison group members were matched on age, sex, ethnicity, indication of prior drug use, number and age of children, treatment history, and criminal history. Given their solid methodology and results, it appears that the risk-reducing effects of family drug courts are maintained over time.

Taken together, there is reason to be optimistic about the benefits of family drug courts. Of all problem-solving courts discussed in this chapter, the findings from studies on family drug courts are the least mixed, and the results are overwhelmingly positive. There are, of course, some notable limitations, such as the lack of randomized controlled trials or meta-analyses, but the research conducted to date suggests that family drug courts reduce recidivism and promote improved outcomes (e.g., reunification, treatment engagement) more than standard court processing for families with substance-involved parents.

Campus Drug Courts

Campus drug courts target college students who demonstrate excessive drug or alcohol use and who are at risk of jeopardizing their student status. These courts use drug court principles of intensive monitoring, treatment, and collaborative stakeholders to help campuses identify and assist college students with substance use issues. The first campus drug court opened at Colorado State University in 2002 as an alternative to suspension from college for students with substance use issues (Dutmers, 2016; Marlowe et al., 2016). Some campus drug courts also include mental health services when substance abuse is indicative of other treatment needs (e.g., trauma, family violence, learning disabilities) (Monchick & Gehring, 2006).

We located little research on campus drug courts. An evaluation of Colorado State University's Back on TRAC (Treatment, Responsibility, and Accountability on Campus) program revealed positive results (Miller, 2008). During a 5-year period, results revealed that approximately 70% of students entering the program went on to earn their university degree, and the recidivism rate for program graduates was reported to be less than 4% (Miller, 2008). A similar program, Maximizing Potential for Academics, Community, and Treatment (MPACT), was established at the University of Alabama in 2013. In MPACT, students who take responsibility for a drug- or alcohol-related offense can have their academic suspension put on hold contingent on their successful completion of the MPACT program. This campus drug court has a dedicated judge and works in conjunction with local law enforcement authorities when cases overlap between the campus judicial board and the criminal justice system (Dutmers, 2016).

Discussion and Next Steps

Recent decades have seen the development of numerous types of problem-solving courts. Given the success of drug courts and the growing body of positive evidence for mental health courts, it is perhaps not surprising that other types of problem-solving courts have been developed. The problem-solving court model has received bipartisan support in Congress (Fruman, 2015; Maron, 2009), and there are calls, along with some funding, to expand these courts.

Earlier in this chapter, we briefly described 13 problem-solving courts that have been developed following the demonstrated success of drug courts and mental health courts. Unfortunately, many of these courts have an extremely limited research base, and several of have no supportive research at all. Throughout this chapter, we only discussed research for some of these courts, including DUI/DWI courts, veterans treatment courts, community courts, family drug courts, domestic violence courts, tribal healing to wellness courts, and campus drug courts. We were unable to locate any meaningful research on the remaining courts, which presents an obvious future direction for researchers.

Some types of problem-solving courts are relatively new and others are both new and small in number, so it may take several years for meaningful research to be conducted. The development of problem-solving courts has clearly outpaced the research. Furthermore, some of these highly specialized courts are not adequately funded, which makes it challenging to sustain the courts and conduct large-scale research. A clear example is the tribal healing to wellness courts, some of which ceased to exist after unimpressive research results and discontinued funding from the Bureau of Justice Assistance. Importantly, however, without a research base, we simply do not know whether these courts are meaningfully reducing recidivism and leading to improvements in other outcome measures. It seems that the development of some of these highly specialized courts is predicated on the assumed success of the problem-solving court model, even though the empirical evidence clearly indicates that some types of problem-solving courts are much more effective than others. As funding becomes more difficult to obtain, providing empirical evidence of a court's utility—using rigorous research designs—will become increasingly important.

One possibility is that the judicial landscape is too saturated with problem-solving courts. Over the years, problem-solving courts have become increasingly specific and designed for very narrow populations of offenders. An important consideration is whether there is a sufficient basis—theoretically and empirically—for these types of specialized courts. Drug courts were developed because there was considerable evidence that standard criminal justice processing was not working for the class of drug-involved offenders; drug-involved offenders have identifiable criminogenic needs, and addressing those needs can effectively reduce recidivism and relapse to drug use. Similar thinking led to the development of mental health courts. Is there a similarly convincing basis to believe that offenders with a gambling disorder or that individuals charged with firearm offenses that did not result in serious physical injury represent distinct classes of offenders with distinct criminogenic needs that are likely to benefit from a specialized problem-solving court? In some ways, it seems that the creation of these highly specialized courts was reactive, with some of these courts being developed for offenders who may not fit neatly within an existing problem-solving court. Perhaps a better use of the limited resources would be to provide more funding to problem-solving courts with a demonstrated history of success, such as drug courts and mental health courts, so that those courts could provide higher quality services to a larger proportion of the target population.

Also, there is considerable overlap among the many types of problem-solving courts. For example, drug courts focus exclusively on offenders with substance use involvement, but other types of problem-solving courts, including mental health courts, veterans courts, co-occurring disorders courts, and community courts, also handle offenders with substance involvement. Furthermore, offenders with mental health disorders are found not only in mental health courts, but also in a range of other types of problem-solving courts. This overlap raises questions about whether (a) problem-solving courts are perhaps too specific and (b) problem-solving courts are truly treating distinct populations of offenders.

Furthermore, as we noted throughout this chapter, most problem-solving courts are based on the drug court model and include many of the same features of drug courts. However, an important empirical question is whether the drug court model is the most effective model for other justice-involved individuals. Rather than simply adopting the drug court model for use with other populations of offenders, it would be more effective for courts and stakeholders to think critically about how to adapt the basic features of the drug court model to better include and serve the needs of the specific offender population being targeted.

The problem-solving courts discussed in this chapter are well-intentioned. Efforts to divert offenders from standard criminal justice processing—when doing so does not increase the risk to public safety and is based on sufficient theoretical and empirical evidence—should be applauded. However, what may be more beneficial is modifying policies so that certain behaviors are excluded from criminal justice jurisdiction in the first place. By the time individuals are in a problem-solving court, they have already penetrated fairly deeply—to Intercept

3—into the criminal justice system (see Munetz & Griffin, 2006). For example, some jurisdictions are reclassifying the act of jumping a turnstile into a ticketable offense instead of a misdemeanor—whereas a misdemeanor leads to some degree of criminal justice processing and potentially a criminal record, a ticket only requires payment of a fine without further justice involvement. Preventing criminal justice involvement through the downward reclassification of certain low-level offenses may be a more effective strategy than creating and maintaining a variety of problem-solving courts to address a wide variety of offenses and offenders.

7
Reentry Courts

Reentry courts were developed in the early 2000s in an attempt to reduce the "revolving door effect" for individuals involved in the justice system. Unlike courts discussed earlier in this volume (e.g., drug courts, mental health courts), reentry courts are a unique problem-solving court in that they are not necessarily treating any behavioral health needs, but rather addressing criminogenic needs that research shows relate to recidivism. These courts help offenders reintegrate into the community by providing intensive monitoring and access to educational, vocational, and social services to aid reentry.

In this chapter, we begin with the history and development of reentry courts. We then discuss the components of reentry courts and highlight a few prototypical models of reentry courts in the United States. We provide an extensive review of the research on reentry courts and highlight some limitations and future directions for the existing literature. We conclude the chapter with a discussion of "What's Next?" as reentry courts continue to gain momentum.

Parole and Probation in the United States

Each year, approximately 640,000 of the more than 1.5 million individuals housed in state and federal correctional facilities are released back into the community (Carson & Anderson, 2016). Indeed, more than 95% of individuals incarcerated in U.S. state prisons will be released back into society at some point (Hughes & Wilson, 2002). In the United States, 4.6 million adults are currently under some form of community supervision, including probation (supervised release, rather than incarceration, following conviction) or parole (supervised release following incarceration) (Kaebel & Bonczar, 2016). At year-end 2015, approximately 1 in 53 adults was under community supervision, with 81% of individuals under community supervision being on probation (Kaebel & Bonczar, 2016). Statistics illustrating failures while under probation or parole are striking. In 2015, 16% of probationers failed under probation by reincarceration (8%), absconding (1%), or failing to meet conditions of supervision (7%) (Kaeble & Bonczar, 2016). Parole failures in 2015 have included reincarceration (14%), absconding (4%), or failing to meet conditions of supervision (1%) (Kaeble &

Bonczar, 2016). One study tracked more than 240,000 offenders on federal community supervision from 2004 to 2010 and found that 37% recidivated within 5 years of commencing supervision; 24% were rearrested, and just under 13% had their supervision revoked (Rhodes, Dyous, Kling, Hunt, & Luallen, 2012). A 2005 study tracked more than 400,000 released prisoners throughout 30 states and found that approximately 68% were rearrested within 3 years of release, with approximatively 57% being rearrested within 5 years of arrest (Durose, Cooper, & Snyder, 2014). Those on probation or parole may be at greater risk for being detected for illegal behavior because of the heightened scrutiny associated with these conditions (Alexander, 2012). As this evidence suggests, adding alternatives to the standard conditions of parole and probation could reduce the rate of failures and challenges to community reintegration. Such changes would affect a large number of justice-involved individuals. For example, there were more individuals incarcerated for probation and parole violations in 2000 than were incarcerated for any reason in 1980 (Alexander, 2012; Travis, 2005).

Incarcerated individuals experience significant and extended isolation from their families and from society. They may face numerous obstacles when released back to society, including difficulties finding housing and employment (Brown, 2016). Some of the challenges faced by returning offenders are direct, including punishments imposed by the courts, parole and probation requirements, and the imposition of fines (Pinard, 2006). There are also significant collateral consequences associated with reentry, generally involving societal restrictions imposed upon individuals with criminal convictions (Brown, 2016). These collateral consequences include employment discrimination, ineligibility for welfare assistance and government-assisted housing, bans on obtaining certain professional licensing, ineligibility for jury service and financial aid, restrictions on voting, and disenfranchisement due to sex offender registration requirements (Focht-Perlberg, 2009; Pinard, 2010). Such consequences can increase the difficulty associated with community reintegration—and they may intensify following longer periods of incarceration (Brown, 2016).

It has been estimated that a substantial proportion of individuals returning from incarceration (more than 20%) receive no formal services to help them reintegrate into society (Thompson, 2004). Those who enter prison tend to have less education, fewer financial resources, and more behavioral and physical health concerns than most Americans. Incarceration can exacerbate these problems, so returning individuals are in particular need of assistance (Miller, 2007). In addition, these individuals often return to communities that lack resources and support systems (Miller, 2006; Pinard, 2006). These obstacles are particularly noteworthy given the significant challenges that returning offenders face when trying to secure housing, employment, and sometimes treatment for substance use or other behavioral health disorders.

The Development of Reentry Courts

Reentry courts were developed to assist in addressing the multiple challenges faced by individuals returning to the community from incarceration. They can support released offenders and link them to community resources, enabling a more effective transition when the likelihood of recidivism and reincarceration is at its highest (Maruna & LeBel, 2003; Travis, 2000). The earliest reentry courts were developed in 2000 and modeled after the first drug court developed in Dade County, Florida (Reno, 2000). Reentry courts extend the drug court model to individuals in the community on probation or parole, and to former inmates who are on parole or supervised released after an early release from prison (Fetsco, 2013). Like drug courts, reentry courts emphasize treatment and rehabilitation. After a prioritization on reentry court development by former U.S. Attorney General Janet Reno and Jeremy Travis, Director of the National Institute of Justice, the Office of Justice Programs (OJP) launched the Reentry Court Initiative (RCI) in 1999.

The RCI was a large-scale reentry initiative developed to "establish a seamless system of offender accountability and support services throughout the reentry process" (Lindquist, Hardison, & Lattimore, 2004, p. 96). After the RCI launch, the OJP began requesting applications from jurisdictions that were interested in piloting reentry courts. Nine pilot sites were selected in California, Colorado, Delaware, Florida, Iowa, Kentucky, New York, Ohio, and West Virginia (Fetsco, 2013). The OJP set forth six elements for the pilot programs: (1) assessment and planning, (2) oversight, (3) management of support services, (4) community accountability, (5) graduated sanctions, and (6) rewards for success (Fetsco, 2013). After incorporating these core elements, each pilot site was free to form its own reentry court program. Most jurisdictions granted authority to the state judicial branch to administer the reentry court program, but a few had the program administered by administrative judges or parole boards (Fetsco, 2013). In addition, each pilot court could select a particular offender population, resulting in programs with varying prioritizations: offenders with mental illness, offenders with a history of domestic violence, and felony offenders sentenced to prison (Fetsco, 2013). Finally, the pilot reentry courts developed differing selection and enrollment methods. Most sites enrolled participants shortly after release. West Virginia and Ohio, however, identified offenders when they were first sentenced, which allowed for comprehensive preparation for reentry prior to the participants' release (Fetsco, 2013).

The success of the RCI reentry court pilot programs led to the signing of the Second Chance Act of 2007 into law in April 2008 (Brown, 2016). The Act, which was passed with bipartisan congressional support, was designed to improve outcomes for returning individuals by authorizing federal grants to support agencies and organizations in developing services intended to reduce recidivism for individuals returning from jails, prisons, and other institutional facilities (Brown, 2016). The Second Chance Act funds various programs that assist justice-involved individuals, including reentry court programs (Brown, 2016). In June 2017, a bipartisan bill was introduced in the US House of Representatives to reauthorize the Act. Proponents of this bill argued that it would help ensure that "federal investment in strategies to reduce recidivism and increase public safety [can] continue for four more years" (Council of State Governments Justice Center, 2017). President Trump signed the bill into law in December 2018.

Reentry Courts: Components and Methodology

Although reentry courts exist at both the state and federal levels, their components are often similar. More has been published on federal reentry courts, however, so they receive more attention in this section. As of 2010, 41 of the 94 federal districts nationwide had (or were expected to have) reentry court programs operated by judges (Meierhoefer & Breen, 2013). Reentry court programs vary in terms of specific methodology and implementation, but most use a team-based model. This team usually includes a judge, a public defender, a prosecuting attorney, and treatment providers; the team works collaboratively to use appropriate incentives and sanctions for participant behavior to help them reenter society more successfully (Beeler, 2013; Brown, 2016). By combining judicial monitoring with community supervision strategies designed to reduce recidivism, the reentry court model seeks to enhance services by partnering with treatment providers, improve compliance through more intensive and individualized supervision, and create more buy-in about the procedural fairness of community supervision (Boar & Walter, 2012).

The judge plays an essential role in reentry court (Hamilton, 2010). In theory, the judge's involvement improves procedural justice, which consequently helps parolees and probationers internalize supervision requirements and increase compliance (Tyler, 1998). Under the reentry court model, the judge engages in open discussion with the reentry court team and participants regarding program requirements, sanctions and incentives, and the purpose of these components (Travis, 2005). The open forum model (as opposed to the typical closed-door parole process) is thought to help enhance the perception of fairness. Reentry courts also often hold ceremonies to celebrate successful completion of the program, during which the judge confers certificates and highlights each participant's growth and achievements (Hamilton, 2010).

Although most reentry courts subscribe to this basic model, there is considerable variation across courts in eligibility requirements, enrollment length, focus, team characteristics, and implementation procedures (Brown, 2016; Meierhoefer & Breen, 2013). Eligibility requirements vary greatly. Some reentry courts only accept volunteer participants, while others *require* that certain offenders participate based on a team decision that there is a need for intensive supervision (Vance, 2011). Some courts do not accept individuals with a substance use history or charges of violent crime, while other reentry courts may require a history of substance use for enrollment. Length of enrollment ranges from 6 months to more than 8 years (Brown, 2016; Hamilton, 2010; Meierhoefer & Breen, 2013).

There is also significant variation in the focus of reentry court programs. Although most courts follow the traditional drug court model, many have specific target populations. Some courts focus on high-risk individuals regardless of any substance use history, while others target individuals who have substance use problems. Other courts set forth risk parameters and seek to enroll high-risk probationers or parolees who fall within those parameters, although some courts and researchers do not specify what makes someone high-risk or what they are at high risk for doing (e.g., reoffending, relapse). Reentry courts see a significant amount of risk variability because many do not have eligibility requirements involving risk or behavioral health. As such, reentry courts often serve a group of participants with varied risks and needs, and they must identify appropriate resources for each participant (Hamilton, 2010). Reentry court teams also vary across programs—some courts consist of a two-member team, while others may have teams of six or more members. Regarding implementation, reentry courts differ in terms of the frequency and duration of hearings, participant meetings, and preparation for court sessions (Brown, 2016).

Most federal reentry courts programs focus on one of the following three populations: (1) those with a substance use history, (2) individuals who have moderate to high risk for reoffending, and (3) those with a history of sexual assault (Meierhoefer & Breen, 2013). The majority of federal reentry courts are reentry drug courts that focus on participants with substance use problems who demonstrate high risk (for reoffending) and high needs (Meierhoefer, 2011). These courts typically target individuals with active substance use problems, mental health or adaptive functioning needs, and risk factors such as previously failed attempts at treatment (Marlowe, 2009). Program participants appear before the court regularly for status meetings, engage in treatment for substance abuse and mental health needs, and receive treatment and vocational support to help maintain a drug-free life and obtain employment (Marlowe, 2009). Many state reentry courts also focus on participants with substance use problems, but also tend to have fewer eligibility requirements and thus serve offenders with a wide range of risks and needs (Hamilton, 2010).

The reentry court model is based on theories of behavioral change using sanctions for failure to comply with program requirements and incentives to reward compliance and good behavior (Beeler, 2013). Generally, reentry court participants are expected to achieve short-term goals and meet basic supervision requirements, such as attending treatment and court sessions. Long-term goals imposed by the court include maintaining abstinence, obtaining and keeping employment, and using effective parenting skills. For failing to comply with basic supervision requirements, such as attending treatment and court hearings, sanctions such as jail or community service may be appropriate. However, for noncompliance due to a positive drug test, referral for additional treatment and counseling may be better indicated. The reentry court model promotes the idea that positive supports in employment, education, and the development of prosocial activities can help shape behaviors over time that are inconsistent with substance use and criminal behavior—and will thus reduce recidivism rates (Beeler, 2013; Marlowe, 2009).

Under this approach, reentry court sanctions should be fair, predictable, and aimed at reducing unwanted behavior. They should also be imposed immediately following that behavior. These courts can also use incentives to reinforce prosocial behaviors, such as attending treatment, seeking and gaining employment, and engaging in active parenting (Beeler, 2013). The primary incentive for most reentry court participants is a reduction in the required supervision length (generally by 1 year) for successful completion (Meierhoefer & Breen, 2013). Programs differ in what is considered to be successful completion, but it usually involves an extended term of sobriety or successful achievement of long-term goals (such as full-time employment) (Beeler, 2013).

Examples of Existing Reentry Courts

Describing the characteristics of some specific reentry courts will illustrate how these courts function. We highlight the courts in the present section because they have been researched and well-documented in the reentry court literature.

Harlem Parole Reentry Court

The Harlem Parole Reentry Court was established in 2001 under a grant from the US Department of Justice, and, in 2009, it was awarded another grant under the Second Chance Act (Boar & Walter, 2012). The program was developed to address the large number of individuals returning to prison within 3 years of release (Langan & Levin, 2002). The court is located in East Harlem, a central location for returning individuals (50% of those paroled in Manhattan are paroled to Upper Manhattan) (Hamilton, 2010). The Harlem Parole Court team consists of a judge, two probation officers, a parole officer, a resource coordinator, two case managers, and administrative staff members. The court assigns smaller caseloads of 40 parolees (compared to the typical caseload of 70 parolees) to facilitate more intensive supervision and to better connect participants to needed treatment and vocational resources. Team members collaborate to provide additional services including "predischarge planning, facilitation of family member engagement, establishment of effective local service partnerships and the provision of in-house services such as mediation, family counseling, and housing assistance" (Hamilton, 2010).

The program involves regular monitoring by the judge and the imposition of sanctions (increased court sessions, extended program length, more drug testing, stricter curfews, and monitoring of electronics) and incentives (recognition from the judge, achievement certificates, relaxed travel restrictions, and other small tokens) to influence behavior. This Harlem Parole Reentry Court is distinctive in its duration (6 months) and its nonvoluntary nature. Participants are inmates housed in one of two transitional facilities after release from prison. The court does not allow participants with serious mental illness or those with a history of sex offending or arson. If a returning individual is selected, program participation is mandatory and a parole officer sets up a prerelease interview to identify risks and needs prior to reentry. The program has two phases. Phase 1 lasts for 2 months and consists of weekly meetings with the parole officer and biweekly meetings with the judge. The reentry court team also meets regularly to discuss any needed adjustments to be applied to the participant's supervision and/or intervention requirements. In Phase 2, which lasts for 4 months, requirements are relaxed and participants are only required to attend biweekly meetings with the parole officer and monthly meetings with the judge. Successful completion of the program culminates in a graduation ceremony where certificates are awarded and participants speak publicly about their challenges and accomplishments with reentry (Hamilton, 2010).

Illinois Second Chance Reentry Program

The Northern Illinois District Court developed a reentry court program in April 2010. Entitled the Second Chance Reentry Program, it focuses on individuals with substance use issues. Probation officers identify high-risk individuals with at least 2 years of supervision remaining and interview them to determine whether they would likely benefit from the Second Chance Program. Candidates with the requisite qualities and characteristics (i.e., formerly incarcerated individuals with a substance abuse issue with at least 2 more years of required court-ordered supervision) are then recommended to the court for admission (Gottschall & Armour, 2011). The stated goal of the program is to help offenders successfully reintegrate into the community and reduce overall criminal recidivism rates. The program is not voluntary—probation officers choose which offenders will be referred to the program, focusing on those with documented substance use problems. The Second Chance team consists of two judges (a district judge and a magistrate judge), a probation officer, attorneys from the US Attorney's Office and the Federal Defender's Office, a substance abuse treatment specialist, and a deputy US Marshall (Vance, 2011). Participants are required to attend 2-hour sessions twice per month. These sessions occur outside of the courtroom in a large conference room where participants and team members gather to discuss progress, challenges, and next steps. The Second Chance Program relies on incentives (typically a reduction in supervision time) and sanctions (usually an increase in supervision time) to influence the behavior of participants. No studies have yet been published regarding its effectiveness, and thus it is not covered in the research section that follows.

Massachusetts Court Assisted Recovery Effort

In May 2006, the United States District Court for the District of Massachusetts implemented the Court Assisted Recovery Effort (CARE) (Vance, 2011). CARE focuses on returning citizens with substance use issues and assists participants in remaining sober and finding lawful employment. The program assumes a strong link between substance use and crime, and it assumes crime will be reduced by decreasing substance use (Brown, 2016). The CARE team consists of a magistrate judge, representatives from probation, a US Attorney, and a Federal Defender. The program takes place in four phases: Early Recovery, Understanding and Taking Responsibility, Healthy Decision-Making, and Relapse Prevention Planning. The Early Recovery phase is the most intensive and requires participants to engage in weekly meetings with the court and enroll in treatment for substance use and mental health. The Understanding and Taking Responsibility phase requires that the participants meet weekly with probation, attend court twice per month, and continue to engage in substance use and mental health treatment. In the third phase, Healthy Decision-Making, participants meet with probation and the court on a biweekly basis and scale back the frequency of substance abuse or mental health treatment. Finally, in the fourth and least intensive phase, Relapse Prevention Planning, the only requirement is that participants attend month meetings with the court and probation officers (Brown, 2016).

Michigan Accelerated Community Entry Program

The Accelerated Community Entry (ACE) Program was developed in 2005 in the United States District Court for the Western District of Michigan (Vance, 2011). It was designed to target medium- to high-risk offenders reintegrating into society in Benton Harbor, Michigan (Brown, 2016). The program's stated purpose is to achieve safer communities by decreasing crime and drug use by high-risk offenders who are most likely to recidivate and be returned to prison, as determined by the Risk Prediction Index (RPI) (ACE Program, 2018). This program seeks to achieve this goal by using procedures found to be effective in drug courts. Court sessions are held on a monthly basis during which legal, logistical, and/or financial issues are discussed. The ACE program team is comprised of judges, probation officers, a federal public defender, a U.S. Attorney, a U.S. Marshal, and staff from a halfway house (Vance, 2011). The ACE program is distinctive in the large geographic area comprising its district. As such, the court sessions are held in a centrally located facility to accommodate participants from across the district (Brown, 2016).

Philadelphia's Supervision to Aid Reentry Program

In 2007, the Federal Probation Office for the Eastern District of Pennsylvania initiated a reentry court program entitled Supervision to Air Reentry (STAR) (Taylor, 2013). By early 2011, the STAR program had 125 current or former participants divided between two reentry courts. To be eligible for the STAR program, returning individuals had to be appraised at medium or high reoffense risk, be on probation in Philadelphia, and have been incarcerated in federal prison. The program targets individuals with a substantial criminal history, often involving violent crimes, who would benefit from employment assistance and other resources. Participation in the STAR program is voluntary; individuals meeting these criteria can choose to participate in the reentry court instead of standard probation. For participants who complete the 52-week program, the reentry court judge will recommend that the original sentencing judge reduce the participant's probation sentence by up to 1 year (Taylor, 2013).

All STAR program participants are required to attend the reentry court sessions held every 2 weeks. These sessions are also attended by the full reentry court team, which includes the federal judge, the probation officers, "an administrative assistant, a reentry coordinator, and representative from the Federal Public Defender's Office, and an Assistant US Attorney" (Taylor, 2013, p. 2). Each participant is called before the judge and asked about recent accomplishments and challenges in reentry, often focusing on domains such as employment, education, family, and healthcare. The reentry court judge provides praise and encouragement for successes and, in response to obstacles, may offer advice or refer participants to community resources. The STAR program team holds regular meetings prior to court sessions during which the progress of each participant is reviewed and the judge is briefed on any significant problems that should be addressed during court. The STAR program also partners with many outside providers, including the Drexel Reentry Project, a comprehensive therapy program designed to meet the needs of offenders reentering the community after incarceration. The STAR program team refers participants to the Drexel Reentry Project for training in life skills, prosocial thinking patterns, and problem-solving.

Research on Reentry Courts

The research on reentry courts differs from research on other problem-solving courts, and it is still in its early stages. Unlike research on other problem-solving courts, there have been few multisite studies or meta-analyses, and the research base has significant limitations. Much of the research focuses on process evaluations or challenges related to implementation rather than outcomes such as rearrest, employment, family functioning, and housing. Overall, the research is largely promising, but researchers note that reentry courts have not been studied sufficiently to draw meaningful conclusions about their effectiveness (Lindquist, Walters, Rempel, & Carey, 2013; Marlowe et al., 2016; Vance, 2011).

Research on State Reentry Courts

The first large-scale evaluation of reentry courts was conducted by the OJP in 2000, just as reentry courts were beginning to develop in the United States. This evaluation was part of the RCI described earlier in this chapter. It included nine reentry courts across the United States. The goal of the RCI was to establish a system of offender accountability and link returning individuals to support services during the reentry process. OJP provided technical assistance to new reentry courts, but no funding was provided for their development (Lindquist et al., 2004). The courts developed as part of the RCI were instructed to (1) improve tracking and supervision of released offenders and provide services to improve rearrest outcomes, (2) assist with reintegration to families and communities, and (3) balance rehabilitation with public safety (Lindquist et al., 2004). All courts included in the RCI had the same core elements: assessment and planning, active court oversight, linkage to support services, accountability, graduated and parsimonious sanctions, and rewards for success (Lindquist et al., 2004). This study evaluating the RCI courts used surveys to gauge perceptions of program effectiveness; no additional outcome measures were obtained. The major findings from this evaluation highlighted the significant variations in program length, service availability, recruitment and target populations, and general court operations (Lindquist, Hardison, & Lattimore, 2003). All sites except one became operational, but they operated on a small scale and encountered significant implementation barriers involving partnering with community agencies for employment and housing services (Lindquist et al., 2004). A follow-up review shows that nearly all of the RCI courts sustained their programs and used information from the earlier evaluation to improve court operations (Lindquist et al., 2013).

Some of the sites that were part of the RCI also conducted their own outcome research. One court in Ohio had a rearrest rate for reentry court participants of 6% during the first year, compared to a national average of approximately 50% (Spelman, 2003). Notably, the sample size of this study was 66 participants, and the study did not include a comparison group. A quasi-experimental study (Farole, 2003) evaluated the Harlem Reentry Court, which provides services to new parolees during the first 6 months of release from state prison. The court's goal is to provide services that help participants secure a job, find stable housing, remain drug-free, and assume familial and personal responsibilities (Farole, 2003). This study compared the first 45 individuals to complete reentry court to a sample of 90 individuals on standard parole, and it did not find significant differences in reincarceration rates between the two groups. Apparently, the Harlem Reentry Court used Farole's study findings to guide organizational and programmatic changes. A subsequent evaluation of the Harlem Reentry Court replicated Farole's study using 300 reentry court participants (completers and noncompleters) and a matched comparison group of more than 600 standard parolees (Hamilton, 2010). This second evaluation showed significantly lower re-arrest and reconviction rates for reentry court participants (both completers and noncompleters), but significantly higher parole revocation and reincarceration rates for reentry court participants.

The evaluation of Project Greenlight was one of the first studies to use a range of outcome variables; it was conducted in New York in 2005, and it serves as a model for methodologically strong research on offender reentry. Project Greenlight was a short-term, prison-based reentry program that relied heavily on research and evidenced-based techniques, particularly cognitive skills training (Wilson & Davis, 2006). Project Greenlight also focused on service linkage; it offered job readiness training and connections to housing, treatment, and social services. The study evaluating Project Greenlight had a large sample ($N = 735$) and used three comparison groups: Project Greenlight, the New York Department of Correction's standard Transitional Services Program, and direct release. Unexpectedly, compared to the other two groups, Project Greenlight participants fared worse on all outcome measures (arrests, felony arrests, and parole revocations) at 1-year follow-up (Wilson & Davis, 2006). It was suggested that these results may be due to variations in integrity, dosage, and duration of the interventions offered (Wilson, 2011). A later study on Project Greenlight considered the follow-up results by participant risk level and found that participants who were lower risk fared better than moderate- or high-risk participants (Wilson & Zozula, 2012). It is possible that the intervention did not show positive results for high-risk individuals because it was not tailored to the specific needs or learning styles of its participants (Wilson, 2011). In other words, the high-risk group may have remained at higher risk despite the best efforts of this program.

The Serious and Violent Offender Reentry Initiative (SVORI) was a federal grant awarded to 69 grantees across the United States during 2002 and 2003. In the years following, several studies were conducted on SVORI grantees. An initial multisite study focusing on implementation found that, 2 years after the grant was awarded, 74% of courts had become fully operational and 31% of those courts reported that it took more than 12 months to be fully implemented (Lattimore, Visher, Winterfield, Lindquist, & Brumbaugh, 2005). A multisite evaluation of 16 reentry courts for adults and juveniles across the country (in Iowa, Indiana, Maryland, Missouri, Maine, Nevada, Ohio, Oklahoma, Pennsylvania, South Carolina, Virginia, and Washington; Lattimore & Visher, 2009) used propensity score matching to evaluate the differences between SVORI and non-SVORI participants across the courts. Results from this study suggest modest improvements in outcomes (substance use, housing, and employment) for adults who participated in reentry programming and no significant differences in outcomes for juveniles (Lattimore & Visher, 2009). Adult SVORI participants exhibited reduced substance use rates, although drug use increased over time for both groups and exceeded 50% at 15 months postrelease (Lattimore & Visher, 2009, 2014). Significant reductions in recidivism for SVORI participants were not observed, but it is possible that this finding is due to different definitions of recidivism held by each court, which complicated these analyses (Lattimore & Visher, 2009, 2014; US Department of Justice, 2010).

A specific analysis of one of the SVORI courts in North Dakota found the same rate of parole revocation in the control and SVORI groups, and it also found that SVORI participants were less likely to be rearrested (Bouffard & Bergeron, 2006). Another study involved a multiyear evaluation on a court in a Midwestern state that began with federal funding from SVORI but later expanded to include a broader sample (Severson, Bruns, Vee, & Lee, 2011). Using propensity score matching, investigators found that participants of this reentry court were more likely to return to prison and returned earlier than non–reentry court participants (Severson et al., 2011). Subsequent additional analyses of these data indicated that reentry participants had a significantly lower likelihood of incurring a new conviction, but there were no significant differences between the two groups on the rates of reincarceration (Veeh, Severson, & Lee, 2017).

The Bureau of Justice Assistance (BJA) awarded more than $250 million in grant funding to help medium- and high-risk offenders reenter society, using findings from evaluations conducted as part of the RCI and SVORI (Lindquist et al., 2013). Grantees were encouraged to use validated assessment tools and evidence-based practices and to carefully track services delivered to participants (Lindquist et al., 2013). The final evaluation will include three components: (1) a process evaluation, (2) an outcome evaluation, and (3) a cost–benefit analysis. The process evaluation has been completed (Lindquist et al., 2013), but we could not locate any publication involving the second and third components. The process evaluation examined courts across eight states (Arkansas, Delaware, Florida, Missouri, New Hampshire, Ohio, Texas, and Virginia). The results showed that many components of these courts were consistent across sites, including the use of substance abuse and employment services, frequent court hearings, periodic urinalysis, and collaborative decision-making among stakeholders about sanctions and rewards for participants (Lindquist et al., 2013). The major differences across sites involved the composition of program participants and the size and voluntariness of the program (Lindquist et al., 2013). Data from qualitative assessments, focus groups, and court observation highlighted numerous implementation challenges, including staffing, determining eligibility criteria, streamlining a referral process, and a limited amount of community resources (Lindquist et al., 2014). Participant interviews reflect generally positive views about the program but revealed service gaps related to housing and transportation (Lindquist et al., 2014). Additionally, participants indicated that they often did not clearly understand the nature of the program prior to agreeing to participate (Lindquist et al., 2014).

A multisite study conducted in 2012 included six reentry courts across California (Administrative Office of the Courts [AOC], 2012). The courts in the study focused on individuals with a history of substance use or mental illness, and participants were enrolled in the court after committing a parole violation. This study found that, after 1 year, the recidivism rate for reentry court participants was significantly lower than California's general recidivism rate for individuals released from state custody (31% vs. 46%, respectively) (AOC, 2012).

Research on Federal Reentry Courts

The first federal reentry court was established in Oregon in 2005 (Vance, 2011). This court appears similar to many other problem-solving courts, although it involved program graduates as peer support at court hearings (Vance, 2011). This program focused on substance use, and participants were eligible for graduation after 1 year of sobriety (Vance, 2011). A retrospective outcome evaluation of the court was conducted in 2008, using court graduates, participants terminated from court, and a sample of standard-condition probationers (Close, Alltucker, & Aubin, 2008). Results showed that reentry court participants (both completers and noncompleters) received more supervision and support services (but also more sanctions) than did standard probationers (Close et al., 2008). Interpretation of these findings was confounded by group differences on several key measures, the absence of a control for time, and the modest sample size ($N = 114$).

The ACE Program in the Western District of Michigan, described earlier, underwent a process evaluation to gauge whether ACE was implemented according to initial program design and whether it followed program policies during the first year of operation (Knollenberg & Martin, 2008). This evaluation indicated that the court and program participants were generally positive about the program, but this study is limited by its qualitative nature and low response rate (Knollenberg & Martin, 2008).

The STAR program in the Eastern District of Pennsylvania, also described earlier, was created in 2007. A process evaluation conducted in 2010, using interview data, notes several key components of the court's effectiveness: the role of the judge, the use of sanctions and incentives, service linkage, and ability to increase offenders' social support (Taylor, 2013). An initial impact evaluation of the STAR program was also conducted comparing 60 STAR participants to standard probationers (Taylor, 2013). This evaluation suggested that participation in the STAR program was not associated with a decreased likelihood of reoffending, but it did correlate with a decreased likelihood of parole revocation; it may have been affected by how sanctions are used in the court to promote compliance and aid participants through the program (Taylor, 2013). Like some of the other studies discussed in this section, the small sample size must be considered a limitation.

The Louisiana 22nd Judicial District Reentry Court received funding from BJA and the Substance Abuse and Mental Health Administration (SAMHSA) and recently conducted a process and early outcome evaluation. This court focuses on high-risk/high-need offenders and features job readiness training prior to release from incarceration (Miller & Khey, 2016). The process evaluation (which used multiple methods of assessment, including specific evaluation instruments) found high levels of program fidelity and identified needs for improvement, including adding trauma-informed care, transportation plans, and medication-assisted treatment. Additional analyses indicated that only 1 of the 31 participants had been reconvicted and returned to prison at a 1-year follow-up, although the sample was small ($N = 31$) (Miller & Khey, 2016).

Correlates of Success in Reentry Courts

Several studies have examined characteristics relevant to success in reentry court. One study evaluated characteristics of attrition across SVORI sites (Listswan, 2008). This study showed that offenders who were unemployed, did not reside with family members, and had higher risk levels were more likely to fail the program during the community reentry phase (Listswan, 2008). In the multiyear evaluation of a Midwestern SVORI site discussed earlier, considerable attention was paid to predictors of success. This evaluation found that participants who returned to prison were younger, had a longer criminal history, and had more frequent positive drug screens than participants who did not return to prison. It also found that individuals who were reconvicted were more likely to be appraised as being higher risk (Severson et al., 2011). Further research showed that program completers had better outcomes and were less likely to return to prison than were noncompleters (Severson, Veeh, Bruns, & Lee, 2012). More recent research, also using SVORI data, considered the role of religion in reentry outcomes (Stansfield, Mowen, O'Conner, & Boman, 2017). This study noted that religious affiliation and a religious community had a strong protective effect on substance use and employment outcomes but no statistically significant relationship to reoffending (Stansfield et al., 2016).

Methodological Limitations of Reentry Court Research

Clearly, the reentry court literature has significant weaknesses that limit our ability to draw firm conclusions about effectiveness. Implementation and organization of the courts vary greatly, thus limiting the ability to generalize findings. The large, multisite evaluations cannot be easily generalized because of this lack of standardization across courts. Such lack of standardization is perhaps understandable as research has not yet established a clear model for reentry courts (Lindquist et al., 2013). Many of the studies highlighted in this chapter have used small samples and did not control for differences between comparison groups. Although randomized control trials are rarely used in problem-solving court research generally, apparently none has been conducted on reentry courts, and only a few truly quasi-experimental studies have been published.

Innovative Practices

As reentry courts have developed across the nation, many have begun to consider using innovative practices to serve distinct populations. One innovation is the faith-based reentry court. In 2002, under directions from the Bush Administration, the Department of Justice provided funding for faith-based organizations to assist in the prevention and treatment of juveniles experiencing problems with offending and substance use (Herz & Walsh, 2004). This prompted discussions about the development of faith-based reentry courts. Faith-based organizations can be a valuable community resource, with some evidence suggesting that religion can serve as a protective factor against recidivism (Branch, 2002). Herz and Walsh (2004) proposed that faith-based programs should partner with reentry courts to provide returning individuals with programming and resources from a religious institution. Such faith-based programming could include mental health treatment, job training, parenting skills training, anger management courses, tutoring, mentoring, and the opportunity to attend prosocial community activities (Herz & Walsh, 2004).

Another proposed innovative practice in reentry courts involves using the reentry court to support previously incarcerated mothers and their children (McGrath, 2012). The recidivism rate among incarcerated mothers reentering society is quite high and negatively impacts many children (Institute on Women and Criminal Justice, 2006). McGrath argues that the traditional parole system has not adequately addressed the reentry needs of previously incarcerated mothers, particularly related to reunification with children. McGrath further suggests that states should expand or adopt reentry court programming to provide support and resources to mothers returning from incarceration and their children. With such mother-focused reentry courts, returning mothers could receive more individual attention, support from community providers, and judicial supervision to help make the transition smoother. This approach, it is suggested, would result in lower recidivism rates, reduced costs, and increased rates of successful family reunification (McGrath, 2012).

Researchers have also proposed the development of specialized sex offender reentry courts that focus on reducing sexual offending recidivism risk (La Fond & Winick, 2003). These researchers assert that ongoing risk management will help decision-makers to appraise risk more accurately and adjust the supervision level accordingly. Like all reentry courts, these courts would be grounded in therapeutic jurisprudence, with judges imposing and adjusting requirements as needed. Individuals under their jurisdiction would commit to engaging in regular treatment as a condition of release, with participants subject to periodic polygraph testing. Such an approach creates incentives for offenders to alter their behavior and beliefs and allows for the effective monitoring of compliance and risk management, which (it is argued) will reduce recidivism (La Fond & Winick, 2003). It is worth noting that polygraph testing is not typically used in problem-solving courts, and a considerable amount of research (which is beyond the scope of this book) has cast significant doubt on the reliability and validity of polygraph testing.

Some federal reentry courts target individuals outside of the substance abuse realm, focusing, for example, on individuals with gang involvement or mental health disorders (Vance, 2011). Another newer model involves a diversion program that targets offenders after they have entered a guilty plea, but prior to sentencing. These programs seek to rehabilitate offenders and improve community safety by changing offender behavior through treatment, sanction alternatives, and incentives (Beeler, 2013). The Conviction and Sentence Alternatives Program in the Central District of California adopted this model. Under this program, the court requires participants to plead guilty and engage in drug and mental health treatment as needed. The program also provides services related to employment and education. If participants successfully complete the program, the court will dismiss their case or they will receive a time-served sentence (Beeler, 2013; US Department of Justice, 2017).

Future Reentry Courts: Recommendations

In 2012, the Center for Court Innovation published the Reentry Court Tool Kit designed to "provide guidance to justice planners in developing or enhancing a reentry court using specific evidenced-based practices and practices that are informed by research" (Boar & Walter, 2012, p. 3). This Tool Kit is one of the few resources available to reentry court leaders and team members that provides guidance on successful development and implementation. It recommends using evidence-based practices, gathering key stakeholders, and mapping community resources. It also addresses how to determine participant eligibility and engage in prerelease communications with enrolled participants. The Tool Kit offers information on reentry court status hearings, the importance of engaging family members, the evaluation of programs, and the hiring of qualified staff. The following table summarizes important aspects of the Tool Kit, with the full Reentry Court Tool Kit available at http://www.courtinnovation.org/sites/default/files/documents/reentry_toolkit.pdf.

How to Begin	
Use evidence-based practices	**Convene primary stakeholders and mapping services**
Rely on rigorous studies and meta-analyses. Use evidenced based practices developed to improve client outcomes, lower recidivism rates, and reduce costs to the justice system. Utilize structured, validated delivery processes. Use available evidence to inform and innovate. Hire planning team to research literature on best practices in reentry. Determine how court will measure participant risks and needs.	Invite leaders from potential partnering agencies and organizations to join task force. Contact local prosecutor to see if they can bring attention to the program and bring relevant stakeholders to the table. Determine target participant population based on community crime and corrections data and feedback from community stakeholders. Identify local resources (housing, substance use treatment, employment, mental health treatment). Map services in relevant geographical area(s). Keep a planning log to track program development to stay on track and create paper trail for grant reporting.

Screening and Assessing Participants	
Determining participant eligibility	**Prerelease participant engagement**
Develop eligibility criteria focused on medium- to high-risk individuals (limit acceptance of low-risk individuals). Utilize actuarial risk and needs assessment tools prior to release, such as the Level of Service Inventory-Revised (LSI-R) or Correctional Offender Management Profiling for Alternative Sanctions (COMPAS). Examples of participant groups include offenders who are: • returning to a specific geographical area • released from a specific correctional facility • housed together • convicted of a certain type of offense (i.e., violent felony) • members of a special offender population (i.e., juveniles) Ensure that staff is trained in administering assessment tools and monitoring participant progress. Develop written protocols for reentry team members.	Prerelease engagement allows for a clinical relationship to be developed prior to release. Prerelease engagement should start 1–2 months prior to release. Use prerelease engagement to give individual attention to the participant, build rapport, reduce recidivism risk, and develop trusting relationship focused on problem solving. Use prerelease engagement to set up referrals in advance to connect participants with outside services and treatment providers. Prerelease engagement allows for participants to be immediately engaged in programming upon release and keep them focused during the risky initial transition period. Consider prerelease questionnaire aimed at identifying participants' strengths, needs, and potential challenges. Ensure participants have a copy of release papers (often used to help released offenders obtain ID).
Participants in the community	**Use of evidence-backed interventions**
After release, have the participant report to parole/probation officer and schedule an intake meeting with the case manager. At the intake meeting, assess the participant's risks/needs using a validated tool and complete a community supervision plan. Make sure the supervision plan is uniquely tailored to the participant (consider age, culture, cognition and education level, interests, hobbies, and previous experiences). Tailor the community treatment plan to the participant's strengths, risks, and needs.	Consider partnering with a cognitive behavioral therapy intervention program. Consider implementing motivational interviewing (a client-centered, strength-based therapy approach designed to help elicit and strengthen client motivation for change). If possible, train reentry court team staff on the basic tenets of motivational interviewing and cognitive behavioral therapy. Partner with outside providers trained in evidenced-based practices. Invite outside providers to reentry court team meetings and encourage regular discussions and open communication. Discuss specific cases with outside providers to tailor treatment to meet participant needs.

Reentry Court Hearings	
Reentry court hearings generally	**Preliminary hearing**
The purpose of hearings is to promote compliance, increase accountability of participants, give positive reinforcement, facilitate respectful communication between the judge and participants, and encourage transparency in supervision process. Hearings may include judge, parole/probation officer, case manager, defense lawyer, prosecution lawyer, and participant. A relaxed hearing atmosphere encourages the development of a positive relationship between the judge and the participant. Consider creating a warm/welcoming environment to encourage rapport and reinforce compliance.	The initial hearing typically occurs within 1 week of a participant's release. The initial hearing should be used to build rapport and introduce the participant to the program requirements and operations. Asking about the participant's goals, strengths, and familial relationships can help develop a trusting relationship. The judge may use this time to suggest resources that could be useful to participant. The judge should make clear the consequences of non-compliance. The judge should encourage self-efficacy on the part of the participant while also establishing the authority of the court and the requirements of the program. Defense and prosecuting attorneys and the parole/probation officer may be involved in initial hearing.
Status hearings	**Enhanced accountability and transparency**
Participants should attend regular status meetings with the judge. Frequency of hearings should be established based on risk/need levels and a participant's compliance/non-compliance. Hearings should occur more frequently at the start of the program (weekly or biweekly) and may become less frequent after the first 3–4 months, depending on a participant's progress. Hearings can be used to engage in problem-solving regarding particular cases, reinforce desired behavior, or make clear the consequences of noncompliance. Status hearings typically begin with a report from the parole/probation officer on a participant's progress. The participant may then respond, after which an informal dialogue takes place among all parties. Status hearings may focus on one or all of the following: problem-solving, reinforcement of prosocial behavior, deterrence of unwanted behavior: • Problem-solving involves identifying the cause of noncompliance, tackling the issue head-on, and fostering motivation for change	Because the reentry team members work so closely together, each partner will be subject to increased scrutiny and accountability. Unlike in standard parole, interaction between reentry court participants and parole/probation officers are often made known to the team (judge, case manager). Increased knowledge of such interactions can help ensure that commitments are upheld and that each team member follows through on his or her responsibility. Scrutiny is also applied to outside providers and any identified issues or shortcomings can be addressed in team meetings.

- Reinforcing prosocial behavior involves praising participants for compliance and accomplishments and providing incentives for desired behavior (such as a gift card)
- Deterrence of unwanted behavior involves the graduated use of sanctions and expressions of disapproval

Consider adding rewards and incentives to the team meeting agenda to ensure that prosocial behavior is rewarded.

Hearings can be used to highlight significant life events of offenders.

Involving family members

Research has shown that the influence of families and friends is often more powerful than that of formal control agents, such as the criminal justice system, in terms of helping offenders lead prosocial lives and avoid recidivating (Meares & Fagan, 2008).

Family and friends can play a key role in the successful reentry of formerly incarcerated individuals by:

- offering emotional and financial support
- serving as prosocial role models
- acting as an early detection system for problem behavior

Reentry courts can tap into this underutilized resource by reaching out to participants' families and friends and having case managers and probation/parole officers engage in regular home visits.

Evaluating the program

Determine whether to have the results evaluated in-house or by an independent researcher.

Use the results of the program evaluation to identify needed modifications and next steps, provide feedback to partners and outside providers, and develop plans for replication and expansion of effective components.

Strive to use the "gold standard" of random assignment where possible; where randomized assignment is not feasible, find a suitable comparison group to conduct a quasi-experimental study.

Consider partnering with the state and local entities that manage criminal justice data and conduct evaluations, and with universities and nonprofit organizations, to help develop an effective evaluation plan.

Staff
The selection and training of staff is essential in developing a reentry court.
Staff should believe in the ability of participants to change and the effectiveness of positive reinforcement.
Staff should also have skills in managing client resistance and holding participants accountable for noncompliance without shaming or condescending.
It is highly recommended that staff are training in motivational interviewing and cognitive behavioral therapy.
Strong, positive interpersonal relationships between participants and staff can be as, or even more, important than the program itself (Domorad & Carey, 2009).
When interviewing potential staff, role-plays can be a useful tool to help determine a candidate's abilities in effective listening, asking open-ended questions, demonstrating a nonjudgmental attitude, and rolling with resistance.

An important step for improving reentry courts will involve addressing the gaps in services they provide. The crux of reentry courts' intervention involves linking participants to services relevant to reentry, including employment and job training, educational services, substance use and/or mental health treatment, housing, financial, and other social services. Research has shown that participants believe transportation, housing, and employment needs are not always met (Lindquist et al., 2014). Other evidence on service gaps has identified a wide variety in the services provided from court to court (Lattimore, Visher, & Steffey, 2011). Although services provided by any reentry court are contingent upon available community resources and the needs of the target population, this variability skews both the research and participants' experience with the court. Directors of reentry courts in this study estimated that they were providing services to a larger percentage of individuals than were actually receiving them (Lattimore et al., 2011). This has important implications for developing reentry courts; it is critical that frequent evaluations be conducted to ensure that participants are receiving services from the community providers partnered with the court. This study also showed that fewer participants than intended actually received a release plan and needs assessment, underscoring the importance of using evidence-based tools to assess need and outline a specific plan to guide reentry. Finally, large discrepancies between program directors' estimation of services provided and participants' reports of services received were observed in the domains of mentorship, counseling, life skills, training, and resumé development (Lattimore et al., 2011). These discrepancies highlight the specific services that reentry court participants may value—and that could be better incorporated into reentry plans. Overall, this study highlights the importance of community partnerships in developing successful reentry courts; without collaboration from community agencies, good communication between agencies and the court, and a willingness from the community to allow reentering citizens to partake in community activities, reentry courts cannot achieve full effectiveness.

Reentry courts are less developed than other kinds of problem-solving courts, particularly in their research base. At this stage, it is important to critically examine the current reentry court model. Existing research shows mixed results about whether reentry courts, as they currently operate, are effective. Several of the studies reviewed in this chapter indicate that reentry courts may decrease rearrest and reconviction rates but increase reincarceration or parole revocations. It is thus possible that reentry courts are a double-edged sword; they provide access to services necessary for successful reentry, but promote intensive supervision and monitoring that may leave participants more vulnerable than their standard parole counterparts to supervision violations. But it should be noted that reentry courts, unlike the drug courts on which they were modeled, are not *treatment* courts in the same respect. Most reentry courts are not providing treatment services for a problem and monitoring individuals for adherence to treatment in the way that drug courts do, and perhaps they should depart from the drug court model as they develop. It is possible that reentry courts would be more effective with a greater emphasis on linkage to services and less focus on intensive monitoring beyond that required in standard probation.

Finally, it seems important that, as reentry courts develop, they adhere more closely to Risk-Need-Responsivity (RNR) principles. Such adherence is particularly important given the mixed research on whether reentry courts improve outcomes or improve some outcomes while compromising others. In this respect, it is important to note that low-risk offenders who are mandated to receive intensive treatment may actually have an increased likelihood of recidivism. Research has demonstrated that placing low-risk individuals in intensive programming can disrupt social support and/or preexisting self-correcting behaviors which can lead to recidivism (Andrews, Bonta, & Hoge, 1990; Lowenkamp, Holsinger, & Latessa, 2005; Lowenkamp, Flores, Holsinger, Makarios, & Latessa, 2010). Furthermore, research indicates that exposing low-risk individuals to medium- or high-risk individuals who may have a negative influence on them can result in an increase in risky thoughts and behaviors (Boar & Walter, 2012). Reentry courts should provide thorough, evidence-based risk–needs assessments and assign services and levels of supervision in accordance with risk level. Furthermore, Project Greenlight's results emphasize the importance of focusing on the risk, needs, and responsivity principles. Reentry courts should thus focus on the indicated populations (moderate- and high-risk individuals), but also tailor interventions to match the needs and learning style of those populations to maximize their effectiveness.

Conclusion

Reentry courts are an important development in the era of problem-solving courts that represent paradigm shifts in the landscape of offender treatment and reintegration. However, the impact of reentry courts and how they function within the criminal justice system requires continued attention. Unlike many of the other problem-solving courts discussed in this book, research on reentry courts is still in its early stages. In terms of research, the next steps should be clear. It is essential that continued empirical research, particularly focused on outcomes, be conducted to determine whether reentry courts are an effective intervention that reduces criminal recidivism and promotes rehabilitative outcomes. It is also important that future research seek to address the significant limitations (e.g., small sample size, absence of appropriate comparison groups, short outcome periods) in extant research. Finally, multisite studies should more clearly evaluate differences in court structure and operations before including multiple courts in large multisite studies. Models for reentry courts and best practice guidelines are less clear than with other problem-solving courts. We have outlined several key components and suggestions for implementation and provided available resources, but clearer guidelines should be established as the literature evolves. After more outcome studies have been conducted, it will be important to conduct systematic literature reviews and meta-analyses to draw more generalized conclusions about the effectiveness of reentry courts.

8

Methodological Challenges in Researching Problem-Solving Courts

Research on problem-solving courts has increased considerably over the past 25 years. Drug courts are by far the most well-researched of the problem-solving courts, and there is an extensive and well-developed body of research on their operation and effectiveness. Research on mental health courts is continuing to grow, and there is reason to be cautiously optimistic about the effects of these courts. However, as discussed in Chapter 6, there is very little research on all other types of problem-solving courts, and we were unable to find any research on several types of these courts.

Conducting process and outcome research on functioning courts can be challenging for a variety of ethical and logistical reasons. In the preceding chapters on drug courts (Chapter 4), mental health courts (Chapter 5), other specialty courts (Chapter 6), and reentry courts (Chapter 7), we noted some of the challenges researchers encounter when studying specific problem-solving courts. In this chapter, we discuss the challenges that are common to research on problem-solving courts more generally.

Randomized Controlled Trials

Among researchers in various disciplines, including the social sciences, the randomized controlled trial (RCT) is considered the gold standard in clinical trials (see Kazdin, 2017; Marczyk, DeMatteo, & Festinger, 2005). In the most basic RCT design, researchers randomly select a sufficiently large sample of individuals to serve as participants and then randomly assign the participants to an experimental condition, in which participants receive the intervention being examined, or a control condition, in which participants receive standard treatment (treatment-as-usual) or a placebo. Through the random selection and random assignment of participants, RCTs minimize participant selection bias and help to reduce the impact of nuisance variables (extraneous variables that are not of interest to the researcher and which can increase the variability of the findings) (Marczyk et al., 2005). By using random assignment, which is the defining feature of experimental RCTs, nuisance variables are distributed unsystematically across study groups, which effectively isolates the intervention being examined in the study. Excluding (or minimizing) experimental confounds by using an RCT permits researchers to draw conclusions about causality regarding the impact of the intervention being studied.

Conducting an RCT in the context of a problem-solving court would involve randomly selecting a sufficiently large number of offenders who are determined to be eligible for the problem-solving court and then randomly assigning those offenders to either standard criminal justice processing (treatment-as-usual) or the problem-solving court. Outcomes of interest for the problem-solving court being examined, such as criminal recidivism, drug use, mental health symptoms, employment, housing, and quality of life, would be measured at specific time points prior to, during, and after the intervention. Using this methodological approach would enable researchers to isolate the effects of the problem-solving court, thereby eliminating competing hypotheses for the observed effects and permitting the researchers to draw defensible causal conclusions about the effects of the court.

For a variety of reasons, conducting RCTs in the context of problem-solving courts, or in most other aspects of the criminal justice system, is quite challenging (DeMatteo, Filone, & LaDuke, 2011; Heck & Roussell, 2007). For example, it is difficult to achieve true random assignment—the hallmark of experimental research—in virtually any criminal justice setting, including problem-solving courts. Randomly assigning offenders to a problem-solving court or standard criminal justice processing raises ethical and legal concerns (Government Accountability Office [GAO], 2005). Legal concerns about equal protection may arise when similarly situated offenders are treated differently by the court. For instance, if an offender is randomly assigned to a control condition, or a treatment condition that involves the provision of fewer resources and services than is typically provided by treatment-as-usual, there is a risk that the offender's equal protection rights may be violated (DeMatteo et al., 2011) (see Chapter 9 for a more detailed discussion of ethical and legal concerns in problem-solving courts). In addition, knowingly providing a high-risk offender with fewer services or less intensive treatment could result in concerns related to public safety. For these and other reasons, many problem-solving court stakeholders, including judges, prosecuting attorneys, and defense attorneys, are understandably reluctant to agree to the random assignment of offenders to various treatment conditions (DeMatteo et al., 2011). As such, most researchers who study problem-solving courts rely on quasi-experimental designs in which they study existing groups without the methodological benefits associated with random assignment. Although quasi-experimental designs can still yield meaningful data, researchers must be cautious when drawing inferences from studies that use those designs because causal inferences may not be justified (Kazdin, 2017; Marczyk et al., 2005).

Despite these challenges, several groups of researchers have successfully conducted RCTs in problem-solving courts. Most of these RCTs have been conducted in drug courts, and these studies have yielded useful data on the operations and effectiveness of drug courts, including outcomes such as relapse to drug use and criminal recidivism. As discussed in Chapter 4, approximately one dozen RCTs have been conducted on drug courts (e.g., Deschenes, Turner, & Greenwood, 1995; Gottfredson & Exum, 2002; Gottfredson, Kearley, Najaka, & Rocha, 2005; Gottfredson, Najaka, & Kearley, 2003; Gottfredson, Najaka, Kearley, & Rocha, 2006; Harrell, Cavanaugh, & Roman, 1998; Marlowe, Festinger, & Lee, 2004; Marlowe, Festinger, Lee, Dugosh, & Benasutti, 2006).

Interestingly, despite the voluminous research on drug courts, including several well-conducted RCTs, meta-analyses, multisite studies, and systematic reviews, the effectiveness of drug courts in reducing criminal recidivism and relapse to drug use is still vigorously debated. The National Association of Drug Court Professionals (NADCP) unequivocally supports the effectiveness of drug courts and other problem-solving courts: "Treatment courts are the most successful intervention in our nation's history for leading people living with substance use and mental health disorders out of the justice system and into lives of recovery and stability" (NADCP, 2018c). Furthermore, in the most recent edition of *Painting the Current Picture*, which provides a comprehensive overview of all available research on problem-solving courts, Marlowe, Hardin, and Fox (2016) concluded that "drug courts are effective and cost-effective" (p. 14).

By contrast, organizations such as the Drug Policy Alliance and the Open Society Foundations are less confident about the effectiveness of drug courts (see Csete & Tomasini-Joshi, 2015), and they also question the effectiveness of other problem-solving courts that have been developed based on the drug court model (see Rowland, 2016). Indeed, the Open Society Foundations concluded that less than 20% of drug court studies relied on rigorous scientific principles (Rowland, 2016); other critics suggest that drug court researchers rely on biased control groups, fail to report data on those participants who did not complete the program, and place too much reliance on self-report data (Fischer, 2003; Rowland, 2016). Other researchers have suggested that drug court graduation rates may be somewhat inflated due to the inclusion of offenders who show little evidence of having a substance use disorder (e.g., DeMatteo, Marlowe, Festinger, & Arabia, 2009; Kleiman et al., 2003). It has also been observed that problem-solving court research is insufficiently independent, as some studies have been conducted on government-funded courts using government funding (Csete & Tomasini-Joshi, 2015). Nevertheless, using accepted standards for assessing the quality of research (see Kazdin, 2017), drug courts appear to be effective and cost-effective in reducing recidivism and relapse to drug use.

Researchers have also conducted RCTs of mental health courts, but we could only find two such studies (see Cosden, Ellens, Schnell, & Yamini-Diouf, 2005; Cosden, Ellens, Schnell, Yamini-Diouf, & Wolfe, 2003). As discussed in Chapter 5, most research studies on mental health courts have involved a quasi-experimental design or a pretest/posttest design. Furthermore, the majority of these studies did not use techniques to account for the impact of nonrandom assignment; for example, propensity score matching can be used to reduce the bias associated with using intact groups (Rosenbaum & Rubin, 1983). Several studies of mental health courts are purely descriptive and do not permit any causal inferences about the effects of mental health courts (see Chapter 5 for a more detailed discussion of research on mental health courts). We were unable to find any research studies that used random assignment for any of the other types of problem-solving courts, including reentry courts, DUI courts, and family drug courts. Furthermore, many studies on these other problem-solving courts did not even use a quasi-experimental design and were instead basic descriptive studies (see Chapter 6 for a discussion of research on other specialty courts).

A key and perhaps obvious recommendation for researchers is to use rigorous research methodology whenever feasible. There is precedent for conducting RCTs in both drug courts and mental health courts, so several groups of researchers have found ways to navigate successfully through the challenges inherent in using random assignment with offenders in courts. Conducting an RCT requires buy-in from all of the problem-solving court stakeholders (judge, defense attorney, prosecutor, etc.), and each stakeholder may have different concerns related to the random assignment of offenders. For example, defense attorneys may believe that their clients are being disadvantaged if they are assigned to an unproven experimental intervention, which could in theory increase the likelihood that their clients may perform poorly in the program and be subject to harsher punishment. Judges and prosecutors may worry about being perceived as too lenient if they permit offenders to be assigned to interventions that involve less supervision and fewer services. Also, requiring court personnel to be blinded to which study conditions the offenders are in may raise concerns that the court is not fully in control. It often requires a leap of faith for stakeholders to agree to random assignment, and not every jurisdiction will have stakeholders who are willing to take such a risk. However, as empirical evidence regarding the positive effects of problem-solving courts continues to grow, stakeholders may perceive less risk in permitting researchers to conduct RCTs in their jurisdictions.

For some types of problem-solving courts, particularly the more recently developed courts, conducting an RCT may be premature. The first step when examining many types of interventions is gathering basic descriptive data on the effects of the intervention. A purely descriptive study does not permit any inferences regarding causality, but it provides preliminary evidence on whether the intervention is associated with improved outcomes, which would provide a foundation and empirical justification for conducting a more rigorous RCT to experimentally isolate the effects of the intervention; this is sometimes referred to as getting inside the "black box" of problem-solving courts (Goldkamp, White, & Robinson, 2001, p. 27). If, however, descriptive research does not provide support for the utility of a particular problem-solving court, there would be less justification for expending the time, money, and resources needed for conducting an experimental study.

If an experimental research design is not possible due to lack of stakeholder buy-in or lack of available resources, the next best design in terms of drawing meaningful inferences about the intervention is quasi-experimental, which involves studying existing groups without the benefit of random assignment. There are also some statistical techniques that can be used when random assignment is not feasible, including propensity score matching or covariate analyses. Given concerns related to participant attrition (discussed later in this chapter), researchers are advised to use intent-to-treat analyses as the primary method of data analysis (see Gupta, 2011; Kazdin, 2017). The intent-to-treat approach controls for crossover and dropout effects because it accounts for all participants who are initially randomized in the study, regardless of whether the participants complete the intervention being examined. As such, intent-to-treat analyses ignore noncompliance, protocol deviations, and attrition (Gupta, 2011). Because no participants are excluded from the statistical analyses, the intent-to-treat approach also provides useful data regarding whether certain types of participants are more likely to fail to complete the program. In addition to intent-to-treat analyses, analyses of successful program completers can be conducted to obtain more nuanced data on those who completed the intervention.

It is important to note that there are other research designs that either closely approximate RCTs or are variations of quasi-experimental designs that may be useful when researching problem-solving courts. For example, using a pretest/posttest design in which problem-solving court participants are assessed upon entry into the court and then at a later timepoint (e.g., scheduled timepoints during the program, at the conclusion of the program, 3 months after program completion) could permit researchers to examine various outcome variables in addition to recidivism, including quality of life, specific targets of treatment, and some dynamic risk factors. If the study also includes offenders in standard criminal justice processing (or some other intervention), comparisons can be made between problem-solving court participants and the other group(s) of any of these outcomes. An interrupted time series analysis, which is a version of quasi-experimental research, is also effective for examining longitudinal data on outcomes that are hypothesized to be affected by participation in the problem-solving court.

Methodological Challenges

Regardless of the methodological design that is used, there are a number of challenges researchers must address when studying problem-solving courts. Due to legal, ethical, public safety, and logistical considerations, even well-designed studies will be challenging to conduct in problem-solving courts. Among the many challenges inherent in problem-solving court research, we focus specifically on those related to the study samples, the differences among problem-solving courts, and the variability in outcome assessment.

Study Samples

Research on problem-solving courts is often marked by high rates of participant attrition and noncompliance. Specifically, participant attrition and noncompliance has hindered research on drug courts (e.g., Latimer, Morton-Bourgon, & Chrétien, 2006), mental health courts (e.g., Cosden et al., 2005; Moore & Hiday, 2006), reentry courts (e.g., Listswan, 2008), and DUI courts (Miller, Curtis, Sonderlund, Day, & Droste, 2015). For longitudinal research, attrition rates can be quite high for several reasons. For example, courts often do not have authority over participants after they have completed the problem-solving court program, so there may be less incentive for participants to continue participating in research. High rates of attrition can threaten the integrity of the research and create bias within a study if those participants who drop out of the study differ systematically from those who continue to receive the intervention (Marczyk et al., 2005). Fortunately, there are several ways to ameliorate attrition bias. For example, as previously discussed, using intent-to-treat analyses can be effective, and statistically demonstrating that the participants who did not complete the study are not systematically different from those who remained in the study should eliminate or at least minimize concerns about attrition bias.

Researchers have developed several ways to reduce or prevent attrition and improve participant compliance, including offering incentives for continued participation and using a detailed tracking system to follow participants. However, managing attrition and compliance is particularly challenging in the context of problem-solving courts. To be eligible for certain problem-solving courts, offenders are required to have specific characteristics—drug use, mental health problems, criminal history, and the like—that may increase the likelihood of attrition or noncompliance. As such, problem-solving court researchers may need to focus less on *preventing* attrition and more on *correcting* attrition. There are several accepted statistical approaches to help researchers correct participant attrition in circumstances when the characteristics related to dropping out of the study are known or unknown (see Miller & Hollist, 2007). Among other steps, problem-solving court researchers should develop a data collection plan that will provide information on the causes of attrition and subsequently rely on available statistical approaches to correct any attrition bias.

Another concern related to study samples in problem-solving courts research is their representativeness (or lack thereof). Much problem-solving court research relies on data from samples that do not accurately represent the composition of the criminal justice system. For example, when compared to the criminal justice population as a whole, there is an observed overrepresentation of female and Caucasian participants in mental health courts (Hiday, Moore, Lamoureaux, & Magistris, 2005; Sarteschi, Vaughn, & Kim, 2011; Steadman & Naples, 2005) and an overrepresentation of female participants in drug courts (Messina, Calhoun, & Warda, 2012). Similarly, minority populations are underrepresented in drug courts compared to the rates of minorities among arrestee, probation, and incarcerated populations (see Marlowe et al., 2016). Given these differences, the results of problem-solving court research may not generalize beyond the study cohorts.

There is also considerable variability in the nature and composition of comparison groups used in problem-solving court research. For example, some studies use program noncompleters as the comparison group, while other studies use a sample of eligible offenders who chose not to participate in the problem-solving court. There are benefits and limitations to both approaches, but the use of different types of comparison groups makes it difficult to compare results across problem-solving courts and to draw broad inferences regarding the effectiveness of these courts. Although researchers often compare drug court participants with offenders who went through traditional criminal justice processing, it is worth noting that there is no universal standard as to what constitutes traditional criminal justice processing due to jurisdictional differences in standard practices. Finally, some problem-solving courts tend to admit less serious offenders (Werkmeister, 2015), which can skew the comparison with offenders who went through traditional criminal justice processing unless affirmative steps are taken to address the between-group differences. Moreover, some problem-solving court participants who fail to successfully complete the program are transferred to a standard criminal docket. If problem-solving courts admit less serious offenders and tend to transfer "problematic" cases, the reported success rates of problem-solving courts may be artificially inflated.

A final concern relates to the sample sizes often seen in problem-solving court research. For many of the studies we reviewed, the most notable limitation was a small sample size, which raises concerns about both internal and external validity. The small samples are perhaps most problematic in longitudinal research, in which (as previously noted) participant attrition over time can be quite significant.

Problem-Solving Court Heterogeneity

Although all problem-solving courts are based on similar foundational principles (e.g., therapeutic jurisprudence, behavioral modification, collaborative justice; see NADCP, 1997), there is considerable variability in how these courts operate. Even among specific types of problem-solving courts, there are notable differences across jurisdictions due to a variety of factors, including funding, available resources, and the acceptability of certain procedures. Problem-solving courts were initially established as experimental programs in a limited number of jurisdictions, so they differ greatly in terms of eligibility requirements and operational procedures. For example, as discussed in Chapter 4, drug courts operate under a variety of models. Some drug courts are pre-plea courts that will result in the dismissal of criminal charges upon an offender's successful completion of the program, others require a guilty plea prior to admission, and still other drug courts admit only offenders on probation. There is also variability among mental health courts in terms of eligibility criteria (e.g., mental health diagnosis), the types and quality of services provided, and the outcomes measured (Honegger, 2015).

As another example, the primary purpose of reentry courts is to link participants to services that will facilitate successful reintegration into the community (e.g., job training, educational services, housing, other social services), yet research suggests that there is considerable variability in the services that are provided to participants across jurisdictions (see Lattimore, Vishner, & Steffey, 2011). Unlike mental health courts or drug courts, which provide services targeted to a specific issue, reentry courts are designed to meet the myriad needs of returning citizens as they reintegrate back into society. These needs span many domains, including substance use, mental health, medical, housing, employment, and family reunification. Responding to such a wide variety of needs is quite challenging, and evidence suggests that there is substantial variability in the services provided (Lattimore et al., 2011). Furthermore, among some reentry courts, there are discrepancies between the perceived and actual amount of services that are provided to participants. Lattimore and colleagues examined this issue by "comparing the percentage of program participants the program directors indicated were receiving a particular service or bundle of services with the percentage of percentage of participants who reported receiving the service of bundle of services," and the results revealed significant variation between the perceptions of the program directors and participants in terms of the services delivered (Lattimore et al., 2011, p. 95).

Variability among problem-solving courts, including the idiosyncratic and often variable operation within a particular court over time, makes it challenging to draw broad, defensible, and generalizable inferences regarding the effectiveness of these courts. Frequently, research does not reflect the diversity among problem-solving courts, and those with an interest in the court and/or the research may draw overly broad conclusions that may not be justified or generalize to other courts. One way to address diversity is to conduct multisite studies across jurisdictions using research methodologies and statistical approaches than can accommodate differences among the courts.

Outcome Assessment

As problem-solving courts continue to proliferate and new types of courts are developed, it is important that researchers and stakeholders consider the differences among the various types of problem-solving courts and delineate the specific research outcomes that should be logically associated with each type of court. Indeed, although research may demonstrate that one type of problem-solving court is effective in improving outcomes, it does not necessarily follow that other problem-solving courts will be similarly effective even if they adhere to similar principles and operations. For example, drugs courts and reentry courts have similar principles and operational protocols, but these courts target very different populations: drug courts target individuals with substance use disorders, while reentry courts target a broader population in terms of criminogenic risk factors and clinical needs. Moreover, for reentry court participants, their recent prolonged incarceration may have changed their existing risks and needs. As such, researchers and stakeholders should not place disproportionate emphasis on successful drug court outcomes when considering the potential impact of reentry courts (see Marlowe & Meyer, 2011). Although all problem-solving courts share the goal of reducing criminal recidivism, each type of court may have goals that are unique to that type of court. As with all research, it is important to specify the outcomes that are being assessed, and those outcomes should be directly relevant to the goals of the particular problem-solving courts being studied.

A related concern is that some problem-solving courts do not systematically collect or maintain the type of data that researchers rely on when conducting process and outcome studies. The lack of comprehensive data is sometimes compounded by the idiosyncratic data systems that are used by some courts; many courts use homegrown data tracking systems that do not lend themselves to conducting meaningful research. Most courts are not designed with research in mind, so there are often many barriers researchers must overcome.

Appropriate Targets of Intervention

The theory behind problem-solving courts is that addressing the root cause of offending behavior will reduce recidivism and improve the offender's quality of life. For example, there is a substantial body of research demonstrating that substance use is associated with antisocial behavior (see Andrews & Bonta, 2010b; Bennett, Holloway, & Farrington, 2008; DeMatteo, Filone, & Davis, 2015). As such, targeting an offender's substance use problem—a demonstrated criminogenic need—should effectively reduce the likelihood of recidivism. But not all problem-solving courts are targeting interventions that have an empirical link with offending behavior.

Mental health courts were developed to address the mental health needs of offenders, and the presumption is that ameliorating mental health symptoms will reduce the likelihood of recidivism. In 1999, the Surgeon General of the United States issued the first report on mental health, which noted that people with mental illness, particularly those with psychotic disorders, are perceived by the public to be more violent and that mental illness is perceived to be linked with unpredictable and violent behavior (US Department of Health and Human Services, 1999). However, as noted in Chapter 1, the relationship between mental illness and risk of offending is neither straightforward nor strong. Mental illness is not one of the Central Eight risk factors of the Risk-Needs-Responsivity model, and a synthesis of available research suggests that there is a modest and indirect relationship between mental illness and offending (Andrews, Bonta, & Wormith, 2006; Skeem, Manchak, & Peterson, 2011). Therefore, the link between mental health and antisocial behavior, particularly violent behavior, may not provide a sufficiently strong rationale for mental health courts.

A review of the MacArthur Violence Risk Assessment Study, which is the largest study examining the relationship between mental illness and violence, may be instructive when considering the rationale underlying mental health courts (Monahan et al., 2001). The MacArthur study examined the prevalence of community violence among individuals with severe mental illness following a stay in an inpatient mental health facility. The researchers for this study followed 951 psychiatric patients after discharge from inpatient psychiatric facilities in Kansas City (Kansas), Worcester (Massachusetts), and Pittsburgh (Pennsylvania). These individuals were diagnosed with a variety of mental health disorders, including schizophrenia (17%), bipolar disorder (13%), major depressive disorder (40%), substance use disorders (24%), and other diagnoses (6%) (Torrey, Stanley, Monahan, & Steadman, 2008). The primary conclusion from the MacArthur study is that individuals with severe mental illness who are discharged from inpatient psychiatric facilities are not significantly more violent or dangerous than individuals in the general community population (Monahan et al., 2001; Torrey et al., 2008).

Monahan et al. (2001) make an important point: regardless of mental illness, violence typically occurs in a social context, and the specific context in which violence occurs must be considered when discussing the relationship between violence and mental illness. They concluded that "patient violence may be most reasonably conceptualized as violence involving people with mental illness rather than a distinct form of irrational behavior" (Monahan et al., 2001, pp. 32–33). This latter point is relevant when thinking about the utility of mental health courts. Should these courts focus on the mental health needs of offenders? Or should they instead pay more attention to other factors, such as community, neighborhood, and peers, that provide the contexts in which violence frequently occurs? However, unlike mental health symptoms, these contextual factors may be difficult to operationalize, measure, and address in a systemic way.

Nevertheless, because mental illness may be indirectly related to offending behavior, the MacArthur study researchers concluded that treating individuals with mental health disorders can lead to an overall reduction in violent behavior and thus serve as an important tool in managing risk (Steadman et al., 1998). Other research has also demonstrated that treating individuals with severe mental illness can reduce the likelihood of violent behavior (e.g., O'Keefe, Potenza, & Mueser, 1997; Swanson et al., 2000).

The MacArthur study findings should be taken into account when thinking about the utility of mental health courts, but it is important to note that the MacArthur study only included individuals whose mental health symptoms were severe enough to require inpatient psychiatric treatment (Torrey et al., 2008). This focus on inpatient settings has two notable implications. First, although the MacArthur study may suggest that there is no significant relationship between severe mental illness and likelihood of violence, it did not investigate the relationship between less severe mental illnesses (which are prevalent in mental health courts) and offending behavior. Second, the MacArthur study evaluated incidences of violence among individuals throughout the first year posttreatment, and perhaps the incidences of violence were lower precisely because these individuals received treatment for their mental illness. Although the MacArthur study raises questions about the strength of the relationship between mental health and violence, it also suggests that treating mental illness can lead to a reduction in violence, which seems to provide a justification for mental health courts. Of course, mental health courts seek to achieve other outcomes that are not related to reoffending per se, such as treatment linkage and improving quality of life, and these goals provide further justification for the continued operation of mental health courts.

This discussion of the relationship between mental illness and violence is intended to examine the rationale for mental health courts and highlight the importance of focusing on relevant outcomes when conducting research in problem-solving courts. Researchers examining the other types of problem-solving courts discussed throughout this book should focus on outcomes that are theoretically relevant to each type of court. There should be a link between the interventions being provided in a specific problem-solving court and the outcome being examined. If, for example, a particular type of problem-solving court is seeking to improve participants' quality of life, then researchers should make sure that quality of life is one of the outcomes being assessed.

Conclusion

Conducting rigorous, high-quality research that yields relevant, valid conclusions is challenging in most contexts, but perhaps even more challenging in the context of problem-solving courts. Given considerations related to judicial fairness, the ethical treatment of offenders, and the differing interests of those involved, examining the effects of problem-solving courts can be complex. The results of problem-solving court research may be carefully scrutinized by other researchers, peer reviewers, the problem-solving court stakeholders, the media, and funding agencies.

In this chapter, we reviewed the types of research designs that are (or should be) used in problem-solving courts, along with some of the more common methodological challenges faced by researchers in problem-solving courts. Although some of the challenges (e.g., attrition) are common to many types of research, other challenges (e.g., within-court and between-court heterogeneity) are distinctive to problem-solving courts. We have offered recommendations for researchers that we hope will guide future efforts to examine the effects of problem-solving courts and summarized these recommendations in two tables (see Tables 8.1 and 8.2). Despite the bipartisan

Table 8.1 Problem-solving courts: research designs, challenges, and recommendations

Research designs	Components	Benefits	Limitations	Recommendations
Randomized controlled trial (RCT)	Randomly selected participants from eligible population Random assignment to treatment group (problem-solving court) and treatment-as-usual group (standard criminal justice processing) Sufficiently large sample (100+ participants)	Gold standard for empirical research Controls for nuisance variables Isolates impact of problem-solving court Excludes or minimizes experimental compounds Allows defensible causal conclusions	Difficult to achieve in criminal justice system Ethical and legal concerns	Obtain buy-in from relevant stakeholders (judge, prosecutor, defense attorney, administrators, case managers) Adhere as closely as possible to components (column 2)
Quasi-experimental design	Examine existing groups without random assignment Consider propensity score matching or covariate analyses Variations include pre/post designs and interrupted time series designs	Easier to conduct than RCT Fewer legal/ethical concerns	Lack of random assignment Not gold standard of research Ability to draw causal inferences is limited	Use statistical techniques such as propensity score matching and covariate analysis to control for lack of random assignment Use intent-to-treat analyses to control for attrition

Table 8.2 Problem-solving courts: study components, challenges, and recommendations

Study components	Challenges	Recommendations
Samples	High attrition rates High noncompliance rates Nonrepresentative samples	Use intent-to-treat analyses Offer incentives for continued participation Utilize detailed tracking system to track participants Collect data on causes of attrition
Heterogeneity of problem-solving courts	Substantial variability of operations and procedures makes it challenging to draw broad and generalizable conclusions Different outcome assessments for each court	Conduct multisite studies Use research techniques and statistical methods to control differences between courts Choose outcomes most relevant to specific type of court being studied
Targets of intervention	Some problem-solving courts target a need that has no clear link to offender behavior	In developing new problem-solving courts, consider whether and how the targeted interventions relate to reoffense/recidivism risk

support problem-solving courts generally receive, they are still entities within the criminal justice system and may be subject to political scrutiny. If high-quality research supports the utility of these courts, those results can be useful in efforts to develop more problem-solving courts and obtain continued funding for existing courts.

9

Ethical and Legal Considerations in Problem-Solving Courts

Currently, thousands of problem-solving courts are operating in state and local jurisdictions across the country (Marlowe, Hardin, & Fox, 2016), and close to 50% of federal districts have problem-solving court programs (Meierhoefer & Breen, 2013). The rapid proliferation of problem-solving courts has led to significant changes in the roles of attorneys and judges and the way they interact in the courtroom. The novel methodology and procedures used by problem-solving courts are substantially different from those used in standard criminal justice processing. As such, as specialty courts continue to spread across the country, the ethical and legal implications of these courts must be considered.

Legal considerations relevant to problem-solving court jurisprudence include plea requirements, competency, and consequences of noncompliance. Problem-solving courts also have the potential to impact certain constitutional rights, including First Amendment protection of free speech, Fourth Amendment rights related to searches and seizures, Sixth Amendment right to counsel, and Fourteenth Amendment substantive due process and equal protection rights. Legal ethics considerations such as informed consent and confidentiality must be addressed in light of the treatment-focused nature of many problem-solving courts. Moreover, due to the heightened involvement of the specialty court judge, problem-solving courts must consider issues related to personal relationships with participants, ex parte communications, and impartiality. In addition, the collaborative approach taken by most problem-solving courts warrants a discussion of the appropriate role of the defense attorney in such courts. It is essential that judges and lawyers consider the legal and ethical implications of these courts and manage any obstacles transparently, so that participants feel confident that their legal rights are protected over any broader interests of the problem-solving court program. A critical aspect of this discussion is procedural justice and the perceptions of defendants regarding fairness in problem-solving courts.

We begin this chapter by reviewing the constitutional considerations relevant to problem-solving courts and how they impact pleadings, consent, and competency. Next, we provide an overview of the ethical issues associated with consent and confidentiality in specialty courts. We then discuss ethical implications regarding the role of the judge in specialty courts, including the potential for coercion and the use of leverage. We also review the role of the defense attorney in problem-solving courts, with a focus on how defense attorneys can effectively represent defendants in light of the team approach adopted by such courts. Finally, we conclude the chapter with a brief discussion of the nature of procedural justice in problem-solving courts.

Constitutional Considerations

Constitutional considerations have taken center stage in standard criminal justice courts, so it is not surprising that constitutional rights need to be considered in the context of problem-solving courts. Indeed, added scrutiny of these rights may be warranted given that specialty court procedures diverge substantially from standard criminal justice processing. For example, involvement in problem-solving court often requires participants to waive their constitutional rights (Boldt, 1998; Casey, 2004; Clarke & Neuhard, 2004; Hoffman, 1999; Mirchandani, 2008; Nolan, 2003; Spinak, 2003).

First Amendment

Two First Amendment issues are implicated in problem-solving courts: violation of the Establishment Clause, and Freedom of Speech (Meyer, 2011; U.S. Const. amend. I; Raine, 2012). The Establishment Clause of the First Amendment to the U.S. Constitution prohibits the state from coercing an individual to engage in a religious activity (*Kerr v. Farrey*, 1996). As such, the procedures used by problem-solving courts may conflict with First Amendment rights when such courts require participants to engage in certain types of treatment programs (e.g., Alcoholics Anonymous [AA] and Narcotics Anonymous [NA]) that have a religious component. Although many 12-step programs such as AA and NA seek to promote tolerance, they typically still require members to give themselves up to a "Higher Being" (Meyer, 2011). Courts have held that, based on the Establishment Clause, it is unconstitutional to require individuals to participate in an AA or NA program (e.g., *Griffin v. Coughlin*, 1996; *Kerr v. Farrey*, 1996; *Inouya v. Kemma*, 2007). However, a court may mandate treatment if a participant has a range of treatment programs from which to choose that includes secular treatment program alternatives (*Destefano v. Emergency Housing Group, Inc.*, 2001; *American United v. Prison Fellowship*, 2007; *O'Conner v. California*, 1994). As such, if a problem-solving court intends to make referrals to 12-step treatment programs, it is important that the court also identifies secular treatment alternatives within the community.

The First Amendment Freedom of Speech and Association Clause may be implicated when problem-solving courts impose area restrictions (prohibiting individuals from being in certain geographical locations) or association restrictions (prohibiting individuals from spending time with certain people) (Meyer, 2011). Courts tend to uphold area restrictions when they are narrowly drawn and reasonable, and this determination is based on several factors, including the size of the restricted area, whether the participant has a legitimate need to be in the restricted area, and the connection between the area and the participant's rehabilitation (e.g., *Andrews v. State*, 2005; *People v. Jungers*, 2005). For example, a Florida appellate court upheld a restriction from areas where there was substantial drug usage (*Johnson v. State,* 1989), and the Louisiana Supreme Court upheld a restriction preventing a defendant from going to the French Quarter of New Orleans (*State v. Morgan*, 1980). Another case provides an example of an impermissible restriction (*State v. Wright,* 2000). In that case, an Ohio appellate court overturned a restriction that required a defendant to avoid any location where alcohol was sold, served, or consumed (*State v. Wright*, 2000).

Association restrictions also tend to be upheld when they are reasonably related to the goals of probation, crime prevention, and public safety (Raine, 2012). For instance, a Georgia appellate court upheld an association restriction requiring a defendant to avoid drug users and drug dealers (*Andrews v. State*, 2005), a California appellate court upheld a requirement that an offender avoid contact with his wife in a case where she was a victim of domestic violence (*People v. Jungers*, 2005), and a Colorado appellate court upheld a requirement that prevented a defendant from associating with his children without supervision (*People v. Forsyth*, 2001). Other permissible association restrictions include prohibiting defendants from associating with motorcycle organizations, Irish clubs, certain gang members, and other individuals with a criminal record (Raine, 2012). An example of a restriction that was deemed overly broad can be found in *Dawson v. State* (1995), where an Alaska appellate court overturned a requirement that a defendant avoid any unsupervised contact with his wife who was actively using drugs. Although the imposition of area and association restrictions is not standard practice in many types of problem-solving courts, courts that use these restrictions should exercise caution to ensure that the restrictions are reasonable.

Fourth Amendment

Under the Fourth Amendment, authorities are prohibited from arresting or searching individuals without probable cause (U.S. Const. amend. IV). However, participants in problem-solving courts often relinquish this right through a search waiver. For example, drug court participants are sometimes required to withstand a search of their person or property, even without cause, to participate in the court (Meyer, 2011). Similarly, probationers, some of whom participate in reentry courts and drug courts, may often be legally searched based on "reasonable suspicion," even without waiving their Fourth Amendment rights (see *Griffin v. Wisconsin*, 1987). Courts have upheld searches of probationers without probable cause by holding that it is acceptable to constrain a probationer's individual rights for the purpose of public safety and mitigating recidivism (see *Payne v. State*, 2005; *State v. Patton*, 2005). Some courts have found that a waiver alone constitutes justification for a search without cause or suspicion (e.g., *State v. Kouba*, 2006; *State v. McAuliffe*, 2005). The U.S. Supreme Court has permitted a search where the probation officer had no reasonable suspicion of criminal behavior, reasoning that the parolee's waiver of his Fourth Amendment rights upon drug court enrollment made such a search constitutional (see *Samson v. California*, 2006). Whether it is constitutional to search individuals *without convictions* based on a search waiver is not yet clear (see *Terry v. Superior Court*, 1999; *United States v. Scott*, 2006). Probationers and parolees may be subject to such searches regardless of whether they are involved in problem-solving courts, but these Fourth Amendment considerations should still be taken into account in the context of problem-solving courts.

The Fourth Amendment is also relevant to the mandatory drug tests often utilized by drug courts. Although drug testing has been found to be appropriate for those on probation or parole due to considerations relating to public safety, conditional drug testing of individuals at pretrial release must comply with the Fourth Amendment, which means that drug testing of such offenders must be reasonable and tailored to the individual (see *Oliver v. United States*, 1996; *State v. Ullring*, 1999; *Steiner v. State*, 2002). Moreover, problem-solving courts are permitted to require that convicted participants refrain from using alcohol (a behavior that is not per se illegal for individuals over age 21) when they find it is reasonably related to that individual's rehabilitation or public safety (see *Payne v. State*, 2005; *State v. Patton*, 2005). Problem-solving courts may also prohibit alcohol use by defendants who have not yet been convicted, assuming that refraining from using alcohol is reasonably related to the defendant's ability to attend a future court date (see *Martell v. County Court*, 1992; *State v. Magnunson*, 2000).

Due Process

Under the Due Process Clause of the Fourteenth Amendment, criminal defendants are entitled to fair treatment and procedural protections by the judicial system (U.S. Const. amend. XIV). There is a risk that problem-solving court participants may not be afforded their procedural due process rights due to several distinctive aspects of problem-solving courts, including the nonadversarial approach, heightened judicial involvement, streamlined judicial hearings, increased monitoring (particularly in drug courts), and the use of sanctions (Boldt, 1998; Meyer, 2011). For instance, a Tennessee court of criminal appeals argued that a mental health court judge who assumed the role of a treatment team leader for court participants will not have the detached objectivity required to adjudicate revocation hearings (*State v. Stewart*, 2010).

The case law regarding procedural due process rights for problem-solving court participants is unsettled. In *Smith v. State* (2003), a Florida District Court held that the legal actors involved in drugs courts must gain a thorough understanding of the nature of these courts and think critically about the best way to serve participants.

> It is essential that lawyers educate themselves as to the availability, requirement, and appropriateness of drug court programs. Only then can they effectively advise their clients.... To ignore the need to learn about the drug court process is to ignore the evolution of the justice system. (p. 404)

Although this opinion addressed drug courts specifically, the sentiment arguably applies to all types problem-solving courts—all involved legal actors must educate themselves about the nature of these courts and determine how to best uphold the due process rights of participants.

The Nonadversarial Nature of Problem-Solving Courts

Problem-solving courts place significant emphasis on collaboration among the legal actors and other stakeholders, often focusing on "teamwork" and cooperation. This collaborative approach raises concerns regarding the defense lawyer's role as a zealous advocate, the lawyer's approach to plea bargaining, and the judge's role in accepting a plea or imposing a sentence (Lane, 2003). Does this "teamwork" approach infringe on a defendant's right to effective counsel or an impartial judge? This section focuses on the *due process* issues associated with the roles of the judges and attorneys in problem-solving courts, and later sections provide a more in-depth discussion of the ethical issues that arise considering the roles of these legal actors in problem-solving court contexts.

Although a criminal defendant must make the decision regarding the plea, it is not unusual (and not unconstitutional) for defense counsel to pressure a defendant to accept a certain plea. However, there may be due process concerns in the "teamwork" approach that underlies the pressure applied to problem-solving court participants. In general, defense lawyers are permitted to push a defendant in a certain legal direction, and defendants can protect themselves from coercion through the procedural safeguard of a claim of ineffective assistance of counsel. However, when a defense attorney is working as part of a team, it may be difficult for the attorney to maintain his or her duty of loyalty to the defendant and avoid (perceived or real) conflicts of interest (Lane, 2003). For example, a defense attorney may enthusiastically encourage a problem-solving court participant to accept a certain plea that may have been developed based on conversations among the entire problem-solving court team. Such a scenario is likely to occur in problem-solving court contexts.

> In a setting in which the defense counsel (legal aid, appointed counsel, counsel from law school clinics), the prosecutor, and the judge are all "regulars," in that they work together daily in the same courtroom, they develop shared goals, attitudes, and rules of conduct that allow the system to work and the participants to work together. (Lane, 2003, p. 966)

Moreover, judges are required to ensure that a plea "represents a voluntary and intelligent choice among the alternative courses of action open the defendant" (*North Carolina v. Alford*, 1970, p. 31). In a problem-solving court, the judge (as the leader of the problem-solving court team) may maintain a perception that a certain treatment or course of action is in the defendant's best interests. Does this perception conflict with a judge's obligation to ensure that a defendant makes a voluntary and intelligent decision regarding his or her plea? Or does the problem-solving court's interest in helping a participant receive needed treatment or support override the judge's interest in ensuring a voluntary and intelligent plea decision? Or did the defendant agree to be overseen by a judge with such a perspective by choosing to participate in the problem-solving court? Problem-solving courts should consider such questions when developing protocol and considering how to best protect participants' due process rights.

Heightened Involvement of Problem-Solving Court Judges

Due process requires that a judge remain impartial and be free of both actual and apparent bias toward any involved party (U.S. Const. amend. XIV; *Turney v. Ohio*, 1927). Judges are expected to recuse themselves if they have obtained extrajudicial or personal knowledge that may impact their ability to be impartial (see *Liteky v. United States*, 1994). The Model Code of Judicial Conduct (Model Code; 2007) addresses judicial impartiality. Model Rule 2.2 sets forth that "[a] judge shall uphold and apply the law and shall perform all duties of judicial office fairly and impartially," and the commentary to the rule adds that a judge must remain "objective" and "open-minded." However, problem-solving court judges play a much more active role than traditional judges, and they often have a significant amount of information about participants, which may raise questions about these judges' abilities to maintain impartiality (Arkfeld, 2007). In addition to on-the-record communications, problem-solving court judges learn about participants through more informal communications, such as staff meetings with the full problem-solving court team, including the defense attorney, prosecutor, treatment providers, and probation staff (Meyer, 2011). Moreover, problem-solving court judges typically have frequent contact with the participant, as well as the participants' family members. This closeness may be a double-edged sword. On one hand, the judge will be aware of family circumstances, outside stressors, and/or substance use problems that could lead to criminal activity, and the judge can use this information to impose a uniquely tailored treatment plan. On the other hand, having such personal information may make it more challenging for a judge to recognize his or her own potential bias, and thus judges may have a difficult time knowing when to recuse themselves from a given case (Arkfeld, 2007).

In a series of studies examining due process issues that arise in problem-solving courts, Lane (2003) found that the judicial activism of problem-solving courts judges varied among different types of problem-solving courts.

> In the drug court study, the question is whether the judge can be impartial; in the community court study, the question is whether the judge can be independent; and in the domestic violence study, the question is how far the judge can go to protect the complainant. (p. 961)

These are important considerations when protecting a defendant's due process right to an impartial judge.

In addressing the issue of impartiality, the Oklahoma Supreme Court held that termination proceedings in a drug court should be assigned to a judge other than the drug court judge where a participant claims potential bias (*Alexander v. State*, 2002). The court reasoned: "Requiring the district court to act as drug court team member, evaluator, monitor, and final adjudicator in a termination proceeding could compromise the impartiality of a district court judge assigned the responsibility of administering a drug court participant's program" (*Alexander v. State*, 2002, p. 115). Other courts, however, have held that a participant's due process rights are not violated if a drug court judge oversees a termination or revocation hearing (e.g., *State v. Belyea*, 2010). To manage this due process concern, problem-solving courts could consider following the recommendation of Meyer regarding drug court participants and afford all participants the ability to request that an alternate judge conduct termination or revocation hearings (Meyer, 2011).

The Right to Termination Hearings in Problem-Solving Courts

Jurisdictions vary in the due process rights accorded to problem-solving court participants with regard to hearings (Raine, 2012). Some state courts have ruled that drug court participants are entitled to the same due process rights accorded to probationers (see *State v. Rogers*, 2006). Probationers' rights include a right to a preliminary and final hearing regarding any revocation, including written notice of the hearing and the alleged violation, rights to testify and confront witnesses, a right to attend the hearing, a right to a neutral arbiter, and a right to receive a written report related to the hearing (*Gagnon v. Scarpelli*, 1973).

The case law is mixed in terms of a problem-solving court participant's right to a revocation hearing. An Illinois appellate court has held that termination from a drug court requires a hearing (*People v. Anderson*, 2005), and a South Carolina appellate court required a hearing *and* notice prior to termination (*State v. Perkins*, 2008). In addition, Indiana and Virginia have held that drug court participants' liberty is at issue as part of their participation, and thus such participants are entitled to termination hearings (see *Gosha v. State*, 2010; *Harris v. Commonwealth*, 2010). However, the New York Court of Appeals (which is the highest court in New York) held that an evidentiary hearing is not required as long as the court determines that there was a legitimate rationale for terminating a participant (*People v. Fiammegta*, 2010).

Many drug courts have also prohibited participants from waiving their substantive due process right to a termination or revocation hearing through contract (see *Staley v. State*, 2003; *State v. LaPlaca*, 2011; *State v. Rogers*, 2006). A Florida district court of appeals held that a defendant could not prospectively waive his future right to a violation hearing upon enrollment in a specialty court (see *Staley v. State*, 2003), and, similarly, the New Hampshire Supreme Court denied a request of a problem-solving court participant to waive his right to a hearing prior to having that right implicated (see *State v. LaPlaca*, 2011).

It is also worth noting that there is no constitutional right to counsel for defendants in preliminary hearings or revocation hearings (see *Gagnon v. Scarpelli*, 1973). Even so, many states have chosen to provide defendants with a right to counsel at these hearings (see *Commonwealth v. Wilcox*, 2006; *State v. Kouba*, 2006; *State v. Matey*, 2006). It has been argued that drug court participants should be accorded the same rights to which probationers are entitled, in addition to the right to counsel in preliminary and revocation hearings, for cases involving a felony offense with a potential sentence of jail time (Meyer, 2011).

These various court decisions should be considered in light of the substantial variation among problem-solving courts. In *State v. Rogers* (2006), the Idaho Supreme Court reasoned that the due process rights to which drug court participants are entitled may differ among jurisdictions due to such diversity: "[I]t must be assumed that each drug court in Idaho operates uniquely and, therefore, the analysis in this case might not be applicable to any other particular drug court program in the state" (p. 881). This notion could apply to all problem-solving courts, given the significant variation among courts of the same type. For example, although there are many mental health courts across the United States, there are distinctive aspects of each court in structure and process. As such, it may be necessary to conduct a separate due process analysis for each court to ensure that participants' rights are protected.

Due Process and the Right to Hearings Regarding Sanctions

As noted throughout this book, it is standard practice for problem-solving court judges to sanction participants in response to noncompliance with program requirements. Outside of the problem-solving court context, probationers and inmates are entitled to certain due process rights when sanctioned for violations, including a hearing in certain cases. Factors that may impact the due process rights of problem-solving court participants when sanctions are imposed include whether the court uses a pre-plea or post-plea model and whether the factual basis underlying the sanction is contested (Raine, 2012). Typically, when a participant enrolls in a problem-solving court, the participant waives the right to a hearing if sanctioned. Courts have held that sanctions imposed in drug courts are governed by contract rules, reasoning that the right to a hearing is waived when a participant "contracts" to engage in a specialty court (see *State v. Rogers*, 2006). Meyer (2011) argues that best practice in drug courts for situations in which a participant is denying that he or she committed the alleged offense would involve providing the participant with a right to notice of the relevant allegations, a right to counsel, a right to testify, and a right to call witnesses and cross-examine opposing witnesses.

Drug Testing in Drug Courts

Although all problem-solving courts employ some form of monitoring, monitoring by drug courts is more invasive because it typically involves drug testing of participants based on urine, hair, or sweat samples. Consequently, due process considerations require that the drug testing mandated by drugs courts meets reliability standards prior to being relied on to discipline participants (Meyer, 2011). Under the Federal Rules of Evidence (FRE), any scientific testing or technique must meet the admissibility standards articulated by the Supreme Court of the United States in *Daubert v. Merrell Dow Pharmaceuticals* (1993). *Daubert* requires the trial court judge to act as a gatekeeper by assessing the scientific validity and reliability of proffered scientific techniques, and the Supreme Court offered four criteria that judges can use in this determination: (1) whether the technique has been subject to peer review and publication, (2) the known error rate of the technique, (3) whether the technique has been scientifically tested (also known as falsifiability), and (4) whether the technique has been generally accepted within the field. Some jurisdictions only require an examination of the last factor—general acceptance of the technique within the field, which provided the admissibility standard in many jurisdictions prior to *Daubert*—to determine whether a technique is admissible (see *Frye v. United States*, 1923).

Drug courts use a variety of techniques to test participants for drug usage, and it is not clear whether all of the techniques are sufficiently reliable to warrant admissibility in court. These techniques include testing of urine, sweat patches, and hair samples. Several tests relying on urine samples have been deemed reliable. Enzyme multiple immunoassay technique (EMIT) has been found to be reliable (*Jones v. State*, 1998; *Lahey v. Kelly*, 1987; *Spence v. Furrier*, 1986), and courts have held that an EMIT test does not need to be confirmed by an independent drug test to meet due process reliability requirements (see *Lahey v. Kelly*, 1987; *Louis v. Department of Corrections*, 2006; *Peranzo v. Coughlin*, 1985). Other forms of urine testing have also been found to be reliable, including fluorescein polarization immunoassay (FPIA) and thin layer chromatography testing (Meyer, 2011; see *Hernandez v. State*, 2003; *People v. Toran*, 1991). However, not all courts are using these methods for testing urine, and many courts rely on methods with questionable reliability, such as test cups or dip sticks (Meyer, 2011). Moreover, the reliability of these methods is undetermined for certain drugs such as methamphetamine (see *Willis v. Roche Biomedical Lab*, 1995).

The reliability of other drug testing techniques is less clear. Some courts use sweat patches to test for drug use. Although such patches are generally considered reliable, some evidence has shown the potential for false positives due to contamination or exposure (see Chawarski et al., 2007; Levisky et al., 2001; *United States v. Alfonzo*, 2003). The reliability of hair analyses is also problematic due to a high likelihood of contamination and an array of methods used to analyze the hair with varying levels of empirical support (see Ropero-Miller et al., 2009; *Thomas v. McBride*, 1998; *Wykoff v. Resig*, 1985).

Drug courts should consider investing in instrumented drug testing techniques and only use noninstrumented tests for screening purposes (Raine, 2012). Courts should conduct a retest with a reliable drug test in situations where a noninstrumented test reveals a positive result but the participant denies drug usage. Moreover, to protect the due process rights of participants, courts should learn about the varying cutoff levels of different drug testing methods, particularly because the cutoff levels of instrumented tests may be lower than those of tests with questionable reliability (Meyer, 2011).

Equal Protection

Equal protection considerations are also relevant in the problem-solving court model. According to the Equal Protection Clause of the Fourteenth Amendment, individuals in similar conditions and circumstances must be treated equally under the law (U.S. Const. amend. XIV). Equal protection concerns may arise in problem-solving courts when only certain individuals are deemed eligible to participate in the program and when such courts are only available in certain jurisdictions.

In the drug court context, the *rational basis equal protection test* is used to determine whether the admission or denial of a participant is constitutional (see *Lomont v. State*, 2006). As such, courts must determine whether the classification of certain individuals as eligible for drug court has a rational relationship with some legitimate government interest. Courts tend to hold that it is acceptable for drugs courts to be available to only certain individuals (see *C.D.C. v. State*, 2001; *Jim v. State*, 2005). For instance, in *Evans v. State* (2008), an appellate court in Georgia held that a drug court's refusal to admit a defendant with HIV did not violate equal protection. The court reasoned that the drug court's decision had a rational basis because the court denied admission on the grounds that the drug court program would not be able to facilitate the complicated medical treatments needed by the participant. Similarly, in *Jim v. State* (2005), a Mississippi appellate court denied a motion to transfer a case to drug court, reasoning that the statute explicitly set forth that no individual had a "right" to participate in a drug court.

Courts have also held that there is no constitutional violation if certain jurisdictions decide not to develop a problem-solving court, even where nearby jurisdictions have such courts. In *State v. Harner* (2004), the Washington Supreme Court held that the lack of availability of a drug court in a certain county—even though such courts were available in adjacent counties—did not constitute a violation of the Equal Protection Clause. The court reasoned that each county must develop programs based on economic resources and the needs of that specific community, and therefore a county's decision to not fund a drug court is considered rationally related to a legitimate government interest. Similarly, in *Lomont v. State* (2006), an Indiana appellate court held that not all Indiana counties were required to have drug diversion programs. Courts have also found that the Equal Protection Clause is not violated when juveniles are placed in problem-solving courts. For example, an Arizona appellate court held that a juvenile drug court participant could not reject his drug court–mandated probation, reasoning that such a requirement was justified considering the state's interest in juvenile rehabilitation and acting as a legal protector in the best interests of the child (*In re Miguel*, 2003).

The Right to Counsel

Under the Sixth Amendment, all defendants in felony or misdemeanor cases in which incarceration is a potential consequence have a right to counsel at all critical stages of the legal proceedings, including sentencing (U.S. Cont. amend. VI). Although individuals on probation and parole are not constitutionally entitled to have counsel present at revocation hearings, the vast majority of states require counsel at revocation hearings for defendants who request legal representation (see *State v. Kouba*, 2006; *State v. Sommer*, 1994). As such, the right to counsel should also apply to similarly situated individuals in problem-solving courts. In some jurisdictions, any significant modification of probation is considered a "critical stage" of legal proceedings that implicates a right to counsel (see *Faretta v. California*, 1975). Meyer (2011) argues that because the sanctioning process in problem-solving courts is substantially similar to probation modification, problem-solving participants should be entitled to defense counsel at any sanctioning proceeding.

How Can Problem-Solving Courts Protect Constitutional Rights of Participants?

Problem-solving courts can take several steps to ensure that their participants' constitutional rights are protected (Meyer, 2011). First, courts can make an effort to educate themselves on the various constitutional and legal implications of the problem-solving court model. Second, courts can inform participants of the conditions involved in enrollment and ensure that the relinquishment of any rights is done knowingly, intelligently, and voluntarily. Third, problem-solving courts can ensure that participants are afforded their due process rights at revocation and termination proceedings, and at sanctioning proceedings when jail is a potential punishment or the defendant denies the allegations. Finally, drug courts in particular can identify secular alternatives to 12-step programs that have a religious undertone, and they can also ensure that drug testing is reliable or confirmed with instrumented techniques (Meyer, 2011).

Ethical Considerations: Confidentiality and Consent

To identify and oversee offenders who are struggling with mental health or substance use disorders, problem-solving courts must obtain certain information about participants. For example, mental health courts require information regarding participants' behavioral health disorders and treatment histories, and drug courts need information related to participants' substance use and drug treatment history. As such, information sharing is an essential element of the problem-solving court model, and without it there can be no collaboration between the criminal justice system and mental health and substance use treatment providers to address the needs of the participants.

Laws Related to Information Sharing

Although both federal and state laws impact information sharing, there are two federal statutes that must be considered in light of collaborations between the criminal justice system and mental health or substance abuse treatment providers (Petrila & Fader-Towe, 2010). The Health Insurance Portability and Accountability Act (HIPAA) sets forth privacy laws to protect individuals' health information, and a section of the Code of Federal Regulations (42 CFR Part 2) addresses the exchange of information regarding substance abuse treatment. Problem-solving courts should consult both of these statutes, in addition to relevant state, county, and local laws, when developing confidentiality and consent policies.

It is worth noting that the ethical principles for many professions, as well as federal and state regulations, reflect the notion that health information related to mental health disorders and substance abuse "is highly personal and most people would prefer it to remain private" (Petrila & Fader-Towe, 2010, p. viii). However, information sharing may be critical to successful collaborations between the criminal justice system and mental health providers, and the exchange of such information can enhance treatment and protect public safety. In sum, it appears that "[t]he federal and state laws generally reflect an attempt to strike a balance between ensuring that private information remains private without compromising the delivery of needed health-care of public safety services" (Petrila & Fader-Towe, 2010, p. viii).

Mental health courts and drug courts both require the exchange of sensitive health information between treatment providers and the court team. Indeed, these courts need such information to determine eligibility for the court, establish an appropriate treatment program, monitor progress, and, in some cases, determine an appropriate termination date. Courts, including problem-solving courts, are not considered "covered entities" under HIPAA and there is some question about whether drug courts constitute "federally assisted programs" under 42 CFR Part 2. Nevertheless, to the extent that problem-solving courts require information related to treatment and monitor treatment compliance of participants, both HIPAA and 42 CFR Part 2 are relevant (Meyer, 2011; Petrila & Fader-Towe, 2010).

Under HIPAA, 42 CFR Part 2, and state and local laws, treatment providers and other covered entities are required to provide healthcare information to courts (including problem-solving courts) when served with a court order (Petrila & Fader-Towe, 2010). These orders should include specifications about the information sought and, consistent with the HIPAA "minimum necessity" principle, should instruct covered entities to disclose the minimum amount of information necessary to satisfy the request (Petrila & Fader-Towe, 2010). States have varying requirements regarding what should be included in a court order for health information, and both HIPAA and 42 CFR Part 2 set forth rules regarding the proper issuance of these court orders (Meyer, 2011). In lieu of a court order, specialty courts can obtain consent from the participants to access their healthcare information (Petrila & Fader-Towe, 2010). Some mental health courts and drug courts require participants to consent to information sharing between the court and treatment providers prior to enrollment (Petrila & Fader-Towe, 2010). However, when specialty courts receive healthcare information related to a potential or current participant, federal confidentiality laws prohibit the court from sharing that information without consent (Petrila & Fader-Towe, 2010).

There are questions regarding whether hearings in drug courts and mental health courts should be open to the public given the potential disclosure of healthcare-related information. Although neither HIPAA nor 42 CFR Part 2 prohibits such hearings from being open, some jurisdictions close these hearings to the public. Some have suggested that health-related discussions should be held in the judge's chambers or at the bench and that only the minimum necessary healthcare-related information be discussed in public hearings (Petrila & Fader-Towe, 2010). For both types of courts, when disclosing such information, treatment providers and problem-solving court teams should ensure they obtain informed consent when necessary and comply with the wishes of the participants and all applicable regulations regarding the confidentiality of medical and mental health records.

Confidentiality and Informed Consent: Best Practices in Problem-Solving Courts

Petrila and Fader-Towe (2010) describe confidentiality and consent considerations that should be taken into account by mental health courts, and Meyer (2011) outlines a similar set of best practices for drug courts. There is substantial overlap between the two sets of guidelines, and these guidelines would apply to any problem-solving court that uses sensitive participant information.

For problem-solving courts to ensure compliance with confidentiality laws and protect participants' interest in confidentiality, it is important that they develop a comprehensive procedure to manage the collection, release, and exchange of participants' information among the court team members and any outside providers with which the courts partner. This procedure should include the use of release forms developed with the assistance of outside counsel, and courts should also stipulate the types of information that may be released to each involved party. Meyer (2011) suggests that problem-solving courts also hire a privacy official to ensure compliance with applicable confidentiality regulations, and they should provide that official with all resources necessary to effectively execute the job.

Problem-solving courts should establish administrative and operational procedures to protect participant information. Specifically, courts should store hardcopy records in secure, locked filing cabinets and maintain electronic records on encrypted computers. Specialty courts should also create a system to ensure the redaction of confidential information and limit the unnecessary disclosure of information. Meyer (2011) also suggests that courts create written documentation of their confidentiality policies and protocol, provide initial and continuing education to team members regarding confidentiality policies, and regularly review confidentiality forms to ensure they comply with current federal and local confidentiality laws. Meyer (2011) also suggests that problem-solving courts adopt a conservative approach toward confidentiality and take all possible precautions to ensure that participants' information is protected. Problem-solving court team members and staff should only disclose information on a need-to-know basis (Petrila & Fader-Towe, 2010).

Problem-solving court participants should be given ample opportunity to read all consent forms related to confidentiality, and courts should also ensure competency prior to obtaining a signature from participants. Determining competency should include an evaluation of literacy, and the consent forms should be read aloud to a participant when necessary. Petrila and Fader-Towe (2010) also suggest that problem-solving courts keep medical and mental health records separate from criminal records whenever possible to avoid unnecessarily making a participant's medical records part of the public record. They also encourage courts to refrain from having any public discussions about participants' medical or mental health status, particularly when such information may be stigmatizing (Petrila & Fader-Towe, 2010).

It is important for problem-solving courts to comply with federal and state confidentiality laws and to be aware of their complexities and nuances. Although problem-solving courts are not considered covered entities under HIPAA, Meyer (2011) suggests that drug courts should comport with some HIPAA-like requirements by executing agreements with the treating healthcare providers (who are covered entities) to share relevant information with the court regarding participants' treatment and using HIPAA-compliant consent forms. Problem-solving courts should also be aware of information that may trigger mandatory or permitted disclosures. Under federal regulations, problem-solving courts are required to disclose information if (1) they receive a valid court order requesting certain information, (2) they become aware of child abuse or neglect, or (3) cause of death needs to be determined (Meyer, 2011). In these situations, confidentiality requirements regarding patient information are exempt, although nonessential information should be redacted whenever possible (Meyer, 2011).

Role of the Judge

The American Bar Association Model Code of Judicial Conduct (Model Code; 2007) sets forth standards regarding the ethical conduct of judges. The Model Code is particularly relevant in problem-solving courts due to their distinctive operational procedures and role in the criminal justice system. In this section, we will refer to specific provisions within the Model Code when considering the ethical responsibilities of problem-solving court judges. Although many jurisdictions have adopted the Model Code, others have adopted their own ethical standards, so problem-solving court judges should of course adhere to the standards applicable in their jurisdiction.

Judicial Independence, Impartiality, and Relationships with Outside Entities

According to Canon I of the Model Code (2007), "A judge shall uphold and promote the independence, integrity, and impartiality of the judiciary, and shall avoid impropriety and the appearance of impropriety." Meyer (2011) argues that this canon serves both to establish a judge's professional responsibility of independence and impartiality *and* to maintain public confidence in the judiciary. Due to the collaborative nature of problem-solving courts and the enhanced knowledge of the problem-solving judiciary, judges in these courts must take extra precautions to ensure they remain independent and impartial (Arkfeld, 2007). However, it has been suggested that collaboration does not violate the judge's duty of independent judgment if the judge retains the authority for the final decision (Meyer, 2011; see *In re Briggs*, 1980; *In re Hughes*, 2004).

Problem-solving courts often establish partnerships with law enforcement entities and outside community organizations and treatment providers (Arkfeld, 2007). When a problem-solving court develops a relationship with law enforcement, such as a probation department, it is essential that the judge retains the role of independent guardian of legal rights (Meyer, 2011). When there are partnerships between specialty courts and community organizations, it is important for courts to specify the nature of the relationship. These partnerships should involve an exchange of information that is limited by necessary, appropriate, informed, and clear standards regarding the exchange of information between the problem-solving court and the community organization.

Personal Engagement with Participants

As noted throughout this book, the judge's personal involvement and engagement with problem-solving court participants is a cornerstone of the model and has been shown to increase the likelihood of participant success (National Association of Dug Court Professionals, 1997). However, this more informal and engaged relationship is not consistent with the typical role of the judge as a detached and impartial overseer. Impartiality does not necessarily imply detachment or disengagement; the key is whether the judge can be fair in his or her dealings with the problem-solving court participants. To ensure ethical behavior, judges in problem-solving courts may try to show equal levels of engagement with all participants and ensure that interactions with participants take place within official judicial proceedings. Moreover, due to the closeness of the relationship with court participants, problem-solving court judges should be mindful of situations where they need to recuse themselves due to an inability to remain impartial (Arkfeld, 2007). Under Model Code rule 2.11, a judge "shall disqualify himself or herself in any proceeding in which the judge's impartiality might reasonably be questioned," such as where "the judge has a personal bias or prejudice concerning a party or a party's lawyer, or personal knowledge of facts that are in dispute in the proceeding" (2007).

Problem-solving court judges may be privy to information regarding participants' criminal behavior, particularly in drug courts in which participants are subject to regular drug testing. As such, an important question is whether specialty court judges have an ethical or legal obligation to report any criminal behavior or other misconduct. Some jurisdictions require by statute that judges report any criminal behavior of which they become aware. However, those states that impose no statutory obligation but that have addressed the issue in case law have held that judges have no ethical responsibility to report criminal behavior they learn about during court hearings.

The role of a problem-solving court judge may be considered in light of the role of the defense counsel. As will be discussed in more detail later, the defense counsel may feel conflicted due to a dual role he or she is expected to play: collaborative member of the problem-solving court team and zealous advocate of the defendant. Arkfeld (2017) suggests that rather than place the defense counsel in a potentially conflicted position, perhaps the better role is for the judge to be the one to pay attention to the need for appropriate treatment, restitution, or other conditions that will address issues that bear on the case and simply allow defenders to remain adversarial, acting as an advocate for the defendant (p. 322).

Judicial Conduct Outside of the Courtroom

According to Canon 2 of the Model Code (2007), "A judge shall perform the duties of judicial office impartially, competently, and diligently." As such, it has been suggested that judges should exercise discretion when considering engaging in non–court-related activities and ensure they appear independent and impartial outside the courtroom (Podgers, 2008). Behavior that appears impartial may have legal repercussions. For instance, one court sanctioned a judge for attending a picnic hosted by an individual with a felony conviction, explaining that "such conduct could be perceived as evidencing sympathy for the convicted individual or disagreement with the criminal justice system that brought about the conviction" and that "such conduct may raise questions concerning the judge's allegiance to the judicial system" (*Matter of Blackman*, 1991, p. 1339). As such, in problem-solving court contexts in which judges develop congenial relationship with participants, it is important that judges remain mindful of the implications of attending social events or engaging in activities outside the courtroom where participants may be in attendance (Meyer, 2011).

Moreover, even though the judge and a participant may have a more personal relationship than is typical in most legal contexts, it would be inappropriate for a judge to provide character testimony of a participant or to write a reference letter on a participant's behalf as such actions call into question a judge's impartiality (Arkfeld, 2007). It might be more appropriate for participants to request such services from the prosecutor because that endorsement may be even more compelling given the prosecutor's role as the defendant's adversary (Meyer, 2011). Due to the enhanced personal engagement between the judge and defendant in problem-solving courts, specialty court judges should take extra caution to ensure they are not being influenced by bias or engaging in behavior that reflects bias. Rule 2.3 of the Model Code (2007) states that judges should not "by words or conduct manifest bias or prejudice, or engage in harassment, including but not limited to bias, prejudice, or harassment based upon race, sex, gender, religion, national origin, ethnicity, disability, age, sexual orientation, marital status, socioeconomic status, or political affiliation." As such, judges should be aware of bias that may impact how they act toward various participants and also make a point to praise and sanction participants in a consistent and uniform matter (Arkfeld, 2007; Meyer, 2011).

Ex Parte Communication

The rules regarding ex parte communications in problem-solving courts are currently in flux, and there is significant variation across jurisdictions. The 2007 revision of the Model Code included specific guidance for problem-solving courts, and a comment to Rule 2.9(A)(5) states:

> A judge may initiate, permit, or consider ex parte communications when authorized by law, such as when serving on therapeutic or problem-solving courts, mental health courts, or drug courts. In this capacity, judges may assume a more interactive role with parties, treatment providers, probation officers, social workers, and others.

As of May 2018, 36 jurisdictions had approved the revised judicial code and 9 jurisdictions were in the process of having their codes reviewed by committees (American Bar Association [ABA], 2018). In those jurisdictions that have not adopted the revised code, ex parte communications are not permitted, with exceptions for communications regarding administrative issues or emergency situations (Meyer, 2011). As such, judges must understand the regulations regarding ex parte communications in their jurisdiction.

There may also be some confusion regarding the rules about information learned in team meetings that take place outside the court room. Under Model Code Rule 2.9(C), "[a] judge shall not investigate facts in a matter independently, and shall consider only the evidence presented and any facts that may properly be judicially noticed" (2007). This rule may come into play in problem-solving court settings where many discussions take place among attorneys, treatment providers, and other staff that may not be recorded and may not occur as part of an official judicial proceeding (Arkfeld, 2007). As such, it is important for problem-solving courts to ensure that both prosecution and defense counsel are present during out-of-court meetings. If a judge learned factual information in a setting where both sides were not represented, there may be grounds for disqualification (Arkfeld, 2007).

Recusal or Disqualification of a Judge

Judges in problem-solving courts can be disqualified if their impartiality can be reasonably questioned (Model Code, 2007, Rule 2.11). Some have suggested that problem-solving court judges may be particularly vulnerable to accusations of bias because they have greater knowledge about participants through their personal engagement and supervisory role (Meyer, 2011). It is also worth noting that information a judge obtains from a treatment provider or other outside entity does not constitute "personal knowledge," which would require recusal, but is governed instead by the regulations on ex parte communication (Model Code, 2007, Rule 2.11(A)(1)).

Role of Defense Counsel

The problem-solving court focus on treatment and rehabilitation has raised some concerns regarding the ethical and professional obligations of defense attorneys (Meekins, 2007). These concerns include (1) possible conflicts of interest, (2) advice provided by judges and treatment providers that may interfere with the defense attorney's ability to play an advisory role, and (3) confusion over what it means to be a "zealous advocate" in the problem-solving court context. It has been argued that defense attorneys feel these dilemmas most acutely.

> Since the inception of the drug court movement in America, arguably no player on the drug court team—be it judge, prosecuting attorney, probation officer or treatment provider—has struggled more with his or her own identify and often conflicted role than the defense attorney. The desires of the treatment team and the drug court client are, at times, conflicting and can seemingly put the defense attorney in a box with no way out. (National Drug Court Institute, 2013, p. 3)

Some have argued that the changes required of defense attorneys in the problem-solving court context are highly problematic, going so far as to assert that they represent an "existential threat to the role of defense counsel" (see Holland, 2010, p. 186). Critics argue that problem-solving courts deprive defendants of legal protection by confusing and marginalizing defense lawyers (Holland, 2010). Lawyers in the problem-solving court context are more likely to develop personal relationships with other legal actors on the team (the prosecuting attorney, the judge), which could impact a defense lawyer's ability to remain a zealous advocate of his or her client with regard to legal decision-making. Defense attorneys also have heightened personal involvement with their clients, which can make failures more difficult emotionally and adversely affect a legal team's physical and mental well-being (Norton, Johnson, & Woods, 2016).

The problem-solving court model requires defense attorneys to relinquish their usual stance of being rigidly adversarial and adjust their client representation to align with the goals of the specialty court. As a result, possible ethical dilemmas and confusion could arise for both the defense attorney and client. Meekins (2007) has argued that questionable practices could arise—including those that may constitute violations of ethical and professional standards—due to this role confusion. Indeed, Meekins (2007) suggests that the collaborative nature of problem-solving courts could result in a precedent of "underzealous representation" by defense attorneys within the broader criminal justice system (p. 79). Given the rapid expansion of problem-solving courts in recent years, Meekins (2007) argues that there is a need for comprehensive and cogent ethical guidelines and standards for defense attorneys working in these contexts.

Model Rules

Lawyers typically adhere to the standards and rules set forth in the American Bar Association's Model Rules of Professional Conduct (Model Rules) (as adopted by individual stated codes) (2016). Although the Model Rules apply to specialty court practice, they do not contain any specific guidance regarding a lawyer's role in a problem-solving court setting (Meekins, 2007). The American Bar Association (1993) has promulgated detailed standards intended to provide guidance for defense attorneys at each stage of the criminal judicial process. Although not mandatory, these standards provide a blueprint for many criminal defense attorneys (Meekins, 2007). Similarly, the National Legal Aid and Defender Association drafted *Blackletter Guidelines* in 1995 that provided guidance to criminal defense attorneys regarding specific responsibilities and case timelines (National Legal Aid and Defender Association, 2001). However, research suggests that defense attorneys have found these comprehensive standards on traditional legal defense practice to be lacking. In a 2001 survey, a majority of respondents reported wanting updated or expanded guidance, and more than 40% of respondents expressed a specific desire for guidelines on the role of defense attorneys in problem-solving courts (Wallace & Carrol, 2004). As such, it appears that specialty court defense standards would provide needed guidance to defense attorneys practicing in such courts and also better protect the rights of problem-solving courts participants (Meekins, 2007).

Notably, the National Drug Court Institute (NDCI, 2001) has argued that the traditional defender role is not compromised by the problem-solving court model. The NDCI published one of the only resources regarding ethical and professional issues for defense attorneys practicing in problem-solving courts, and it concluded that, for the most part, the traditional model of legal advocacy for defense attorneys can be reconciled with drug court operations (NCDI, 2001). The NDCI acknowledged that the professional roles of judges and attorneys are adjusted in the drug court context and that "practitioners in drug courts need heightened ethical sensitivity" (NDCI, 2001, pp. 58–59). However, the report ultimately concluded that "the proper exercise of the roles of judge or lawyer in drug court need not conflict with the professionals' ethical obligations" (NDCI, 2001, pp. 58–59). The NDCI published a follow-up manual for defense attorneys practicing in drug courts that more explicitly highlighted ethical concerns that may arise. In this manual, the NDCI (2003) stated that "the proper role of the defense attorney remains ambiguous" in the drug court context and indicated that drug court jurisprudence may, at times, conflict with ethical guidelines (p. 4).

Specific Ethical Issues Relevant to Defense Attorneys

Meekins (2007) provides the most comprehensive overview of the ethical implications for defense attorneys in problem-solving courts, and we were unable to find many other sources on the topic. As such, this section will pull significantly from Meekins's (2007) scholarship. Meekins (2007) highlighted five major ethical issues that may arise for defense attorneys working in problem-solving court contexts: conflicts of interest, zealous representation, competent representation, appropriate communication with the defendant, and decision-making responsibilities.

Conflicts of Interest

In problem-solving courts, it is possible that the court's interests and the client's interests may conflict. In such instances, to whom does the defense attorney owe a duty of loyalty? In a traditional court context, a defense attorney would not disclose information to the court or the opposing attorney without the client's consent or without being required to make such a disclosure. However, in the problem-solving court model, the participant's best interests are valued more than his or her stated interests. For instance, in a drug court, a participant's sobriety may be prioritized over the best possible legal outcome for the participant's case. As such, disclosing certain information may seem necessary with regard to the client's prescribed treatment and ultimate success in the problem-solving court, even though such a disclosure would not typically be made in standard criminal justice processing (Meekins, 2007). This dilemma may be particularly notable in staff conferences during which the defense attorney may be expected to play the role of both advocate for his or her client and representative of the court (Arkfeld, 2007). A defense attorney may be uncertain about where to draw the line in disclosing privileged client information (Meekins, 2007). The Model Rules is also implicated. Model Rule 1.7(a)(2) (2004) prohibits legal representation when that representation may be "materially limited by the lawyer's responsibilities to another client, a former client or a third person or by a personal interest of the lawyer." This rule may be particularly relevant in specialty courts that emphasize collaboration and the development of a united team (Meekins, 2007).

Another conflict of interest lies in the relationships defense attorneys may have with broader communities. Some problem-solving courts, including community courts, may hire defense attorneys on a full-time basis and expect them to attend community meetings as representatives of the court or endorse the virtues of certain specialty courts to community members. As a result, the community may see the defense attorney as an extension of the court or law enforcement instead of as an impartial legal advocate who represents the court participants. This perception cuts against the typically held view of defense attorneys as partisan advocates of their clients (Meekins, 2007).

The NDCI (2001) report suggested that the separate roles and responsibilities of the individual problem-solving court team members are not divided and that the presumption of cooperation does not violate ethical rules. However, the NDCI report cautioned defense attorneys to remain aware of team relationships that might impair their ability to remain loyal to their clients. In the NDCI's follow-up publication, *Critical Issues for Defense Attorneys in Drug Courts* (2003), the organization recognized the problematic nature of having a defense attorney reveal client confidences to the court without permission and concluded that the attorney should establish clear boundaries with the court regarding disclosures of client information.

Zealous Representation

Although there is no specific rule in the Model Rules (2004) requiring that a lawyer zealously advocate on behalf of his or her clients, the preamble to the Model Rules sets forth that a lawyer should "zealously assert the client's position." Indeed, several state codes and defense attorney guidelines have adopted a requirement of zealous advocacy in client representation (Freedman & Smith, 2004). This "zealous advocacy" concept underlies the adversarial nature of the American legal system. In problem-solving courts, how zealous an attorney should be is unclear because these settings replace traditional adversarial proceedings with team collaboration.

There are several instances in a problem-solving court context when a defense attorney may not act as a zealous advocate. For example, in a drug court, the judge may ask a defendant about his or her drug use. Although in a traditional court the defense attorney may object to these questions as potentially incriminating, in a problem-solving court the defense attorney may actually encourage the defendant to volunteer the requested information. Moreover, a defense attorney in a problem-solving court may be expected to encourage the client to engage in court-mandated treatment or other conditions even when the defendant expresses reluctance (Meekins, 2007). A defense attorney appointed by a specialty court may struggle to advocate zealously due to a fear of losing future appointments within the court, even sensing that adhering to the nonadversarial approach of the problem-solving court is in the attorney's economic interest because it may lead to future cases or employment opportunities within that particular court (Meekins, 2007).

Is has been suggested that the confusion regarding the role of zealous advocacy in problem-solving court jurisprudence jeopardizes client interests (see Holland, 2010; Meekins, 2007). Specifically, critics argue that a client's constitutional rights and liberty could be at risk when a problem-solving court—rather than a defense attorney—asserts itself as the entity best suited to identify and treat clients' interests and needs (Meekins, 2007; Smith, 2003). In standard criminal justice processing, litigants observe their attorneys engage in zealous advocacy on their behalf, which includes maintaining a respectful and clear distance from the judge. However, in the problem-solving court context, participants witness the key legal actors (attorneys from both sides and the judge) collaborating to pursue an overall objective (Feinblatt & Denckla, 2001). This process can be particularly problematic if one of the litigants does not agree with the objective being sought. To alleviate this concern, some jurisdictions require that defense attorneys describe the problem-solving court protocol to their clients and explain how it could influence conventional advocacy rules (Meekins, 2007).

There is also concern about "underzealous representation" becoming the norm in the legal profession (Meekins, 2006, p. 111). According to this line of thinking, underzealousness could lead community members to lose trust that lawyers will act with a certain degree of professionalism and commitment (Meekins, 2007). However, it is important to note that the traditional adversarial system has been criticized by some legal scholars who argue that it does not promote justice and fairness (see Frankel, 1980; Kessel, 1992; Simon, 2000). Indeed, these critics assert that lawyers can often be partisan and overzealous and that problem-solving court jurisprudence could be a solution to the issues that arise out of these practices. Standard criminal justice processing has also been criticized under the theory of therapeutic jurisprudence. According to this model, many laws that deal with mental health issues often produce outcomes that actually exacerbate mental health issues rather than alleviate them or serve a therapeutic purpose (see Wexler, 2006; Winick, 2003). Moreover, the actions of legal actors, including lawyers and judges, can impact the mental health and overall well-being of individuals in the criminal justice system with whom they come into contact (Winick, 2003).

Competent Representation

Model Rule 1.1 states that "competent representation requires the legal knowledge, skill, thoroughness, and preparation reasonably necessary for representation" (Model Rules, 2004, Rule 1.1). This rule is particularly relevant in the problem-solving court context because the procedures and operations of problem-solving courts differ from those used in traditional courts. Consequently, attorneys may not be familiar with the methods used in problem-solving courts and may lack the requisite training and knowledge about a problem-solving court's operations and protocol. Meekins (2007) suggests that, ideally, the defense attorney would act as an integrated team member of the court, attend trainings on the methodological underpinnings of the problem-solving court, and develop an understanding of the underlying mental health, drug abuse, or other specialized needs targeted by the court. However, many defense attorney agencies manage large caseloads and lack financial resources, which often prevents them from obtaining such training or knowledge (Holland, 2010; Meekins, 2007).

A defense attorney in a problem-solving court may also struggle to comply with Model Rule 1.1 because these courts sometimes require expedited decision-making and specialized knowledge. If an attorney lacks the time, knowledge, or resources necessary to adequately represent a defendant and help the defendant make the required decisions, the competence of the attorney's representation may be problematic (Meekins, 2007). According to a comment to Model Rule 1.1, the "required attention and preparation [of an attorney] are determined in part by what is at stake" (Model Rules, 2004, Rule 1.1 comments). As Meekins (2007) points out, the stakes are high in problem-solving courts when the constitutional rights of criminal defendants are at issue. Indeed, the decision to participate in the specialty court carries with it significant implications because it can involve the waiver of certain constitutional rights and the risk of serious sanctions, including incarceration, if a participant fails to comply with the program requirements (Meekins, 2007).

A defense attorney may also struggle to adhere to Model Rule 1.1 due to the nature of many problem-solving courts. Problem-solving courts are a relatively nascent development in the criminal justice system and, in many ways, are still in the "experimental" phase (Casey, 2004). As such, these courts often make administrative and methodological adaptations in response to empirical evidence, which can result in changes to treatment providers and case management. Keeping up with these changes may be difficult for defense attorneys managing large caseloads, even when doing so is necessary to provide competent representation (Meekins, 2007).

In terms of a defense attorney's ability to provide competent representation under Model Rule 1.1, some have argued that there is little difference between specialty courts and traditional courts (Meekins, 2007). Indeed, some plea bargains in traditional courts are offered with a short time frame for a defendant to make a decision. Moreover, defense attorneys in traditional courts may also be required to conduct a thorough investigation into a specific legal matter about which they are not familiar. In such cases, some argue, it appears the defense attorney must overcome the same obstacles in both specialty and traditional courts when it comes to providing a defendant with competent legal representation (Meekins, 2007).

Meekins (2007) asserts, however, that problem-solving court participants may suffer heightened consequences from subpar representation. As such, defense attorneys in problem-solving courts may need to conduct a more in-depth analysis of the requirements imposed by the court and the various impacts those requirements may have on a participant. For instance, when a mental health court requires participants to engage in mental health treatment, the participant's attorney should consider the likelihood that such a treatment will work, obstacles the participant may encounter in complying with treatment, and the impact of the treatment on the participant's risk of future offending. Such considerations are beyond the scope of what is typically considered in traditional court contexts, where attorneys tend to consult other defense attorneys about a judge's sentencing tendencies and can more easily request a continuance to further investigate a matter.

Communications Between Defense Attorneys and Defendants

According to Model Rule 1.4 (2004), a lawyer should engage in prompt and reasonable communication with the client regarding the client's objectives and the status of relevant matters of importance, and the lawyer should also explain matters to the client in such a way that the client can make an informed decision about the representation. This obligation may be somewhat unclear in specialty courts due to the team approach. For example, problem-solving court participants may rely on team members other than the defense attorney, such as treatment providers, case managers, and the judge. Because these various specialty court team members are often heavily involved in the case, participants may be more inclined to rely on the advice and guidance of these individuals. Such reliance may also occur because a defense attorney's representation occurs in pre-hearing conference meetings that do not include defendants. As such, participants may not witness the advocacy made on their behalf by their defense attorneys (Meekins, 2007).

Moreover, the specialty court judge plays a more central role in terms of communicating with the client. Indeed, in many problem-solving courts, the hearings involve communications between the judge and the participant where the judge imposes rewards or sanctions and provides advice and guidance as necessary (Nolan, 2003). It is not unusual for attorneys to be absent from such conversations at court hearings. Meekins (2007) points out that, as a result of this protocol, "clients may not believe their defense attorney is necessary, or may confuse the roles of the judge and attorney, viewing the judge as the legal advocate and counselor" (p. 116).

Ultimate Decision-Making Power

Although an attorney is permitted to consult with his or her client and provide guidance about the best course of action, Model Rule 1.2 sets forth that an attorney in criminal cases shall "abide by a client's decisions" regarding "a plea to be entered, whether to waive jury trial and whether the client will testify" (Model Rules, 2004, Rule 1.2). Many attorneys ascribe to a model of client-centered lawyering under which defendants make all relevant case decisions, even decisions regarding strategy (see Kruse, 2006). Under this model, a defendant's autonomy is valued and his or her decisions are respected, even when not necessarily considered in the defendant's self-interest. This client-centered approach does not always comport with problem-solving court models in which the central focus is typically the participants' best interests. In specialty courts, the various members of the team work together to determine an approach that will best meet a participant's needs. Defense attorneys who typically ascribe to client-centered lawyering may struggle to adopt the teamwork approach used in problem-solving courts that is focused more on determining the course of action that is in the participants' best interest (Meekins, 2007).

Procedural Justice and Problem-Solving Courts

Procedural justice refers to defendants' rights to be treated respectfully in the justice system (trust), to have their voice heard in a dispute (standing), and to have court authorities make fair decisions regarding their case (neutrality) (Lind & Tyler, 1988). Research suggests that when procedural justice is present, justice-involved individuals exhibit an increase in behavior that is law-abiding and compliant with legal authorities (Lind & Tyler, 1988; Tyler, 2006). As noted throughout this chapter, problem-solving courts adhere to procedures that fall outside of standard criminal justice processing. As such, it is worthwhile to consider problem-solving court participants' perceptions regarding procedural justice in these courts.

Perceptions of procedural justice in problem-solving courts are complex and varied due to the diverse nature of these courts (Canada & Watson, 2013; Dollar, Ray, Hudson, & Hood, 2018; Rossman, Roman, & Zweig, 2011). However, although limited, recent research on procedural justice in problem-solving courts has identified a few trends. Several studies have found that most problem-solving court defendants feel they are treated fairly and with respect (Dollar et al., 2018; Gottfredson, Kearley, Najaka, & Rocha, 2007; Poythress, Petrila, McGaha, & Boothroyd, 2002; Redlich & Han, 2014; Rossman et al., 2011; Wales, Hiday, & Ray, 2010). In mental health courts, studies have shown that participants perceive receiving greater procedural justice than do those in court-assisted outpatient care (Munetz, Ritter, Teller, & Bonfine, 2014). In addition, studies have found that procedural justice in mental health courts is associated with a decrease in symptomatology (Kopelovich, Yanos, Pratt, & Koerner, 2013), an increase in coping skills (Ray & Dollar, 2014), and overall compliance and follow-through with program requirements (Redlich & Han, 2014). Research on procedural justice in drug courts has yielded similar findings. A large-scale, longitudinal study of 23 drug courts found that participants in drug courts perceived greater levels of procedural justice than did those in standard criminal justice processing and that higher perceptions of procedural justice correlated with increased compliance and lower recidivism rates (Rossman et al., 2011).

Some studies have examined how defendants' perceptions of procedural justice were impacted by actors other than the judges in problem-solving courts. Several studies found that case managers, probation officers, and attorneys within mental health courts also impacted defendant's perceptions of procedural justice (Marlowe, Festinger, Dugosh, & Lee, 2005; Marlowe, Festinger, & Lee, 2004; Wales et al., 2010) and that defendants' perceptions of procedural justice are substantially impacted by interactions with these non-judge actors (Canada & Watson, 2013). Interestingly, a recent longitudinal study of several problem-solving courts (including drug courts and mental health courts) found that defendants perceived case managers as providing more procedural justice than judges (Dollar et al., 2018). In a recent study examining racial and ethnic disparities in perceptions of procedural justice among problem-solving court participants, Atkin-Plunk, Peck, and Armstrong (2019) concluded that African American participants perceive significantly less procedural justice than Caucasian participants, but they also found that procedural justice perceptions did not have an impact on recidivism rates.

Conclusion

Ethical and legal implications must be considered at every stage of the criminal justice process. But they are especially relevant in the problem-solving court context because these courts are representative of a major paradigm shift taking place within the criminal justice system. As we shift toward a new model of rehabilitative justice, it is essential to ensure that participants' constitutional and legal rights are protected and that judicial and legal actors are able to effectively and ethically uphold their duties. This chapter has addressed the ethical, constitutional, and legal issues that can arise within problem-solving court jurisprudence and provides guidance on how to ensure that participants' rights are upheld, providing more comprehensive discussion of various viewpoints on particular issues where appropriate. It is important that problem-solving courts address four issues in particular as part of their establishment and operation. These are (1) the constitutional issues related to problem-solving courts and their impact on pleadings, consent, and competency; (2) the ethical considerations associated with these courts, including how to manage federal and local privacy laws related to consent and confidentiality; (3) the role of the problem-solving court judge and the complications that can arise based on the team model and the development of personal relationships with participants; and (4) the role of the defense counsel in problem-solving courts and how it differs from the standard approach of zealous advocacy.

10

Problem-Solving Courts

Present Status and Future Directions

The two primary goals of this book involve providing information in two important areas related to problem-solving courts: relevant information on their current status and recommendations for future research, practice, and policy. We aim to help inform practitioners, researchers, trainees, administrators, and policymakers about the development and nature of problem-solving courts and how they function within the criminal justice system. We also discuss the current research on problem-solving courts, including methodological considerations and gaps in the literature, in an attempt to provide researchers with information relevant to conducting methodologically rigorous research in this field. As part of this discussion, we have considered (1) the development of problem-solving courts in the United States; (2) the various types of problem-solving courts, their operation, and the existing empirical support; (3) the relevant legal and ethical concerns; and (4) the methodological issues associated with researching such courts. In this chapter, we review this discussion and offer recommendations that follow on the future directions of problem-solving justice in reference to research, practice, and policy.

Present Status of Problem-Solving Courts

Individuals with behavioral health disorders, including substance abuse and mental illness, are substantially overrepresented in the criminal justice system (Casey & Rottman, 2005; Honegger, 2015; James & Glaze, 2006; Lamb & Weinberger, 1998). Indeed, a significant portion of community members with mental illness will have contact with the criminal justice system at some time in their lives, and there are very high rates of substance abuse in criminal justice-involved populations (see DeMatteo, Filone, & Davis, 2015).

One response to the overrepresentation of such individuals has involved reform in criminal justice processing, with more emphasis on treatment and rehabilitation. Problem-solving courts are one of the most salient examples of the paradigm shift toward rehabilitative alternatives to standard prosecution. The philosophical foundation of the shift toward greater rehabilitative emphasis within the law has been strongly bolstered by *therapeutic jurisprudence*, which advocates a multidisciplinary approach to improving the behavioral health of those subject to legal proceedings, particularly within the criminal justice system (Wexler & Winick, 1991, 1996; Winick, 2000, 2005; Winick & Wexler, 2003).

The rehabilitative approaches employed by problem-solving courts have been termed *problem-solving justice*, and those approaches are described as having six distinct principles: enhanced information, community engagement, collaboration, individualized justice, accountability, and data-based evaluation (see Berman, 2009; Wolf, 2007). The principle of *enhanced information* refers to the need to obtain more information than is usually available to courts and attorneys in an effort to promote better-informed decisions regarding rehabilitation. Under the *community engagement* principle, problem-solving courts seek connections with local community members, interest groups, and neighborhood coalitions to help identify, prioritize, and solve criminal justice challenges. The *collaboration* principle brings together stakeholders in the criminal system (judges, prosecutors, defense attorneys, probation and parole officers, law enforcement) and community-based partners (treatment providers, neighborhood coalitions, schools, hospital). *Individualized justice* involves the use of evidence-based risk–need assessment to identify specific services tailored to the participant's criminogenic needs (e.g., substance abuse, employment, education, family problems). *Accountability* refers to using careful monitoring and the imposition of sanctions when indicated to improve participants' performance within justice contexts. The *data-based evaluations* principle suggests that problem-solving justice should involve ongoing collection of relevant data to evaluate the effectiveness of programs, gauge the impact of specific treatments, and engage in continuous improvements.

Future Directions: Recommendations for Problem-Solving Courts

In this section, we synthesize the information discussed in the first nine chapters into a series of recommendations for problem-solving courts. These recommendations are offered in three domains: establishing a court, expanding and operating a court, and empirical, ethical, and legal considerations relevant to these courts.

Establishing a Problem-Solving Court

These considerations arise when a jurisdiction does not have a problem-solving court but is considering starting one. This may arise in the context of having existing smaller initiatives consistent with problem-solving justice—or it may begin even prior to that.

Use the Sequential Intercept Model (SIM) as a foundation for understanding the operation of a problem-solving court. The SIM provides a conceptual framework for problem-solving courts by identifying five "intercepts" at which community-based rehabilitative alternatives can be provided in lieu of standard criminal justice processing (Munetz & Griffin, 2006). Problem-solving courts are an example of an Intercept 3 diversion because this intercept encompasses an individual's contact with jails, prisons, courts, forensic mental health assessments, and commitments. Problem-solving courts at this stage divert individuals with serious mental illness, substance abuse, and those who belong to certain populations with increased risk of justice involvement, such as veterans. These courts adhere to the principles of therapeutic jurisprudence and provide programming and targeted treatment to address the needs of these specific populations (see Hora, Schma, & Rosenthal, 1999). The SIM can also provide guidance in determining whether the court's jurisdiction might include other intercepts and (through the use of cross-system mapping; see Chapter 7) assist with the cross-disciplinary conceptualization, planning, evaluation, and modification of problem-solving courts.

Establish and operate a problem-solving court at the intercept providing the best fit for the establishing jurisdiction. Problem-solving courts are most often based at Intercept 3 (jails and courts). But considering the other SIM intercepts (Intercept 1: law enforcement and emergency responders; Intercept 2: initial detention and hearing; Intercept 4: Reentry from incarceration; Intercept 5: community corrections), it is noteworthy that problem-solving justice has been used across this entire range. Some of these interventions closely resemble the problem-solving court, while others have used problem-solving approaches to modify existing rehabilitative alternatives to standard criminal justice processing.

At Intercept 1, *crisis intervention training* (CIT) training is a promising practice with empirical support in which police officers and other first responders are trained in recognizing mental health symptoms and diverting individuals to hospitals rather than arresting them (DeMatteo, LaDuke, Locklair, & Heilbrun, 2013; Reuland, 2004). CIT and prearrest diversion programs could be expanded by incorporating some of the principles of problem-solving courts described earlier and by modifying these programs to include minimal monitoring and follow-up to ensure a more stable connection to services. Such an approach would enhance an already existing program rather than starting a new one, which could offer a more efficient use of community resources.

Postarrest diversion at Intercept 2 is an intervention that is underutilized and does not yet have a significant research foundation (see DeMatteo et al., 2013), but it holds some promise for the expansion of problem-solving courts, either through earlier enrollment (e.g., identification and screening during initial detention and hearings, incorporating pre-plea problem-solving court models) or community diversion when indicated. Another potential expansion at this intercept would involve adapting the problem-solving court model for individuals found incompetent to stand trial. For example, Philadelphia has a track within its state-level mental health court for defendants who are incompetent to stand trial; the court monitors defendants' competency status as they receive treatment and restoration services. A similar approach could be used in problem-solving courts.

Reentry courts at Intercepts 4 and 5 have proliferated rapidly, with mixed results reflected in the literature. Such reentry courts could serve at least two distinct purposes. First, for particular populations, they could be operated with a treatment/rehabilitative focus that is substantially similar to problem-solving courts at Intercept 3. This would involve selecting a particular focus (e.g., mental health, substance abuse) and facilitating the provision of relevant services at a level and intensity beyond that provided by standard community supervision. Second, for individuals going through reentry who have more generalized needs, perhaps because they present a higher risk for reoffending, these courts could benefit individuals and communities by increasing support during reentry, creating new community partnerships, and serving individuals who might otherwise be ineligible for such services or at such intensity. Many communities have specialized probation and parole services for individuals with treatment needs, but increasing the available services through community partnerships and involving judges as part of monitoring could lower recidivism risk and (when indicated) improve mental health outcomes.

Expanding and Operating a Problem-Solving Court

We have observed in earlier chapters that there is substantial variation in how existing problem-solving courts are operated. The recommendations in this section would promote somewhat more uniform operation but still respect the distinctive needs associated with the particular jurisdiction.

Expand Strategically

Limited resources are frequently cited as a justification for the decision not to establish a problem-solving court, but many of the problem-solving principles we have discussed throughout this book could be implemented through minor alternations of existing programs or venues. Pilot testing might involve implementing a single docket or limited schedule (e.g., 1 day per week) of problem-solving court services. It is noteworthy that establishing or expanding a problem-solving court requires a philosophical shift among all stakeholders toward a more rehabilitative (vs. punitive) model of criminal justice, and pilot testing can help gauge both feasibility and acceptance.

Given the incremental increase in exposure to therapeutic jurisprudence in law schools, judicial training, and continuing legal education, we anticipate that the ideas associated with problem-solving justice will become better established within our legal system. But another essential component involves collaboration. We recognize that problem-solving courts are most often established and led by judges, but their successful operation requires the collaboration of prosecutors and defense attorneys, probation officers and service providers, and the participants served by these courts. The shift to such a model can be difficult, and the time and effort needed to "recalibrate" one's approach to criminal justice in the problem-solving context should not be underestimated.

The public relations associated with such a shift also need attention. The clear identification of who is eligible, how they are selected, what the rewards for success and the consequences for noncompliance might be, and how participation might affect families and crime victims are among the considerations associated with the development or expansion of problem-solving courts. Addressing these issues requires outreach to and interaction with various segments of the community. When there is also a clear plan for gathering data on process and outcome as part of a larger plan for evaluating effectiveness, then it is clearer that problem-solving courts stress personal accountability. As discussed throughout this book, these courts are designed to enhance public safety, save taxpayer dollars, and provide needed rehabilitative services. One additional point: the proliferation of certain kinds of specialty courts has greatly outpaced the relevant research—so, whenever possible, it is preferable to establish a problem-solving court of a type that is already well-supported empirically.

Problem-solving courts have their limitations, as we discuss in previous chapters. One such limitation involves a combination of geography and resources. Many jurisdictions have developed and now operate problems-solving courts—but communities that are more remote or with fewer resources are typically not among them. As a result, even problem-solving courts that exist in high numbers, such as drug courts, are only serving a small segment of offenders who may benefit from such programs. The lack of sufficient numbers of problem-solving courts may reflect limitations on resources, differences in underlying philosophy, the absence of perceived need, or some combination of these considerations. None of these is a compelling reason to avoid seriously considering the development of a problem-solving court, but "serious consideration" is not necessarily followed by adoption; it may be that some jurisdictions do not have the need or resources, even with the interdisciplinary planning that is available through cross-system mapping (see Chapter 7).

Use the Risk-Need-Responsivity Model to Conceptualize, Assess, Plan, and Intervene

The development of problem-solving courts is associated with the idea that providing treatment as an alternative to incarceration—while targeting certain behavioral health problems or other influences that are relevant to reoffense risk—will reduce rates of reoffending and mitigate the "revolving door" phenomenon within the criminal justice system for individuals with specific needs. The Risk-Need-Responsivity (RNR) model provides a framework for conceptualizing offenders' distinctive risk and needs by considering risk, need, and responsivity. This in turn raises some important questions that should be addressed by every problem-solving court: (1) What are the reoffense risk levels of individuals under the court's jurisdiction? (2) What are their associated needs for reducing reoffense risk? (3) What are the available services that provide the interventions relevant to these needs? (4) Are these services delivered at a level at which participants are likely to respond favorably? (5) What is the approach for appraising risk, needs, and court outcomes for the purpose of evaluating relevance and effectiveness? As problem-solving courts continue to be established throughout the United States, an important step involves the consistent use of RNR, established process and measures, and uniformly defined outcomes (e.g., rearrest, service utilization) for the purpose of program evaluation and subsequent dissemination of the findings (e.g., technical reports, peer-reviewed publications). The creation of a broad empirical foundation is essential for jurisdictions that are developing or modifying problem-solving courts.

Applying RNR in this fashion leads to another important consideration. Individuals who are low risk, with limited criminogenic needs, probably do not need the added intensity of a problem-solving court. We are aware of the potential political consequences to a rehabilitation-oriented program or court that can result from a single outcome involving a client committing an act of serious violence toward others. In light of that awareness, it is tempting to select low-risk individuals and offer interventions that address primarily behavioral health needs. Although such an approach is understandable in one sense, it would involve a misuse of public resources in a larger respect. Problem-solving courts are firmly located within the criminal justice system, and they still have public protection as a primary mission. If an individual does not need additional services or monitoring to help protect public safety, then it seems far preferable to have noncriminogenic behavioral health needs addressed through the mental health system rather than the criminal justice system.

Likewise, selecting high-risk individuals may invoke more political risk than a particular jurisdiction or system can tolerate. Certainly, there is solid empirical evidence that such individuals need serious and intensive intervention; whether such an intervention is delivered as part of a problem-solving court involves questions of accountability, philosophy, risk, and benefit that are difficult (but necessary and important) for all problem-solving court jurisdictions to address.

It may be, therefore, that the best candidates for problem-solving courts are medium-risk individuals who also have substantial behavioral health or other specialized needs. Such individuals are less likely to be involved in further offending than are their higher risk counterparts, but they have greater needs and potential for risk reduction than do low-risk individuals. This kind of overall calculation cannot be made, however, without explicitly thinking in terms of the risk and needs of potential clients for the specialty court, and jurisdictions with problem-solving courts—or those that are considering the establishment of a problem-solving courts—are encouraged to address this important topic.

Recognize Variability in Jurisdictional Needs, Resources, and Problem-Solving Courts

Operate a "best fit" court relative to jurisdiction needs. One of the frequent observations throughout this book has involved the variations within each type of problem-solving court. Drugs courts were developed to address the dramatic increase in drug-related offenses, for example, and consistently view drug dependence as a disease that warrants a rehabilitative response. But there are substantial operational differences among drug courts. Some drug courts are diversionary and result in the dismissal of the offender's charges upon successful completion of the program, others require a formal finding of guilt before admitting a participant, and yet others include only probation revocation cases. Similarly, mental health courts focus on the contribution of mental health symptoms to offending and endorse the notion that the criminal justice system can protect the public by providing needed mental health treatment to offenders with specific needs. As with drug courts, there is substantial variation in the organization and operation of mental health courts. Like drug courts, mental health courts may ascribe to one of three models: preadjudication, postadjudication, and probation-based. Although both mental health courts and drugs courts employ a nonadversarial, multidisciplinary team approach to providing supervision and treatment to participants, the composition and size of these teams varies by court. These courts also vary with regard to referral systems, eligibility criteria, the number and strength of community partnerships, the use of rewards and sanctions, and the intensity of monitoring.

Use Widely Accepted Aspects of Problem-Solving Courts

Problem-solving courts also have common elements that are important to incorporate. Unlike courts that provide standard criminal justice processing, most problem-solving courts have the following common elements: (1) a docket consisting of individuals with specific needs; (2) a committed judge who is highly involved in the process and oversees the relevant hearings and meetings; (3) defense and prosecution attorneys willing to engage in a collaborative, rehabilitation-focused legal process; (4) a nonadversarial approach that involves joint decision-making by the judge, attorneys, treatment providers, and any other relevant stakeholders; (5) voluntary participation, involving agreement to comply with a treatment plan as a condition of participation in the court; (6) regular monitoring by the court of participants' progress and compliance; and (7) a sentence reduction or dismissal of charges for individuals who successfully complete the program (see Moore & Hiday, 2006). These common elements are likely associated with much of the effectiveness of problem-solving courts. Of note: even when these common elements are all present, there is still room for the flexibility that can allow the best possible fit with the needs and resources of each jurisdiction.

Be Aware of the Existing Research Base Supporting Problem-Solving Courts

Strong empirical research supports drug courts and, to a lesser extent, mental health courts, but research on other types of problem-solving courts is limited in volume and less consistent in its findings. Drug courts have been the focus of numerous research studies, program evaluations, multisite studies, and meta-analyses, and the research demonstrates that they are reasonably effective in reducing the risk of criminal recidivism among drug-involved offenders. There is also substantial research demonstrating that drug courts are effective in terms of reducing the risk of drug relapse and favorably affecting other important outcomes (e.g., mental health functioning, incarceration rates, access to treatment and other services). The research on other kinds of problem-solving courts is less conclusive. Unlike drug court research, the evidence for mental health courts includes few meta-analyses, systematic reviews, or large-scale studies—and there is notably less research on all other types of problem-solving courts. We should be cautiously optimistic about mental health courts (growing evidence indicates that mental health courts reduce criminal recidivism risk) while remaining aware of the mixed empirical evidence on whether such courts effectively connect participants to treatment and improve mental health outcomes.

This book also addresses the development of 13 other types of problem-solving courts developed in the wake of drug and mental health courts. These include veterans' courts, DUI/DWI courts, family drug courts, co-occurring disorders courts, gambling courts, community courts, truancy courts, domestic violence courts, gun courts, homelessness courts, prostitution courts, tribal wellness courts, and campus drug courts. Research on these courts is far less developed than the research on drug courts and mental health courts, and some of these courts have not been researched at all. As such, it is premature at this point to reach firm conclusions regarding these other types of problem-solving courts. Establishing a research base is necessary to gauge whether these courts can effectively reduce recidivism and have a positive impact on other outcomes. The broad proliferation of varied problem-solving courts also raises the possibility that the criminal justice system is saturated with courts that are increasingly specific and tailored to relatively narrow populations of offenders. Do we need specific courts for individuals with gambling disorders or gun offenses? Are there factors that meaningfully distinguish these offenders to the extent that they need a narrowly tailored intervention that can only be delivered through a specialty court?

Reentry Courts Are Distinct

We consider reentry courts separately from other problem-solving courts because they typically do not focus on an identified behavioral health need or distinct population. Instead, as discussed in Chapter 7, they usually help offenders reintegrate into the community through monitoring and the provision of educational, vocational, and social services, all of which are relevant to reoffending. (Earlier, we noted that reentry courts actually could function more like conventional problem-solving courts by selecting a more distinct population based on behavioral health needs or life experience, but that has apparently not occurred with any frequency.) In addition, although most problem-solving courts involve interventions at Intercept 3 (jails, prisons, and courts), reentry courts focus their efforts at Intercepts 4 (reentry) and 5 (community corrections). The research on reentry courts is still in its early stages. There have been few multisite studies or meta-analyses, and the extant research has significant limitations (e.g., small sample sizes, absence of appropriate comparison groups, short outcome periods). The limited available research suggests that reentry courts may be effective, but there is insufficient research to allow us to draw meaningful conclusions about the impact of these courts. Research is particularly needed with reentry courts, given their placement in the criminal justice sequence and the likelihood that their numbers will continue to grow in the next few years.

Empirical, Ethical, and Legal Considerations

Our third domain of recommendations involves empirical research, ethical considerations, and legal parameters.

Meaningful Research Must Overcome Methodological Challenges

Numerous challenges arise when attempting to conduct rigorous empirical research on problem-solving courts, as we discuss in Chapter 8. Although the randomized controlled trial (RCT) is considered the gold standard in clinical trials, it can be difficult to use this design in conducting research on problem-solving courts. There are various reasons for this, including fairness (actual and perceived), the ethical treatment of offenders, and the differing interests of various stakeholders. Additional research challenges include attrition of participants, within-court and between-court differences, identifying uniform outcome variables, and obtaining relevant samples (including comparison samples). If an RCT design is not feasible for a given study, then the best alternative is a quasi-experimental design (one that uses existing groups without random assignment) in conjunction with statistical techniques such as propensity score matching and covariate analyses. Chapter 8 includes a table with recommendations for researchers investigating problem-solving courts.

Consider Ethical and Legal Implications

Because problem-solving courts represent a substantial paradigm shift within the criminal justice system, the ethical and legal implications of these new courts must be considered carefully. Our criminal justice system incorporates the guarantee of certain legal rights to criminal offenders. These rights must be recognized and respected, even in slightly modified form, in the rehabilitative justice model to which problem-solving courts subscribe. Problem-solving court jurisprudence requires attention to plea requirements, competency, informed consent, sanctions in response to noncompliance, and confidentiality. Constitutional rights must also be considered because problem-solving courts may have implications for the First Amendment protection of free speech, Fourth Amendment rights related to searches and seizures, Sixth Amendment right to counsel, and Fourteenth Amendment substantive due process and equal protection rights. Legal actors in problem-solving courts also must evaluate their responsibilities in this more collaborative approach to criminal justice because these courts call for a considerable shift in roles for the judge, prosecutor, and defense attorney.

Include Underrepresented Defendants as Problem-Solving Courts Expand

Most current problem-solving courts provide services to a limited proportion of eligible offenders. That is perhaps as it should be; given the absence of an empirical justification for some types of courts and the limited research on most types of problem-solving courts, we do not call for the widespread adoption of problem-solving justice in lieu of standard criminal justice processing at present. But even the more targeted shift involving a growing number of problem-solving courts should address the present underrepresentation of minority populations in problem-solving courts (see Marlowe, Hardin, & Fox, 2016). A better understanding of the causes of this underrepresentation, combined with effective strategies to address it, is important for reasons involving basic fairness and equal access.

Conclusion

This book has provided a summary of the salient issues associated with problem-solving justice and the specialty courts that have been developed and operated in the United States during the past three decades. There is little doubt that this approach reflects an innovative reconceptualization of the strong punitive emphasis associated with the criminal justice system, with the potential for balancing individual need, public safety, and fiscal efficiency. Yet the enthusiasm for this approach must be tempered with the importance of conceptual clarity, respect for individual rights, and empirical evidence about effectiveness. We hope that the material provided in this book can serve to promote the needed expansion of problem-solving justice balanced by the associated empirical, ethical, and legal considerations needed for its responsible implementation.

Cases

Alexander v. State, 48 P.3d 110 (Okla. Crim. App. 2002).
Americans United v. Prison Fellowship, 509 F.3d 406 (8th Cir. 2007).
Andrews v. State, 623 S.E.2d 247 (Ga. Ct. App. 2005).
CDC v. State, 821 So. 2d 1021 (Ala. Crim. App. 2001).
Daubert v. Merrell Dow Pharmaceuticals, 509 U.S. 579 (1993).
Dawson v. State, 894 P.2d 672 (Alaska Ct. App. 1995).
Destafano v. Emergency Housing Group, Inc., 247 F.3d 397 (2d Cir. 2001).
Evans v. State, 667 S.E.2d 183 (Ga. Ct. App. 2008).
Faretta v. California, 422 U.S. 806 (1975).
Frye v. United States, 293 F. 1013 (D.C. Cir. 1923).
Gagnon v. Scarpelli, 411 U.S. 778 (1973).
Gosha v. State, 927 N.E.2d 942 (Ind. Ct. App. 2010).
Griffin v. Coughlin, 673 N.E.2d 98 (N.Y. 1996).
Griffin v. Wisconsin, 483 U.S. 888 (1987).
Harris v. Commonwealth, 689 S.E.2d 713 (Va. 2010).
Hernandez v. State, 116 S.W.3d 26 (Tex. Crim. App. 2003).
Inouya v. Kemma, 504 F.3d 705 (9th Cir. 2007).
In re Briggs, 595 S.W.2d 270 (Mo. 1980).
In re Hughes, 874 So. 2d 746 (La. 2004).
In re Miguel, 63 P.3d 1065 (Ariz. Ct. App. 2003).
Jim v. State, 911 So. 2d 658 (Miss. Ct. App. 2005).
Johnson v. State, 547 So. 2d 1048 (Fla. Dist. Ct. App. 1989).
Jones v. State, 548 A.2d 35 (D.C. Cir. 1998).
Kerr v. Farrey, 95 F.3d 471 (7th Cir. 1996).
Lahey v. Kelly, 518 N.E.2d 135 (N.Y. 1987).
Liteky v. United States, 510 U.S. 540 (1994).
Lomont v. State, 852 N.E.2d 1002 (Ind. Ct. App. 2006).
Louis v. Department of Corrections, 437 F.3d 697 (8th Cir. 2006).
Martell v. County Court, 854 P.2d 1327 (Colo. Ct. App. 1992).
Matter of Blackman, 591 A.2d 1339 (N.J. 1991).
North Carolina v. Alford, 400 U.S. 30 (1970).
O'Conner v. California, 855 F.Supp. 202 (C.D. Cal. 1994).
Oliver v. United States, 682 A.2d 186 (D.C. Cir. 1996).
Payne v. State, 615 S.E. 2d 564 (Ga. Ct. App. 2005).
People v. Anderson, 833 N.E.2d 390 (Ill. App. Ct. 2005).

People v. Fiammegta, 923 N.E.2d 113 (N.Y. 2010).
People v. Forsythe, 43 P.3d 652 (Colo. Ct. App. 2001).
People v. Jungers, 25 Cal. Rptr. 3d 873 (Ct. App. 2005).
People v. Toran, 580 N.W.2d 595 (Ill. App. Ct. 1991).
Peranzo v. Coughlin, 608 F. Supp. 1504 (S.D.N.Y 1985).
Robinson v. California, 370 U.S. 660 (1962).
Samson v. California, 547 U.S. 843 (2006).
Smith v. State, 840 So. 2d 404 (Fla. Dist. Ct. 2003).
Spence v. Furrier, 807 F.2d 753 (8th Cir. 1986).
Staley v. State, 851 So.2d 805 (Fla. Dist. Ct. App. 2003).
State v. Belyea, 999 A.2d 1080 (N.H. 2010).
State v. Harner, 103 P.3d 738 (Wash. 2004).
State v. Kouba, 709 N.W. 2d 299 (Minn. Ct. App. 2006).
State v. LaPlaca, 27 A.3d 719 (N.H. 2011).
State v. Magnunson, 606 N.W. 2d 536 (Wis. 2000).
State v. Matey, 891 A.2d 592 (N.H. 2006).
State v. McAuliffe, 125 P.3d 276 (Wyo. 2005).
State v. Morgan, 389 So. 2d 364 (La. 1980).
State v. Patton, 119 P.3d 250 (Ore. Ct. App. 2005).
State v. Perkins, 661 S.E.2d 366 (S.C. Ct. App. 2008).
State v. Rogers, 170 P.3d 881 (Idaho 2006).
State v. Ullring, 741 A.2d 1045, 1045 (Me. 1999).
State v. Sommer, 878 P.2d 1007 (N.M. Ct. App. 1994).
State v. Stewart, No. W2009-00980-CCA-R3-CD, 2010 VL 3293920 (Tenn. Crim. App. 2010).
State v. Wright, 739 N.E.2d 1172 (Ohio Ct. App. 2000).
Steiner v. State, 763 N.E. 2d 1024 (Ind. Ct. App. 2002).
Terry v. Superior Court, 86 Cal. Rptr. 2d 653 (Ct. App. 1999).
Thomas v. McBride, 3 F. Supp. 989 (N.D. 1998).
Tumey v. Ohio, 273 U.S. 510 (1927).
United States v. Alfonso, 248 F.Supp.2d 193 (D. Mass. 2003).
United States v. Scott, 450 F.3d 863 (9th Cir. 2006).
Willis v. Roche Biomedical Lab, 61 F.3d 313 (5th Cir. 1995).
Wisconsin v. Loomis, 881 N.W.2d 749 (Wis. 2016).
Wykoff v. Resig, 613 F.Supp. 1504 (N.D. Ind. 1985).

References

ACE Program. (2018). *Accelerated Community Entry Program* [Brochure]. Western District of Michigan: United States Probation and Pretrial Services.

Administrative Office of the Courts. (2012). *A preliminary look at California parolee reentry courts.* Retrieved November 4, 2017, from http://www.courts.ca.gov/documents/AOCBriefParolee0612.pdf.

Alexander, M. (2012). *The new Jim Crow: Mass incarceration in the age of colorblindness.* New York: New Press.

Almquist, L., & Dodd, E. (2009). *Mental health courts: A guide to research-informed policy and practice.* New York: Council of State Governments Justice Center.

American Bar Association. (1993). *Standards for criminal justice: Prosecution and defense function.* Retrieved May 19, 2018, from https://www.americanbar.org/groups/criminal_justice/standards/DefenseFunctionFourthEdition-TableofContents.html.

American Bar Association. (2004). *Model rules of professional conduct.* Retrieved May 19, 2018, from https://www.americanbar.org/groups/professional_responsibility/publications/model_rules_of_professional_conduct/model_rules_of_professional_conduct_preamble_scope.html.

American Bar Association. (2008). *Model code of judicial conduct* (2007). Retrieved May 19, 2018, from https://www.americanbar.org/content/dam/aba/migrated/judicialethics/ABA_MCJC_approved.authcheckdam.pdf.

American Bar Association. (2018). *Jurisdictional adoption of revised model code of judicial conduct.* Retrieved May 19, 2018, from https://www.americanbar.org/groups/professional_responsibility/resources/judicial_ethics_regulation/map.html.

American Psychiatric Association. (1994). *Diagnostic and statistical manual of mental disorders* (4th ed.). Washington, DC: Author.

Andrews, D. A., & Bonta, J. (2001). *Level of Service Inventory-Revised (LSI-R): User's manual.* North Tonawanda, NY: Multi-Health Systems.

Andrews, D. A., & Bonta, J. (2010a). Rehabilitating criminal justice policy and practice. *Psychology, Public Policy, and Law, 16,* 39–55.

Andrews, D. A., & Bonta, J. (2010b). *The psychology of criminal conduct* (5th ed.). Newark, NJ: LexisNexis.

Andrews, D. R., Bonta, J., & Hoge, R. D. (1990). Classification for effective rehabilitation: Rediscovering psychology. *Criminal Justice and Behavior, 17,* 19–52.

Andrews, D. A., Bonta, J., & Wormith, J. S. (2004). *LS/CMI: The level of service/case management inventory.* Toronto, Ontario, Canada: Multi-Health Systems.

Andrews, D. A., Bonta, J., & Wormith, J. S. (2006). The recent past and near future of risk and/or need assessment. *Crime and Delinquency, 52,* 7–27.

Andrews, D. A., & Dowden, C. (2006). Risk principle of case classification in correctional treatment: A meta-analytic investigation. *International Journal of Offender Therapy and Comparative Criminology, 50,* 88–100.

Andrews, D. A., Zinger, I., Hoge, R. D., Bonta, J., Gendreau, P., & Cullen, F. T. (1990). Does treatment work? A psychologically informed meta-analysis. *Criminology, 28,* 369–404.

Antonowicz, D. H. (2005). The Reasoning and Rehabilitation Program: Outcome evaluations with offenders. In M. McMurran & J. McGuire (Eds.), *Social problem solving and offenders: Evidence, evaluation and evolution* (pp. 163–182). Chichester, UK: Wiley.

Antonowicz, D. H., & Ross, R. R. (2005). Social problem solving deficits in offenders. In M. McMurran & J. McGuire (Eds.), *Social problem solving and offenders: Evidence, evaluation and evolution* (pp. 91–102). Chichester, UK: Wiley.

Anumba, N., DeMatteo, D., & Heilbrun, K. (2012). Social functioning, victimization, and mental health among female offenders: Targets of gender-responsive treatment. *Criminal Justice and Behavior, 39*, 1204–1218.

Aos, S., Miller, M., & Drake, E. (2006). *Evidence-based public policy options to reduce future prison construction, criminal justice costs, and crime rates.* Olympia: Washington State Institute for Public Policy. Retrieved September 26, 2018, from http://www.wsipp.wa.gov/ReportFile/952/Wsipp_Evidence-Based-Public-Policy-Options-to-Reduce-Future-Prison-Construction-Criminal-Justice-Costs-and-Crime-Rates_Full-Report.pdf.

Arkfeld, L. C. (2007). Ethics for the problem-solving court judge: The new ABA Model Code. *Justice System Journal, 28*(3), 317–323.

Ashford, J. (2004). Treating substance abusing parents: A study of the Pima County family drug court approach. *Juvenile and Family Court Journal, 55*, 27–37.

Atkin-Plunk, C. A., Peck, J. H., & Armstrong, G. S. (2019). Do race and ethnicity matter? An examination of racial/ethnic differences in perceptions of procedural justice and recidivism among problem-solving court clients. *Race and Justice, 9*, 151–179.

Baglivio, M. T. (2009). The assessment of risk to recidivate among a juvenile offending population. *Journal of Criminal Justice, 37*, 596–607.

Baillargeon, J., Binswanger, I. A., Penn, J. V., Williams, B. A., & Murray, O. J. (2009). Psychiatric disorders and repeat incarcerations: The revolving prison door. *American Journal of Psychiatry, 166*, 103–109.

Baldwin, J. M. (2014). The veterans treatment court concept in practice: Issues for practitioners. *Perspectives: The Journal of the American Probation and Parole Association, 38*, 74–92.

Baldwin, J. M. (2015). Whom do they serve? A national examination of veterans treatment court participants and their challenges. *Criminal Justice Policy Review, 28*, 514–554.

Balyakina, E., Mann, C., Ellison, M., Sivernell, R., Fulda, K. G., Sarai, S. K., & Cardarelli, R. (2014). Risk of future offense among probationers with co-occurring substance use and mental health disorders. *Community Mental Health Journal, 50*, 288–295.

Barrett, E. L., Indig, D., Sunjic, S., Sannibale, C., Sindicich, N., Rosenfeld, J., . . . Mills, K. (2015). Treating comorbid substance use and traumatic stress among male prisoners: A pilot study of the acceptability, feasibility, and preliminary efficacy of Seeking Safety. *International Journal of Forensic Mental Health, 14*, 45–55.

Basquill, M., Nezu, C. M., Nezu, A. M., & Klein, T. L. (2004). Aggression-related hostility bias and social problem solving deficits in adult males with mental retardation. *American Journal on Mental Retardation, 109*, 255–263.

Bazelon Center for Mental Health Law. (2003). Criminalization of people with mental illnesses: The role of mental health courts in system reform. *Jail Suicide/Mental Health Update, 12*, 1–8, 10–11.

Beck, A. J., & Shipley, B. E. (1989). *Recidivism of prisoners released in 1983.* Washington, DC: US Department of Justice, Office of Justice Programs, Bureau of Justice Statistics.

Beck, A. T. (1976). *Cognitive therapy and the emotional disorders.* New York: International Universities Press.

Beeler, H. (2013). Federal reentry courts and other new models of supervision. *Federal Lawyer, 60,* 55–60.

Belenko, S. (1998). Research on drug courts: A critical review. *National Drug Court Institute Review, 1,* 1–42.

Belenko, S. (1999). Research on drug courts: A critical review: 1999 update. *National Drug Court Institute Review, 2,* 1–58.

Belenko, S. (2001). *Research on drug courts: A critical review: 2001 update.* New York: National Center on Addiction and Substance Abuse at Columbia University.

Belenko, S. (2002a). Drug courts. In C. G. Leukefeld, F. Tims, & D. Farabee (Eds.), *Treatment of drug offenders: Policies and issues* (pp. 301–318). New York: Springer.

Belenko, S. (2002b). The challenges of conducting research in drug treatment court settings. *Substance Use and Misuse, 37,* 1635–1664.

Belenko, S., DeMatteo, D., & Patapis, N. (2007). Drug courts. In D. W. Springer & A. R. Roberts (Eds.), *Handbook of forensic mental health with victims and offenders: Assessment, treatment, and research* (pp. 385–423). New York: Springer.

Belenko, S., Fabrikant, N., & Wolff, N. (2011). The long road to treatment models of screening and admission into drug courts. *Criminal Justice and Behavior, 38,* 1222–1243.

Belenko, S., Patapis, N., & French, M. T. (2005). *Economic benefits of drug treatment: A critical review of the evidence for policy makers.* Philadelphia: Treatment Research Institute.

Belenko, S., & Peugh, J. (2005). Estimating drug treatment needs among state prison inmates. *Drug and Alcohol Dependence, 77,* 269–281.

Bennett, T., Holloway, K., & Farrington, D. (2008). The statistical association between drug misuse and crime: A meta-analysis. *Aggression and Violent Behavior, 13,* 107–118.

Berenson S. (2010). The movement toward veterans courts. *Journal of Poverty Law and Policy, 44,* 37–42.

Berman, G. (2009). Problem-solving justice and the moment of truth. In P. Higgins & M. B. Mackinem (Eds.), *Problem-solving courts: Justice for the twenty-first century?* (pp. 1–11). Santa Barbara, CA: Praeger.

Berman, G., & Feinblatt, J. (2001). Problem-solving courts: A brief primer. *Law & Policy, 23,* 125–140.

Berman, G., & Feinblatt, J. (2002). *Judges and problem solving courts.* New York: Center for Court Innovation.

Berman, G., & Feinblatt, J. (2005). *Good courts: The case for problem-solving justice.* New York: New Press.

Bertman-Pate, L., Burnett, D., Thompson, J., Calhoun, C., Deland, S., & Fryou, R. (2004). The New Orleans Forensic Aftercare Clinic: A seven year review of hospital discharged and jail diverted clients. *Behavioral Sciences and the Law, 22,* 159–169.

Bhati, A., Roman, J. K., & Chalfin, A. (2008). *To treat or not to treat: Evidence on the prospects of expanding treatment to drug-involved offenders.* Washington, DC: Urban Institute.

Blonigen, D. M., Bui, L., Elbogen, E. B., Blodgett, J. C., Maisel, N. C., Midboe, A. M., . . . Timko, C. (2016). Risk of recidivism among justice-involved veterans: A systematic review of the literature. *Criminal Justice Policy Review, 27,* 812–837.

Blue-Howells J. H., Clark S. C., van den Berk-Clark C., & McGuire, J. F. (2013). The US Department of Veterans Affairs Justice programs and the sequential intercept model: Case examples in national dissemination of intervention for justice-involved veterans. *Psychological Services, 10,* 48–53.

Boar, D., & Walter, C. (2012). *Reentry court tool kit: A guide for reentry court practitioners* (Center for Court Innovation Guide). Retrieved July 8, 2018, from http://www.courtinnovation.org/sites/default/files/documents/reentry_toolkit.pdf

Boldt, R. C. (1998). Rehabilitative punishment and the drug court movement. *Washington University Law Review, 76,* 1206–1300.

Boles, S., Young, N. K., Moore, T., & DiPirro-Beard, S. (2007). The Sacramento Dependency Drug Court: Development and outcomes. *Child Maltreatment, 12,* 161–171.

Bonta, J., & Andrews, D. A. (2007). Risk-need-responsivity model for offender assessment and rehabilitation. *Rehabilitation, 6,* 1–22.

Bonta, J., Blais, J., & Wilson, H. A. (2014). A theoretically informed meta-analysis of the risk for general and violent recidivism for mentally disordered offenders. *Aggression and Violent Behavior, 19,* 278–287.

Bonta, J., Law, M., & Hanson, K. (1998). The prediction of criminal and violent recidivism among mentally disordered offenders: A meta-analysis. *Psychological Bulletin, 123,* 123–142.

Boothroyd, R. A., Mercado, C. C., Poythress, N. G., Christy, A., & Petrila, J. (2005). Clinical outcomes of defendants in mental health court. *Psychiatric Services, 56,* 829–834.

Boothroyd, R. A., Poythress, N. G., McGaha, A., & Petrila, J. (2003). The Broward Mental Health Court: Process, outcomes, and service utilization. *International Journal of Law and Psychiatry, 26,* 55–71.

Borum, R., Deane, M. W., Steadman, H., & Morrissey, J. (1998). Police perspectives on responding to mentally ill people in crisis: Perceptions of program effectiveness. *Behavioral Sciences and the Law, 16,* 393–405.

Bouffard, J. A., & Bergeron, L. E. (2006). Reentry works: The implementation and effectiveness of a serious and violent offender reentry initiative. *Journal of Offender Rehabilitation, 44,* 1–29.

Bouffard, J. A., & Richardson, K. A. (2007). The effectiveness of drug court programming for specific kinds of offenders: Methamphetamine and DWI offenders versus other drug involved offenders. *Criminal Justice Policy Review, 18,* 274–293.

Bouffard, J. A., Richardson, K. A., & Franklin, T. (2010). Drug courts for DWI offenders? The effectiveness of two hybrid drug courts on DWI offenders. *Journal of Criminal Justice, 38,* 25–33.

Branch, A. Y. (2002). *Faith and action: Implementation of the national faith-based initiative for high-risk youth.* Philadelphia, PA: Public/Private Ventures.

Breckenridge, J. F., Winfree, L. T., Maupin, J. R., & Clason, D. L. (2000). Drunk drivers, DWI "drug court" treatment, and recidivism: Who fails? *Justice Research and Policy, 2,* 87–105.

Brennan, T., & Oliver, W. L. (2000). *Evaluation of reliability and validity of COMPAS scales: National aggregate sample.* Traverse City, MI: Northpointe Institute for Public Management.

Broner, N., Lattimore, P., Cowell, A., & Schlenger, W. (2004). Effects of diversion on adults with co-occurring mental illness and substance use: Outcomes from a national multisite study. *Behavioral Sciences and the Law, 22,* 519–541.

Broner, N., Mayrl, D., & Landsberg, G. (2005). Outcomes of mandated and nonmandated New York City diversion for offenders with alcohol, drug, and mental disorders. *Prison Journal, 85,* 18–49.

Brown, K. (2016). The missing pieces in federal reentry courts: A model for success. *Drexel Law Review, 8*, 397–423.

Bruns, E. J., Pullmann, M. D., Weathers, E. S., Wirschem, M. L., & Murphy, J. K. (2012). Effects of a multidisciplinary family treatment drug court on child and family outcomes: Results of a quasi-experimental study. *Child Maltreatment, 17*, 218–230.

Bureau of Justice Statistics. (2002). *Drugs and crime facts: Drug law violations*. Washington, DC: US Department of Justice, Office of Justice Programs, Bureau of Justice Statistics. Retrieved September 26, 2018, from: https://www.bjs.gov/content/dcf/duc.cfm.

Bureau of Justice Statistics. (2005). *Drugs and crime facts: Drug law violations*. Washington, DC: US Department of Justice, Office of Justice Programs, Bureau of Justice Statistics. Retrieved September 26, 2018, from https://www.bjs.gov/content/dcf/duc.cfm.

Burgoyne, B., & Tyson, G. (2013). An evaluation of the "Think First" program. *Australian and New Zealand Journal of Criminology, 46*, 88–100.

Burns, P. J., Hiday, V. A., & Ray, B. (2013). Effectiveness 2 years postexit of a recently established mental health court. *American Behavioral Scientist, 57*, 189–208.

Bush, J., Glick, B., & Taymans, J. (1997, revised 1998). *Thinking for a change: Integrated cognitive behavior change program*. National Institute of Corrections. Washington, DC: US Department of Justice. Retrieved July 29, 2017, from https://nicic.gov/t4c

Callahan, L., Steadman, H. J., Tillman, S., & Vesselinov, R. (2013). A multi-site study of the use of sanctions and incentives in mental health courts. *Law and Human Behavior, 37*, 1–9.

Canada, K., & Watson, A. (2013). "Cause everybody likes to be treated good": Perceptions of procedural justice among mental health court participants. *American Behavioral Scientist, 57*, 209–230.

Canales, D. D., Campbell, M. A., Wei, R., & Totten, A. E. (2014). Prediction of general and violent recidivism among mentally disordered adult offenders: Test of the Level of Service/Risk-Need-Responsivity (LS/RNR) instrument. *Criminal Justice and Behavior, 41*, 971–991.

Carey, S. M., Allen, T. H., & Einspruch, E. L. (2012). *San Joaquin DUI monitoring court process and outcome evaluation* (final report). Portland, OR: NPC Research. Retrieved October 2, 2018, from http://npcresearch.com/wp-content/uploads/San_Joaquin_DUI_Court_Evaluation_0912.pdf

Carey, S. M., Fuller, B. E., & Kissick, K. (2008). *Michigan DUI courts outcome evaluation*. Lansing: Michigan Supreme Court. Retrieved November 6, 2017, from https://council.legislature.mi.gov/Content/Files/sdtcac/mi_dui_outcome_eval_final_report_0308.pdf

Carey, S. M., Herrera Allen, T., Einspruch, E. L., Mackin, J. R., & Marlowe, D. (2015). Using behavioral triage in court-supervised treatment of DUI offenders. *Alcoholism Treatment Quarterly, 33*, 44–63.

Carey, S. M., Mackin, J. R., & Finigan, M. W. (2012). What works? The ten key components of drug court: Research-based best practices. *Drug Court Review, 8*, 6–42.

Carey, S. M., Sanders, M. B., Waller, M. S., Burrus, S. W. M., & Aborn, J. A. (2010a). *Marion County Fostering Attachment Treatment Court process, outcome and cost evaluation* (final report). Portland, OR: NPC Research. Retrieved November 17, 2017, from https://npcresearch.com/wp-content/uploads/Marion_Byrne_Final_06101.pdf.

Carey, S. M., Sanders, M. B., Waller, M. S., Burrus, S. W. M., & Aborn, J. A. (2010b). *Jackson County Community Family Court process, outcome, and cost evaluation* (final report).

Portland, OR: NPC Research. Retrieved November 17, 2017, from https://npcresearch.com/wp-content/uploads/Jackson_Byrne_06101.pdf.

Carson, E. A., & Anderson, E. (2016). *Prisoners in 2015*. Washington, DC: US Department of Justice, Office of Justice Programs, Bureau of Justice Statistics.

Cary, P. (2011). The fundamentals of drug testing. In D. B. Marlowe & W. G. Meyer (Eds.), *The drug court judicial benchbook* (pp. 113–138). Alexandria, VA: National Drug Court Institute.

Case, B., Steadman, H., Dupuis, S., & Morris, L. (2009). Who succeeds in jail diversion programs for persons with mental illness? A multi-site study. *Behavioral Sciences and the Law, 27*, 661–674.

Casey, P. M., & Rottman, D. B. (2005). Problem-solving courts: Models and trends. *Justice System Journal, 26*, 35–56.

Casey, T. (2004). When good intentions are not enough: Problem-solving courts and the impending crisis of legitimacy. *Southern Methodist University Law Review, 57*, 1459–1519.

Castellano, U., & Anderson, L. (2013). Mental health courts in America: Promise and challenges. *American Behavioral Scientist, 52*, 163–173.

Cavanaugh, M. R., & Franklin, T. W. (2012). Do DWI courts work? An empirical evaluation of a Texas DWI court. *Journal of Offender Rehabilitation, 51*, 257–274.

Center for Substance Abuse Treatment. (2000). *Linking substance abuse treatment and domestic violence services: A guide for treatment providers* (TIP No. 25). Rockville, MD: US Department Health and Human Services.

Chadwick N., DeWolf A. H., & Serin R. C. (2015). Effectively training community supervision officers: A meta-analytic review of the impact on offender outcome. *Criminal Justice and Behavior, 42*, 977–989.

Chawarski, M. C., Fiellin, D. A., O'Connor, P. G., Bernard, M., & Schottenfeld, R. S. (2007). Utility of sweat patch testing for drug use monitoring in outpatient treatment for opiate dependence. *Journal of Substance Abuse Treatment, 33*, 411–415.

Child, H., & McIntyre, D. (2015). Examining the relationships between family drug court program compliance and child welfare outcomes. *Child Welfare, 94*, 67–87.

Child Welfare League of America. (1990). *Crack and other addictions: Old realities and new challenges*. Washington, DC: Author.

Chiu, T. (2010). *It's about time: Aging prisoners, increasing costs, and geriatric release*. New York: Vera Institute of Justice.

Christy, A., Clark, C., Frei, A., & Rynearson-Moody, S. (2012). Challenges of diverting veterans to trauma informed care: The heterogeneity of Intercept 2. *Criminal Justice and Behavior, 39*, 461–474.

Christy, A., Poythress, N. G., Boothroyd, R. A., Petrila, J., & Mehra, S. (2005). Evaluating the efficiency and community safety goals of the Broward County Mental Health Court. *Behavioral Sciences and& the Law, 23*, 227–243.

Chuang, E., Moore, K., Barrett, B., & Young, M. S. (2012). Effect of an integrated family dependency treatment court on child welfare reunification, time to permanency and re-entry rates. *Children and Youth Services Review, 34*, 1896–1902.

Cissner, A. (2009). *The drug court model and persistent DWI*. New York: Center for Court Innovation. Retrieved November 6, 2017, from http://www.courtinnovation.org/sites/default/files/dwi_court_evaluation.pdf

Clark, S., McGuire, J., & Blue-Howells, J. (2010). Development of veterans treatment courts: Local and legislative initiatives. *Drug Court Review, 7*, 171–208.

Clarke, C., & Neuhard, J. (2004). From day one: Who's in control as problem solving and client-centered sentencing take center stage. *New York University Review of Law & Societal Change, 29*, 11–55.

Close, D., Alltucker, K., & Aubin, M. (2008). *The District of Oregon Reentry Court: Evaluation, policy recommendations, and replication strategies*. United States Probation Office, District of Oregon. Retrieved July 18, 2018, from http://www.orp.uscourts.gov/documents/ReentryCourtDoc.pdf

Cloyes, K. G., Wong, B., Latimer, S., & Abarca, J. (2010). Time to prison return for offenders with serious mental illness released from prison: A survival analysis. *Criminal Justice and Behavior, 37*, 175–187.

Cocozza, J. J., & Shufelt, J. L. (2006, June). *Juvenile mental health courts: An emerging strategy.* National Center for Mental Health and Juvenile Justices. Retrieved June 11, 2017, from https://www.ncmhjj.com/wp-content/uploads/2013/07/2006_Juvenile-Mental-Health-Courts1.pdf

Commaroto, L., Jewell, T., & Wilder, A. (2011). *Rochester Veterans Court: An expanded service of the Rochester Drug Court: Evaluation summary report.* Rochester, NY: Coordinated Care Services.

Compton, M., Bahora, M., Watson, A., & Oliva, J. (2008). A comprehensive review of extant research on crisis intervention team (CIT) programs. *Journal of the American Academy of Psychiatry and the Law, 36*, 47–55.

Compton, M., & Chien, V. (2008). Factors related to knowledge retention after crisis intervention team training for police officers. *Psychiatric Services, 59*, 1049–1051.

Compton, M., Demir Neubert, B., Broussard, B., McGriff, J., Morgan, R., & Oliva, J. (2011). Use of force preferences and perceived effectiveness of actions among crisis intervention team police officers and non-CIT officers in an escalating psychiatric crisis involving a subject with schizophrenia. *Schizophrenia Bulletin, 37*, 737–745.

Coons, P. M., & Bowman, E. S. (2010). *Psychiatry in Indiana: The first 175 years.* New York: iUniverse.

Cosden, M., Ellens, J., Schnell, J., & Yamini-Diouf, Y. (2005). Efficacy of a mental health treatment court with assertive community treatment. *Behavioral Sciences and the Law, 23*, 199–214.

Cosden, M., Ellens, J., Schnell, J., Yamini-Diouf, Y., & Wolfe, M. (2003). Evaluation of a mental health treatment court with assertive community treatment. *Behavioral Sciences and the Law, 21*, 415–427.

Council of State Governments. (2005). *A guide to mental health court design and implementation.* New York: Author.

Council of State Governments Justice Center. (2011). *Mental health courts: A guide to research-informed policy and practice.* Retrieved June 11, 2017, from http://consensusproject.org/jc_publications/mental-health-courts-a-guide-to-research-informed-peolicy-and-practice

Council of State Governments Justice Center. (2017). *Bill to reauthorize second chance act introduced in US House of Representatives.* Retrieved January 28, 2018, from https://csgjusticecenter.org/jc/bill-to-reauthorize-second-chance-act-introduced-in-u-s-house-of-representatives/

Covington, S. S., & Bloom, B. E. (2006). Gender responsive treatment and services in correctional settings. *Women and Therapy, 29*(3/4), 9–33.

Crancer, A. (2003). *An analysis of Idaho's Kootenai county DUI court.* Washington, DC: National Highway Traffic Safety Administration. Retrieved November 6, 2017, from http://s3.amazonaws.com/zanran_storage/www.isc.idaho.gov/ContentPages/24306314.pdf

Criminal Justice Council of the Judiciary. (2016). *Report on Delaware's problem-solving courts.* Retrieved June 10, 2017, from http://courts.delaware.gov/AOC/docs/CJCJ_Final_Report.pdf

Criminal Justice/Mental Health Consensus Project. (2005). *Mental health courts: A national snapshot.* New York: Council of State Governments Justice Center.

Csete, J., & Tomasini-Joshi, D. (2015). *Drug courts: Equivocal evidence on a popular intervention.* New York: Open Society Foundations.

Cullen, F., & Gendreau, P. (1989). The effectiveness of correctional rehabilitation. In L. Goodstein & D. L. MacKenzie (Eds.), *The American prison: Issues in research policy* (pp. 23–44). New York: Plenum.

Cusack, K. J., Morrissey, J. P., Cuddeback, G. S., Prins, A., & Williams, D. M. (2010). Criminal justice involvement, behavioral health service use, and costs of forensic assertive community treatment: A randomized trial. *Community Mental Health Journal, 46*, 356–363.

D'Amico, E. J., Edelen, M. O., Miles, J. N., & Morral, A. R. (2008). The longitudinal association between substance use and delinquency among high-risk youth. *Drug and Alcohol Dependence, 93*, 85–92.

DeMatteo, D., Filone, S., & Davis, J. (2015). Substance use and crime. In B. L. Cutler & P. A. Zapf (Eds.), *APA handbook of forensic psychology: Vol. I. Individual and situational influences in criminal and civil contexts* (pp. 325–349). Washington, DC: American Psychological Association.

DeMatteo, D., Filone, S., & LaDuke, C. (2011). Methodological, ethical, and legal considerations in drug court research. *Behavioral Sciences and the Law, 29*, 806–820.

DeMatteo, D., LaDuke, C., Locklair, B. R., & Heilbrun, K. (2013). Community-based alternatives for justice-involved individuals with severe mental illness: Diversion, problem-solving courts, and reentry. *Journal of Criminal Justice, 41*, 64–71.

DeMatteo, D. S., Marlowe, D. B., & Festinger, D. S. (2006). Secondary prevention services for clients who are low risk in drug court: A conceptual model. *Crime and Delinquency, 52*, 114–134.

DeMatteo, D., Marlowe, D. B., Festinger, D. S., & Arabia, P. L. (2009). Outcome trajectories in drug court: Do all participants have serious drug problems? *Criminal Justice and Behavior, 36*, 354–368.

Denckla, D., & Berman, G. (2001). *Rethinking the revolving door: A look at the mental health courts.* New York: Center for Court Innovation.

Deschenes, E. P., Turner, S., & Greenwood, P. W. (1995). Drug court or probation? An experimental evaluation of Maricopa County's drug court. *Justice System Journal, 18*, 55–73.

Desmarais, S. L., Van Dorn, R. A., Telford, R. P., Petrila, J., & Coffey, T. (2012). Characteristics of START assessments completed in mental health jail diversion programs. *Behavioral Sciences and the Law, 30*, 448–469.

Diamond, P. M., Wang, E. W., Holzer, C. E., III, Thomas, C., & Cruser, D. A. (2001). The prevalence of mental illness in prison. *Administration and Policy in Mental Health, 29*, 21–40.

Dirks-Linhorst, P. A., & Linhorst, D. M. (2012). Recidivism outcomes for suburban mental health court defendants. *American Journal of Criminal Justice, 37*, 76–91.

Dishion, T. J., & Andrews, D. W. (1995). Preventing escalation in problem behaviors with high-risk young adolescents: Immediate and 1-year outcomes. *Journal of Consulting and Clinical Psychology, 63*, 538–548.

Ditton, P. M. (1999). *Mental health and treatment of inmates and probationers* (Bureau of Justice Statistics Special Report No. NCJ 174463). Washington, DC: US Department of Justice, Office of Justice Programs.

Dollar, C. B., Ray, B., Hudson, M. K., & Hood, B. J. (2018). Examining changes in procedural justice and their influence on problem-solving court outcomes. *Behavioral Sciences and the Law, 36*, 32–45.

Domorad, F., & Carey, M. (2009). Implementing evidence based practices. *Center of Public Policy.* Retrieved January 28, 2018, from http://www.cepp.com/documents/Implementing%20Evidence%20Based%20Practices.pdf

Dorf, M. C., & Fagan, J. A. (2003). Community courts and community justice. *American Criminal Law Review, 40*, 1501–1511.

Douds, A. S., Ahlin, E. M., Howard, D., & Stigerwalt, S. (2017). Varieties of veterans' courts: A statewide assessment of veterans' treatment court components. *Criminal Justice Policy Review, 28*, 740–769.

Douglas, K. S., Skeem, J. L. (2005). Violence risk assessment: Getting specific about being dynamic. *Psychology, Public Policy, and Law, 11*, 347–383.

Dowden, C., & Andrews, D. A. (1999). What works for female offenders: A meta-analytic review. *Crime and Delinquency, 45*, 438–452.

Dowden, C., & Andrews, D. A. (2000). Effective correctional treatment and violent reoffending: A meta-analysis. *Canadian Journal of Criminology, 42*, 449–467.

Dowden, C., & Brown, S. L. (2002). The role of substance abuse factors in predicting recidivism: A meta-analysis. *Psychology, Crime, and Law, 8*, 243–264.

Drake, E. K., Aos, S., & Miller, M. G. (2009). Evidence-based public policy options to reduce crime and criminal justice costs: Implications for Washington State. *Victims and Offenders, 4*, 170–196.

Dupont, R., & Cochran, S. (2000). Police response to mental health emergencies: Barriers to change. *Journal of the American Academy of Psychiatry and the Law, 28*, 338–344.

Dupont, R., Cochran, S., & Pillsbury, S. (2007). *Crisis intervention team core elements.* Memphis, TN: University of Memphis.

Durkin, M., Cheesman, F., Maggard, S., Rottman, D., Sohoni, T., & Rubio, D. (2009). *Process evaluation of the Philadelphia Community Court.* Williamsburg, VA: National Center for State Courts. Retrieved November 6, 2017, from http://pacrimestats.info/PCCDReports/EvaluationResearch/Completed%20Research/Courts/Specialty%20Courts/Process%20Evaluation.pdf

Durose, M. R., Cooper, A. D., & Snyder, H. N. (2014). *Recidivism of prisoners released in 30 states in 2005: Patterns from 2005 to 2010.* Washington, DC: US Department of Justice, Office of Justice Programs, Bureau of Justice Statistics.

Dutmers, J. M. (2016). Campus drug courts: How universities may be best equipped to tackle crime and substance abuse in young adults. *Law and Psychology Review, 41*, 191–208.

D'Zurilla, T. J., & Goldfried, M. R. (1971). Problem solving and behavior modification. *Journal of Abnormal Psychology, 78*, 107–126.

D'Zurilla, T. J., & Nezu, A. M. (2007). *Problem-solving therapy: A positive approach to clinical intervention* (3rd ed.). New York: Springer.

D'Zurilla, T. J., Nezu, A. M., & Maydeu-Olivares, A. (2002). *Social problem solving inventory–revised (SPSI–R)*. North Tonawanda, NY: Multi-Health Systems.

Eckberg, D. A. (2001). *Hennepin County Community Justice Project: Summary report of short-term evaluation.* Minneapolis, MN: Hennepin County District Court Research Department. Retrieved December 7, 2017, from http://www.mncourts.gov/mncourtsgov/media/assets/documents/4/reports/Community_Evaluation_(2001).pdf

Eibner, C., Morral, A. R., Pacula, R. L., & MacDonald, J. (2006). Is the drug court model exportable? The cost-effectiveness of a driving-under-the-influence court. *Journal of Substance Abuse Treatment, 31*, 75–85.

Eisen, S. V. (1996). Behavior and symptom identification scale (BASIS- 32). In L. I. Sederer & B. Dickey (Eds.), *Outcomes assessment in clinical practice* (pp. 65–69). Baltimore, MD: Williams and Wilkins.

Eno Louden, J., & Skeem, J. (2011). Parolees with mental disorder: Toward evidence-based practice. *Bulletin of the Center for Evidence-Based Corrections, 7*, 1–9.

Erickson, S., Campbell, A., & Lamberti, J. (2006). Variations in mental health courts: Challenges, opportunities, and a call for caution. *Community Mental Health Journal, 42*, 335–344.

Faraci, S. M. (2004). Slip slidin' away? Will our nation's mental health court experiment diminish the rights of the mentally ill? *Quinnipiac Law Review, 22*, 811–848.

Farole, D. J., Jr. (2003). *The Harlem Parole Reentry Court evaluation: Implementation and preliminary impacts.* New York: Center for Court Innovation. Retrieved November 4, 2017, from https://www.courtinnovation.org/pdf/harlem_reentry_eval.pdf

Farole, D. J., Jr. (2006). *The challenges of going to scale: Lessons from other disciplines for problem-solving courts.* Retrieved June 3, 2017, from http://www.courtinnovation.org/sites/default/files/Lessons.pdf.

Farole D. J., Jr., Puffett, N., Rempel, M., & Byrne, F. (2005). Applying problem-solving principles in mainstream courts: Lessons for state courts. *Justice System Journal, 26*, 57–75.

Fass, T. L., Heilbrun, K., DeMatteo, D., & Fretz, R. (2008). The LSI-R and the COMPAS: Validation data on two risk-needs tools. *Criminal Justice and Behavior, 35*, 1095–1108.

Feinblatt, J., & Denckla, D. (2001, January). What does it mean to be a good lawyer? Prosecutors, defenders and problem-solving courts. *Judicature*, 208–214.

Fell, J. C., Tippetts, S., & Lanston, E. (2008). *An evaluation of the process and impact of three Georgia DUI courts.* Washington, DC: National Highway Traffic Safety Administration. Retrieved November 6, 2017, from http://www.nhtsa.gov/staticfiles/nti/pdf/811450.pdf

Ferguson, A., McAuley, K., Hornby, H., & Zeller, D. (2008). *Outcomes from the last frontier: An evaluation of the Anchorage mental health court.* South Portland, Maine: Hornby Zeller Associates.

Ferguson, A. M., Ogloff, J. R. P., & Thomson, L. (2009). Predicting recidivism by mentally disordered offenders using the LSI-R: SV. *Criminal Justice and Behavior, 36*, 5–20.

Festinger, D. S., DeMatteo, D. S., Marlowe, D. B., & Lee, P. A. (2005). Expungement of arrest records in drug court: Do clients know what they're missing? *Drug Court Review, 5*, 1–21.

Festinger, D. S., Marlowe, D. B., Lee, P. A., Kirby, K. C., Bovasso, G., & McLellan, A. T. (2002). Status hearings in drug court: When more is less and less is more. *Drug and Alcohol Dependence, 68*, 151–157.

Fetsco, D. M. (2013). An emerging use of judicial resources in the struggle to reduce the recidivism of released offenders. *Wyoming Law Review, 13*, 593–594.

Finigan, M., Carey, S. M., & Cox, A. (2007). *The impact of a mature drug court over 10 years of operation: Recidivism and costs* (final report). Portland, OR: NPC Research. Retrieved September 6, 2017, from http://npcresearch.com/wp-content/uploads/10yr_STOP_Court_Analysis_Final_Report.pdf

Fischer, B. (2003). Doing good with a vengeance: A critical assessment of the practices, effects, and implications of drug treatment courts in North America. *Criminology and Criminal Justice, 3*, 227–248.

Focht-Perlberg, J. A. (2009). Two sides of one coin—Reaping the harm and reducing recidivism: A case for restorative justice in reentry in Minnesota and beyond. *Hamline Journal of Public Law and Policy, 31*, 219–229.

Ford, M. (2015, June 8). *America's largest mental hospital is a jail.* Retrieved June 3, 2017, from https://www.theatlantic.com/politics/archive/2015/06/americas-largest-mental-hospital-is-a-jail/395012/

Ford, M. (2017, May 23). What Trump's ideal justice department would look like. *The Atlantic.* Retrieved November 7, 2017, from https://www.theatlantic.com/politics/archive/2017/05/trump-budget-justice-department/527871/

Frailing, K. (2010). How mental health courts function: Outcomes and observations. *International Journal of Law and Psychiatry, 33*, 207–213.

Frankel, M. E. (1980). *Partisan justice* (p. 18). New York: Hill and Wang.

Frantzen, D. (2015). *Evaluation of the Bexar County Veterans Treatment Court.* San Antonio: Texas A & M University. Retrieved November 6, 2017, from https://www.bexar.org/1085/Veterans-Treatment-Court

Frazer, M. S. (2006). *The impact of the community court model on defendant perceptions of fairness: A case study at the Red Hook Community Justice Center.* New York: Center for Court Innovation. Retrieved November 6, 2017, from www.courtinnovation.org/sites/default/files/Procedural_Fairness.pdf

Freedman, M. H., & Smith, A. (2004). *Understanding lawyers' ethics.* Durham, NC: LexisNexis.

Friedmann, P. D., Taxman, F. S., & Henderson, C. E. (2007). Evidence-based treatment practices for drug-involved adults in the criminal justice system. *Journal of Substance Abuse Treatment, 32*, 267–277.

Fruman, A. (2015). *In 2016 race, drug courts get second look.* Retrieved June 2, 2017, from http://www.msnbc.com/msnbc/amid-2016-election-drug-courts-get-closer-look.

Gallas, E. (2004). Endorsing religion: Drug courts and the 12-step recovery support program. *American University Law Review, 53*, 1063–1102.

Gavett, G. (2012). *Cook County Jail's impending mental health crisis.* Retrieved June 3, 2017, from http://www.pbs.org/wgbh/pages/frontline/social-issues/cook-county-jails-impending-mental-health-crisis/.

Gendreau, P., & Andrews, D. A. (1990). Tertiary prevention: What the meta-analyses of the offender treatment literature tell us about what works. *Canadian Journal of Criminology, 32*, 173–184.

Gendreau, P., & Ross, R. R. (1987). Revivification of rehabilitation: Evidence from the 1980s. *Justice Quarterly, 4*, 349–407.

Gifford, E. J., Eldred, L. M., Vernerey, A., & Sloan, F. A. (2014). How does family drug treatment court participation affect child welfare outcomes? *Child Abuse and Neglect, 38*, 1659–1670.

Glaze, L., & James, D. (2006). *Mental health problems of prison and jail inmates.* Washington, DC: US Department of Justice, Office of Justice Programs, Bureau of Justice Statistics.

Goff, A., Rose, E., Rose, S., & Purves, D. (2007). Does PTSD occur in sentenced prison populations? A systematic literature review. *Criminal Behaviour and Mental Health, 17,* 152–162.

Golden, L. S., Gatchel, R. J., & Cahill, M. A. (2006). Evaluating the effectiveness of the National Institute of Corrections' "Thinking for a Change" program among probationers. *Journal of Offender Rehabilitation, 43,* 55–73.

Goldkamp, J. S., & Irons-Guynn, C. (2000). *Emerging judicial strategies for the mentally ill in the criminal caseload: Mental health courts in Fort Lauderdale, Seattle, San Bernardino, and Anchorage.* Retrieved April 10, 2017, from https://www.ncjrs.gov/pdffiles1/bja/182504.pdf.

Goldkamp, J. S., Weiland, D., Collins, M., & White, M. (1996). *Role of drug and alcohol abuse in domestic violence and its treatment: Dade county's domestic violence court experiment* (final report). Philadelphia: Crime and Justice Research Institute. Retrieved November 6, 2017, from https://www.ncjrs.gov/App/Publications/abstract.aspx?ID=163410

Goldkamp, J. S., White, M. D., & Robinson, J. B. (2001). Do drug courts work? Getting inside the drug court black box. *Journal of Drug Issues, 31,* 27–72.

Gottfredson, D., & Exum, L. (2002). The Baltimore City Drug Court: One-year results from a randomized study. *Journal of Research on Crime and Delinquency, 39,* 337–356.

Gottfredson, D. C., Kearley, B. W., Najaka, S. S., & Rocha, C. M. (2005). The Baltimore City drug treatment court: 3-year self-report outcome study. *Evaluation Review, 29,* 42–64.

Gottfredson, D. C., Kearley, B. W., Najaka, S. S., & Rocha, C. M. (2007). How drug treatment courts work: An analysis of mediators. *Journal of Research in Crime and Delinquency, 44,* 3–35.

Gottfredson, D. C., Najaka, S. S., & Kearley, B. W. (2003). A randomized study of the Baltimore City Drug Treatment Court: Results from the two-year follow-up. *Criminology and Public Policy, 2,* 171–196.

Gottfredson, D. C., Najaka, S. S., Kearley, B. W., & Rocha, C. M. (2006). Long-term effects of participation in the Baltimore City drug treatment court: Results from an experimental study. *Journal of Experimental Criminology, 2,* 67–98.

Gottlieb, K. (2005). Process and outcome evaluations in four tribal wellness courts. Retrieved November 6, 2017, from https://www.ncjrs.gov/pdffiles1/nij/grants/231167.pdf

Gottschall, J., & Armour, M. (2011). Second chance: Establishing a reentry program in the Northern District of Illinois. *DePaul Journal of Social Justice, 3,* 31–44.

Gover, A. R., Brank, E. M., & MacDonald, J. M. (2007). A specialized domestic violence court in South Carolina: An example of procedural justice for victims and defendants. *Violence Against Women, 13,* 603–626.

Gover, A. R., MacDonald, J. M., & Alpert, G. P. (2003). Combating domestic violence: Findings from an evaluation of a local domestic violence court. *Criminology and Public Policy, 3,* 109–132.

Government Accountability Office. (2005). *Adult drug courts: Evidence indicates recidivism reductions and mixed results for other outcomes.* Washington, DC: Author.

Government Accountability Office. (2011). *Adult drug courts.* Washington, DC: Author.

Green, B. L., Furrer, C. J., Worcel, S. D., Burrus, S. W. M., & Finigan, M. W. (2007). How effective are family treatment drug courts? Results from a four-site national study. *Child Maltreatment 12*, 43–59.

Green, B. L., Furrer, C. J., Worsel, S. D., Burrus, S. V. M., & Finigan, M. W. (2009). Building the evidence base for family drug treatment courts: Results from recent outcome studies. *Drug Court Review, 6*, 53–82.

Green, M., & Rempel, M. (2012). Beyond crime and drug use: Do adult drug courts produce other psychosocial benefits? *Journal of Drug Issues, 42*, 156–177.

Griffin, P. A., & DeMatteo, D. (2009). Mental health courts: Cautious optimism. In P. Higgins & M. B. Mackinem (Eds.), *Problem-solving courts: Justice for the twenty-first century?* (pp. 91–113). Santa Barbara, CA: Praeger.

Griffin, P. A., Steadman, H. J., & Petrila, J. (2002). The use of criminal charges and sanctions in mental health courts. *Psychiatric Services, 53*, 1285–1289.

Grommon, E., Hipple, N. K., & Ray, B. (2017). An outcome evaluation of the Indianapolis community court. *Criminal Justice Policy Review, 28*, 220–237.

Guerin, P., & Pitts, W. J. (2002). *Evaluation of the Bernalillo County metropolitan DWI/drug court: Final report.* Albuquerque, NM: The University of New Mexico, Institute for Social Research & Center for Applied Research and Analysis. Retrieved November 6, 2017, from http://isr.unm.edu/reports/2002/evaluation-of-the-bernalillo-county-metropolitan-dwidrug-court-final-report.pdf

Guerin, P., & Watkins, E. (2009). *Dona Ana County magistrate court DWI/drug court outcome study.* Albuquerque, NM: University of New Mexico. Retrieved November 6, 2017, from https://nmsc.unm.edu/reports/2009/DACMC_DWIDrugCourt_FinalReport_v1_063009-1.pdf

Gupta, S. K. (2011). Intent-to-treat concept: A review. *Perspectives in Clinical Research, 2*, 109–112.

Gutierrez, L., & Bourgon, G. (2012). Drug treatment courts: A quantitative review of study and treatment quality. *Justice Research and Policy, 14*, 47–77.

Hakuta, J., Soroushian, V., & Kralstein, D. (2008). *Do community courts transform the justice response to misdemeanor crime?* New York: Center for Court Innovation. Retrieved April 8, 2017, from http://www.courtinnovation.org/sites/default/files/Midtown_Downtown.pdf.

Hall, D. L., Miraglia, R. P., Lee, L. W. G., Chard-Wierschem, D., & Sawyer, D. (2012). Predictors of general and violent recidivism among SMI prisoners returning to communities in New York State. *Journal of the American Academy of Psychiatry and the Law, 40*, 221–231.

Hall, R. C. W. (1995). Global assessment of functioning: A modified scale. *Psychosomatics, 36*, 267–275.

Hamilton, Z. (2010). *Do reentry courts reduce recidivism? Results from the Harlem Parole Reentry Court.* New York: Center for Court Innovation. Retrieved November 4, 2017, from http://www.courtinnovation.org/sites/default/files/Reentry_Evaluation.pdf

Han, W., & Redlich, A. D. (2015). The impact of community treatment on recidivism among mental health court participants. *Psychiatric Services, 67*, 384–390.

Hanlon, T. E., Nurco, D. N., Bateman, R. W., & O'Grady, K. E. (1998). The response of drug abuser parolees to a combination of treatment and intensive supervision. *Prison Journal, 78*, 31–44.

Hanson, R. K., Bourgon, G., Helmus, L., & Hodgson, S. (2009). The principles of effective correctional treatment also apply to sexual offenders: A meta-analysis. *Criminal Justice and Behavior, 36*, 865–891.

Hardin, C., & Fox, C. (2011). Getting started. In D. B. Marlowe & W. G. Meyer (Eds.), *The drug court judicial benchbook* (pp. 19–43). Alexandria, VA: National Drug Court Institute.

Harrell, A., Cavanagh, S., & Roman, J. (1998). *Findings from the evaluation of the DC Superior Court Drug Intervention Program* (final report). Washington, DC: The Urban Institute. Retrieved from http://www.urban.org/sites/default/files/publication/66316/409041-Findings-from-the-Evaluation-of-the-D-C-Superior-Court-Drug-Intervention-Program.PDF

Harrell A., & Goodman, A. (1999). *Review of specialized family drug courts: Key issues handling child abuse and neglect cases.* Washington, DC: Department of Justice. Retrieved November 6, 2017, from https://www.ncjrs.gov/pdffiles1/nij/grants/179281.pdf

Harrison, P. M., & Beck, A. J. (2003). *Prisoners in 2002* (NCJ 200248). Washington, DC: US Department of Justice, Office of Justice Programs, Bureau of Justice Statistics.

Harrison, P. M., & Karberg, J. C. (2004). *Prison and jail inmates at midyear 2003* (NCJ 203947). Washington, DC: US Department of Justice, Office of Justice Programs, Bureau of Justice Statistics.

Hasselbrack, A. M. (2001). Opting in to mental health courts. *Corrections Compendium, 26*(10), 4–25.

Hayward, J., McMurran, M., & Sellen, J. (2008). Social problem solving in vulnerable adult prisoners: Profile and intervention. *Journal of Forensic Psychiatry and Psychology, 19*, 243–248.

Heck, C. N., & Roussell, A. (2007). Record keeping and statistics. In J. E. Lessenger & G. F. Roperd (Eds.), *Drug courts* (pp. 401–413). New York: Springer.

Heilbrun, K. (2009). *Evaluation for risk of violence in adults.* New York: Oxford University Press.

Heilbrun, K., DeMatteo, D., King, C., Thornewill, A., & Phillips, S. (2016). Risk-reducing interventions for justice-involved individuals: A critical review. In B. H. Bornstein & M. K. Miller (Eds.), *Advances in psychology and law* (Vol. 2, pp. 271–304). New York: Springer.

Heilbrun, K., DeMatteo, D., Strohmaier, H., & Galloway, M. (2015). The movement toward community-based alternatives to criminal justice involvement and incarceration for people with severe mental illness. In P. Griffin, K. Heilbrun, E. Mulvey, D. DeMatteo, & C. Schubert (Eds.), *The Sequential Intercept Model and criminal justice: Promoting community alternatives for individuals with serious mental illness* (pp. 1–20). New York: Oxford University Press.

Heilbrun, K., DeMatteo, D., Yasuhara, K., Brooks-Holliday, S., Shah, S., King, C., . . . Laduke, C. (2012). Community-based alternatives for justice-involved individuals with severe mental illness: Review of the relevant research. *Criminal Justice and Behavior, 39*, 351–419.

Heilbrun, K., Yasuhara, K., & Shah, S. (2010). Approaches to violence risk assessment: Overview and critical analysis. In R. Otto & K. Douglas (Eds.), *Handbook of violence risk assessment* (pp. 1–17). New York: Routledge.

Herinckx, H. A., Swart, S. C., Ama, S. M., Dolezal, C. D., & King, S. (2005). Rearrest and linkage to mental health services among clients of the Clark County mental health court program. *Psychiatric Services, 56*, 853–857.

Herz, D. C., & Walsh, J. E. (2004). Faith-based programs for reentry courts: A summary of issues and recommendations. *Juvenile and Family Court Journal, 55*, 15–25.

Hiday, V. A., Moore, M. E., Lamoureaux, M., & de Magistris, J. (2005, Spring/Summer). North Carolina's mental health court. *Popular Government*, 24–30. Retrieved May 31, 2017, from http://www.iog.unc.edu/pubs/electronicversions/pg/pgspsm05/article3.pdf

Hiday, V., & Ray, B. (2010). Arrests two years after exiting a well-established mental health court. *Psychiatric Services, 61*, 463–468.

Hiday, V. A., Wales, H. W., & Ray, B. (2013). Effectiveness of a short- term mental health court: Criminal recidivism one year postexit. *Law and Human Behavior, 37*, 401–411.

Hiller, M., Saum, C., Taylor, L., Watson, C., Hayes, W., & Samuelson, B. (2009). Waukesha Alcohol Treatment Court (WATC): Process and outcomes. Philadelphia: Temple University, Dept. of Criminal Justice. Retrieved November 6, 2017, from http://www.dwicourts.org/wp-content/uploads/2016/09/WATC_Outcome_Evaluation-final-draft.pdf

Hoff, R., Baranosky, M., Buchanan, J., Zonana, H., & Rosenheck, R. (1999). The effects of a jail diversion program on incarceration: A retrospective cohort study. *Journal of the American Academy of Psychiatry and the Law, 27*, 377–386.

Hoffman, M. B. (1999). Drug court scandal. *North Carolina Law Review, 78*, 1437–1532.

Holbrook, J. G., & Anderson, S. (2011). Veterans courts: Early outcomes and key indicators for success. *Widener Law School Legal Studies Research Paper, Series, 11*, 1–52.

Holland, P. (2010). Lawyering and learning in problem-solving courts. *Washington University Journal of Law and Policy, 34*, 185–238.

Hollin, C. R., McGuire, J., Hounsome, J. C., Hatcher, R. M., Bilby, C. A. L., & Palmer, E. J. (2008). Cognitive skills behavior programs for offenders in the community: A reconviction analysis. *Criminal Justice and Behavior, 35*, 269–283.

Honegger, L. N. (2015). Does the evidence support the case for mental health courts? A review of the literature. *Law and Human Behavior, 39*, 478–488.

Hora, P. F., Schma, W. G., & Rosenthal, J. T. A. (1999). Therapeutic jurisprudence and the drug treatment court movement: Revolutionizing the criminal justice system's response to drug abuse and crime in America. *Notre Dame Law Review, 74*, 439–538.

Houck, K. D. F., & Loper, A. B. (2002). The relationship of parenting stress to adjustment among mothers in prison. *American Journal of Orthopsychiatry, 72*, 548–558.

Huddleston, C. W., & Marlowe, D. B. (2011). *Painting the current picture: A national report on drug courts and other problem solving court programs in the United States.* Alexandria, VA: National Drug Court Institute.

Hughes, T., & Wilson. D. J. (2002). *Reentry trends in the United States*. Washington, DC: US Department of Justice, Bureau of Justice Assistance.

Husband, S. D., & Platt, J. J. (1993). The cognitive skills component in substance abuse treatment in correctional settings: A brief review. *Journal of Drug Issues, 23*, 31–42.

Inciardi, J. A., Martin, S. S., & Butzin, C. A. (2004). Five-year outcomes of therapeutic community treatment of drug-involved offenders after release from prison. *Crime and Delinquency, 50*, 88–107.

Institute on Women and Criminal Justice. (2006). *Hard hit: The growth in the imprisonment of women, 1977–2004.* Women's Prison Association. Retrieved from http://csdp.org/research/HardHitReport4.pdf

James, D. J., & Glaze, L. E. (2006). *Mental health problems of prison and jail inmates* (NCJ-213600). Washington, DC: US Department of Justice, Office of Justice Programs, Bureau of Justice Statistics.

Johnson, R. S., Stolar, A. G., McGuire, J. F., Clark, S., Coonan, L. A., Hausknecht, P., & Graham, D. P. (2016). US veterans' court programs: An inventory and analysis of national survey data. *Community Mental Health Journal, 52*, 180–186.

Johnson, R. S., Stolar, A. G., McGuire, J. F., Mittakanti, K., Clark, S., Coonan, L. A., & Graham, D. P. (2017). Predictors of incarceration of veterans participating in US veterans' courts. *Psychiatric Services, 68*, 144–150.

Jolley, J. M., & Kerbs, J. J. (2010). Risk, need, and responsivity: Unrealized potential for the international delivery of substance abuse treatment in prison. *International Criminal Justice Review, 20*, 280–301.

Justice for Vets. (2015). *Veterans treatment court locations.* Retrieved November 6, 2017, from http://www.justiceforvets.org/veterans-treatment-court-locations

Kaeble, D., & Bonczar, T. P. (2016). *Probation and parole in the United States, 2015.* Washington, DC: US Department of Justice, Office of Justice Programs, Bureau of Justice Statistics.

Kaeble, D. K., & Glaze, L. (2016). *Correctional populations in the United States, 2015.* Washington, DC: US Department of Justice, Office of Justice Programs, Bureau of Justice Statistics.

Karafin, D. L. (2008). *Community courts across the globe: A survey of goals, performance, measures, and operations.* New York: Center for Court Innovations. Retrieved November 6, 2017, from http://www.courtinnovation.org/sites/default/files/community_court_world.pdf

Katz, S. 2009. *Expanding the community court model: Testing community court principles in the Bronx Centralized Courthouse.* New York: Center for Court Innovation. Retrieved November 6, 2017, from www.courtinnovation.org/sites/default/files/BCS_Impact.pdf

Kazdin, A. E. (2017). *Research design in clinical psychology* (5th ed.). New York: Pearson Education.

Keator, K. J., Callahan, L., Steadman, H. J., & Vesselinov, R. (2013). The impact of treatment on the public safety outcomes of mental health court participants. *American Behavioral Scientist, 57*, 231–243.

Kessel, G. V. (1992). Adversary excesses in the American criminal trial. *Notre Dame Law Review, 67*, 403–550.

Kierkus, C. A., & Johnson, B. R. (2015). *Michigan DWI/Sobriety Court Ignition Interlock evaluation: 2015 report.* Lansing: Michigan State Court Administrative Office. Retrieved November 6, 2017, from http://responsibility.org/wp-content/uploads/2015/06/2015-Michigan-DWISobriety-Court-Ignition-Interlock-Evaluation.pdf

Kilmer, B., & Sussell, J. (2014). *Does San Francisco's Community Justice Center reduce criminal recidivism?* RAND Corporation. Retrieved November 6, 2017, from http://dev.courtinnovation.org/sites/default/files/documents/RAND_CJC.pdf

Kim, K., Becker-Cohen, M., & Serakos, M. (2015). *The processing and treatment of mentally ill persons in the criminal justice system: A scan of practice and background analysis.* Washington, DC: Urban Institute.

King, M. (2008). Non-adversarial justice and the coroner's court: A proposed therapeutic, restorative, problem-solving model. *Journal of Law and Medicine, 16*, 442–457.

Kinsler, P. J., & Saxman, A. (2007). Traumatized offenders: Don't look now, but your jail's also your mental health center. *Journal of Trauma and Dissociation, 8*, 81–95.

Kleiman, M. A. R., Tran, T. H., Fishbein, P., Magula, M. T., Allen, W., & Lacy, G. (2003). *Opportunities and barriers in probation reform: A case study of drug testing and sanctions*. Berkeley, CA: University of California, California Policy Research Center.

Knollenberg, L., & Martin, V. A. (2008). Community reentry following prison: A process evaluation of the accelerated community entry program. *Federal Probation, 72*, 54–60.

Knudsen K. J., & Wingenfeld, S. (2015). A specialized treatment court for veterans with trauma exposure: Implications for the field. *Community Mental Health Journal, 52*, 127–135.

Kopak, A. M., Hoffman, N. G., & Proctor, S. L. (2016). Key risk factors for relapse and re-arrest among substance use treatment patients involved in the criminal justice system. *American Journal of Criminal Justice, 41*, 14–30.

Kopelovich, S., Yanos, P., Pratt, C., & Koerner, J. (2013). Procedural justice in mental health courts: Judicial practices, participant perceptions, and outcomes related to mental health recovery. *International Journal of Law and Psychiatry, 36*, 113–120.

Kroner, D. G., & Mills, J. F. (2001). The accuracy of five risk appraisal instruments in predicting institutional misconduct and new convictions. *Criminal Justice and Behavior, 28*, 471–489.

Kruse, K. (2006). Fortress in the sand: The plural values of client centered representation. *Clinical Law Review, 12*, 369–370.

Kubiak, S., Tillander, L., Comartin, E., & Ray, B. R. (2012). *Statewide mental health court outcome evaluation: Aggregate report*. Lansing: Michigan Department of Community Health.

La Fond, J. Q., & Winick, B. J. (2003). Sex offender reentry courts: A cost effective proposal for managing sex offender risk in the community. *Annals of the New York Academy of Sciences, 989*, 300–323.

Lamb, H. R. (1984). Deinstitutionalization and the homeless mentally ill. *Hospital and Community Psychiatry, 35*, 899–907.

Lamb, H. R., & Weinberger, L. E. (1998). Persons with severe mental illness in jails and prisons: A review. *Psychiatric Services, 49, 483–492.*

Lamb, H. R., Weinberger, L. E., Marsh, J. S., & Gross, B. H. (2007). Treatment prospects for persons with severe mental illness in an urban county jail. *Psychiatric Services, 58*, 782–786.

Lamberti, J. S., Weisman, R., & Faden, D. I. (2004). Forensic assertive community treatment: Preventing incarceration of adults with severe mental illness. *Psychiatric Services, 55*, 1285–1293.

Lamberti, J., Weisman, R., Schwarzkopf, S., Price, N., Ashton, R., & Trompeter, J. (2001). The mentally ill in jails and prisons: Towards an integrated model of prevention. *Psychiatric Quarterly, 72*, 63–77.

Landenberger, N. A., & Lipsey, M. W. (2005). The positive effects of cognitive-behavioral programs for offenders: A meta-analysis of factors associated with effective treatment. *Journal of Experimental Criminology, 1*, 451–476.

Lane, E. (2003). Due process and problem-solving courts. *Fordham University Law Journal, 30*, 955–1026.

Lang, J. (2011). *What is a community court? How the model is being adapted across the United States.* Washington, DC: US Department of Justice, Office of Justice Programs, Bureau of Justice Assistance. Retrieved November 6, 2017, from www.courtinnovation.org/sites/.../What%20is%20a%20Community%20Court.pdf

Langan, P. A., & Levin, D. J. (2002). Recidivism of prisoners released in 1994. *Federal Sentencing Reporter, 15*, 58–65.

Lapham, S. C., C'de Baca, J., McMillan, G. P., & Lapidus, J. (2006). Psychiatric disorders in a sample of repeat impaired-driving offenders. *Journal of Studies on Alcohol, 65*, 707–713.

Latessa, E. J., Sullivan, C., Blair, L., Sullivan, C. J., & Smith, P. (2013). *Final report: Outcome and process evaluation of juvenile drug courts.* Cincinnati, OH: Center for Criminal Justice Research, University of Cincinnati. Retrieved September 6, 2017, from https://www.ncjrs.gov/pdffiles1/ojjdp/grants/241643.pdf

Latimer, J., Dowden, C., & Muise, D. (2005). The effectiveness of restorative justice practices: A meta-analysis. *The Prison Journal, 85*, 127–144.

Latimer, J., Morton-Bourgon, K., & Chrétien, J.-A. (2006). *A meta-analytic examination of drug treatment courts: Do they reduce recidivism?* Ottawa, Ontario, Canada: Research and Statistics Division, Canada Department of Justice. Retrieved September 6, 2017, from http://www.justice.gc.ca/eng/rp-pr/csj-sjc/jsp-sjp/rr06_7/rr06_7.pdf

Lattimore, P. K., & Visher, C. A. (2009). *The multi-site evaluation of SVORI: Summary and synthesis*. (Report No. NJC 230421). National Criminal Justice Reference Service. Retrieved January 20, 2018 from https://www.ncjrs.gov/pdffiles1/nij/grants/230421.pdf

Lattimore, P. K., & Visher, C. A. (2014). The impact of prison reentry services on short-term outcomes: Evidence from a multisite evaluation. *Evaluation Review, 37*, 274–313.

Lattimore, P. K., Visher, C. A., & Steffey, D. M. (2011). Measuring gaps in reentry service delivery through program director and participant reports. *Justice Research and Policy, 13*, 77–100.

Lattimore, P. K., Visher, C. A., Winterfield, L., Lindquist, C., & Brumbaugh, S. (2005). Implementation of prisoner reentry programs; Findings from the Serious and Violent Offender Reentry Initiative multi-site evaluation. *Justice Research and Policy, 7*, 87–109.

Lee, C. G., Cheesman F., Rottman D., Swaner R., Lambson S., Rempel M., & Curtis R. (2013). *A comprehensive evaluation of the Red Hook Community Justice Center.* Williamsburg, VA: National Center for State Courts. Retrieved November 6, 2017, from www.ncsc.org/RH_Exec_Summary

Levisky, J. A., Bowerman, D. L., Jenkins, W. W., Johnson, D. G., Levisky, J. S., & Karch, S. B. (2001). Comparison of urine to sweat patch test results in court ordered testing. *Forensic Science International, 122*(1), 65–68.

Lind, E. A., & Tyler, T. R. (1988). *The social psychology of procedural justice.* New York: Plenum.

Lindquist, C., Ayoub, L. H., Dawes, D., Harrison, P., Malsch, A. M., Walters, J. H., . . . Carey, S. C. (2014). *The national institute of justice's evaluation of second chance act adult reentry courts: Staff and client perspectives on reentry courts from year 2.* National Criminal Justice Reference Service. Retrieved November 4, 2017, from http://www.courtinnovation.org/sites/default/files/documents/NIJ_Second_Chance_Act_Year_2_summary_report_0814.pdf

Lindquist, C., Hardison, J., & Lattimore, P. K. (2003). *Reentry court process evaluation* (Phase 1). Research Triangle Park, NC: Research Triangle Institute. Retrieved November 14, 2017, from https://www.ncjrs.gov/pdffiles1/nij/grants/202472.pdf

Lindquist, C., Hardison, J., & Lattimore, P. K. (2004). The reentry court initiative: Court-based strategies for managing released prisoners. *Justice Research and.Policy, 6*, 97–118.

Lindquist, C., Walters, J., Rempel, M., & Carey, S. (2013). *The National Institute of Justice's evaluation of second chance act adult reentry courts: Program characteristics and preliminary themes from year 1* (Report No. NJC 241400). National Criminal Justice Reference Service. Retrieved November 4, 2017, from https://www.ncjrs.gov/pdffiles1/nij/grants/241400.pdf

Lindsay, W. R., Hamilton, C., Moulton, S., Scott, S., Doyle, M., & McMurran, M. (2011). Assessment and treatment of social problem solving in offenders with intellectual disability. *Psychology, Crime and Law, 17*, 181–197.

Lipsey, M. W. (2009). The primary factors that characterize effective interventions with juvenile offenders: A meta-analytic review. *Victims and Offenders, 4*, 124–147.

Lipsey, M. W., Chapman, G., & Landenberger, N. A. (2001). Cognitive-behavioral programs for offenders. *The Annals of the American Academy of Political and Social Science, 578*, 144–157.

Lipsey, M. W., & Cullen, F. T. (2007). The effectiveness of correctional rehabilitation: A review of systematic reviews. *Annual Review of Law and Social Science, 3*, 297–320.

Lipsey, M. W., Landenberger, N. A., & Wilson, S. J. (2007). Effects of cognitive-behavioral programs for criminal offenders. *Campbell Systematic Reviews, 6*, 1–27.

Listswan, S. J. (2008). Reentry for serious and violent offenders: An analysis of program attrition. *Criminal Justice Policy Review, 20*, 154–169.

Little, G., & Robinson, K. (1986). *How to escape your prison: A moral reconation therapy workbook*. Memphis, TN: Eagle Wing Books.

Liu, S., & Redlich, A. (2015). Intercept 3: Jails and courts. In P. A. Griffin, K. Heilbrun, E. P. Mulvey, D. DeMatteo, & C. A. Schubert (Eds.), *The Sequential Intercept Model and criminal justice: Promoting community alternatives for individuals with serious mental illness* (pp. 78–94). New York: Oxford University Press.

Logan, T. K., Hoyt, W., McCollister, K. E., French, M. T., Leukefeld, C., & Minton, L. (2004). Economic evaluation of drug court: Methodology, results, and policy implications. *Evaluation and Program Planning, 27*, 381–396.

Lowenkamp, C. T, Flores, A., Holsinger, A., Makarios, M., & Latessa, E. (2010). Intensive supervision programs: Does program philosophy and the principles of effective interventions matter? *Journal of Criminal Justice, 38*, 368–375.

Lowenkamp, C. T., Holsinger, A. M., & Latessa, E. J. (2005). Are drug courts effective: A meta-analytic review. *Journal of Community Corrections, 15*, 5–11.

Lowenkamp, C. T., Hubbard, D., Makarios, M. D., & Latessa, E. J. (2009). A quasi-experimental evaluation of thinking for a change: A "real-world" application. *Criminal Justice and Behavior, 36*, 137–146.

Lowenkamp, C. T., & Latessa, E. J. (2002). *Validating the Level of Service Inventory Revised in Ohio's community based correctional facilities*. Division of Criminal Justice, University of Cincinnati. Retrieved July 29, 2017, from https://www.uc.edu/content/dam/uc/ccjr/docs/articles/ticc04_final_complete.pdf.

Lowenkamp, C. T., Latessa, E. J., & Holsinger, A. M. (2006). The risk principle in action: What have we learned from 13,676 offenders and 97 correctional programs? *Crime and Delinquency, 52*, 77–93.

Lowenkamp, C. T., Latessa, E. J., & Smith, P. (2006). Does correctional program quality really matter? The impact of adhering to the principles of effective intervention. *Criminology and Public Policy, 5*, 575–594.

Lurigio, A. J. (2008). The first 20 years of drug treatment courts: A brief description of their history and impact. *Federal Probation, 72*, 13–17.

Luskin, M. L. (2013). More of the same? Treatment in mental health courts. *Law and Human Behavior, 37*, 255–266.

Lynch, S. M., Heath, N. M., Mathews, K. C., & Cepeda, G. J. (2012). Seeking safety: An intervention for trauma-exposed incarcerated women. *Journal of Trauma and Dissociation, 13*, 88–101.

MacDonald, J. M., Morral, A. R., Raymond, B., & Eibner, C. (2007). The efficacy of the Rio Hondo DUI court: A 2-year field experiment. *Evaluation Review, 31*, 4–23.

Mahoney, B., & Carlson, A. (2007). *The Seattle Community Court: Start-up, initial implementation, and recommendations concerning future development.* Denver, CO: The Justice Management Institute. Retrieved November 6, 2017, from www.courtinnovation.org/SeattleCommunityCourt_ExecutiveSummary10_07.pdf

Malkin, V. (2003). Community courts and the process of accountability: Consensus and conflict at the Red Hook Community Justice Center. *The American Criminal Law Review, 40*, 1573–1593.

Marczyk, G., DeMatteo, D., & Festinger, D. (2005). *Essentials of research design and methodology.* Hoboken, NJ: Wiley.

Marlowe, D. B. (2002). Effective strategies for intervening with drug abusing offenders. *Villanova Law Review, 47*, 989–1026.

Marlowe, D. B. (2009). Evidence-based sentencing for drug offenders: An analysis of prognostic risks and criminogenic needs. *Chapman Journal of Criminal Justice, 1*, 167–201.

Marlowe, D. B. (2011). Applying incentives and sanctions. In D. B. Marlowe & W. G. Meyer (Eds.), *The drug court judicial benchbook* (pp. 139–157). Alexandria, VA: National Drug Court Institute.

Marlowe, D. B. (2014). Drug courts. In N. el-Guebaly, G. Carra, & M. Galanter (Eds.), *Textbook of addiction treatment: International perspectives* (pp. 1149–1165). New York: Springer.

Marlowe, D. B., DeMatteo, D. S., & Festinger, D. S. (2003). A sober assessment of drug courts. *Federal Sentencing Reporter, 16*, 153–157.

Marlowe, D. B., Festinger, D. S., Arabia, P. L., Croft, J. R., Patapis, N. S., & Dugosh, K. L. (2009). A systematic review of DWI court program evaluations. *Drug Court Review 1*, 11–57.

Marlowe, D. B., Festinger, D. S., Dugosh, K., & Lee, P. (2005). Are judicial status hearings a "key component" of drug court? Six and twelve months outcomes. *Drug and Alcohol Dependence, 79*, 145–155.

Marlowe, D. B., Festinger, D. S., & Lee, P. A. (2003). The role of judicial status hearings in drug court. *Offender Substance Abuse Report, 3*, 33–46.

Marlowe, D. B., Festinger, D. S., & Lee, P. A. (2004). The judge is a key component of drug court. *Drug Court Review, 4*(2), 1–34.

Marlowe, D. B., Festinger, D. S., Lee, P. A., Dugosh, K. L., & Benasutti, K. M. (2006). Matching judicial supervision to clients' risk status in drug court. *Crime and Delinquency, 52*, 52–76.

Marlowe, D. B., Hardin, C. D., & Fox, C. L. (2016). *Painting the current picture: A national report on drug courts and other problem-solving courts in the United States*. Alexandria, VA: National Drug Court Institute.

Marlowe, D. B., & Meyer, W. G. (Eds.) (2011). *The drug court judicial benchbook*. Alexandria, VA: National Drug Court Institute.

Maron, D. F. (2009, Oct. 6). Drug courts appeal to democrats and republicans. *Newsweek*. Retrieved June 2, 2017, from http://www.newsweek.com/drug-courts-appeal-democrats-and-republicans-81225.

Marquant, T., Sabbe, B., Van Nuffel, M., & Goethals, K. (2016). Forensic assertive community treatment: A review of the literature. *Community Mental Health Journal, 52*, 873–881.

Martin, S. S., Butzin, C. A., Saum, S. A., & Inciardi, J. A. (1999). Three-year outcomes of therapeutic community treatment for drug-involved offenders in Delaware. *Prison Journal, 79*, 294–320.

Maruna, S., & LeBel, T. (2003). Welcome home? Examining the reentry court concept from a strengths-based perspective. *Western Criminology Review, 4*, 91–107.

McCoy, C. (2003). The politics of problem-solving: An overview of the origins and development of therapeutic courts. *American Criminal Law Review, 40*, 1513–1534.

McCuan, R., Prins, S., & Wasarhaley, N. (2007). Resources and challenges: Corrections and mental health collaborations. *Corrections Today, 69*, 18–19.

McGrath, E. (2012). Reentry courts: Providing a second change for incarcerated mothers and their children. *Family Court Review, 50*, 113–127.

McGuire, J. (2005). Social problem solving: Basic concepts, research, and applications. In M. McMurran & J. McGuire (Eds.), *Social problem solving and offenders: Evidence, evaluation and evolution* (pp. 3–30). Chichester, UK: Wiley.

McGuire, J., Bilby, C. A. L., Hatcher, R. M., Hollin, C. R., Hounsome, J., & Palmer, E. J. (2008). Evaluation of structured cognitive–behavioural treatment programmes in reducing criminal recidivism. *Journal of Experimental Criminology, 4*, 21–40.

McGuire J., Clark S., Blue-Howells, J., & Coe, C. (2013). *An inventory of VA involvement in veterans courts, dockets and tracks* (VA Veterans Justice Programs white paper). Alexandria, VA: Justice for Vets. Retrieved November 6, 2017, from http://www.justiceforvets.org/sites/default/files/files/An%20Inventory%20of%20VA%20involvement%20in%20Veterans%20Courts.pdf

McGuire, M., & Hatcher, R. (2001). Offence-focused problem solving: Preliminary evaluation of a cognitive skills program. *Criminal Justice and Behavior, 28*, 564–587.

McKim, W. A., & Hancock, S. D. (2013). *Drugs and behavior: An introduction to behavioral pharmacology* (7th ed.). New York: Pearson Prentice Hall.

McLellan, A. T., Luborsky, L., Woody, G. E., & O'Brien, C. P. (1980). An improved diagnostic evaluation instrument for substance abuse patients: The Addiction Severity Index. *Journal of Nervous and Mental Disease, 168*, 26–33.

McMullin, R. E. (2000). *The new handbook of cognitive therapy techniques*. New York: W. W. Norton.

McMurran, M., Egan, V., Blair, M., & Richardson, C. (2001). The relationship between social problem solving and personality in mentally disordered offenders. *Personality and Individual Differences, 30*, 517–524.

McMurran, M., Fyffe, S., McCarthy, L., Duggan, C., & Latham, A. (2001). "Stop & think!" Social problem solving therapy with personality-disordered offenders. *Criminal Behaviour and Mental Health, 11*, 273–285.

McMurran, M., Egan, V., & Duggan, C. (2005). Stop & think! Social problem-solving therapy with personality-disordered offenders. In M. McMurran & J. McGuire (Eds.), *Social problem solving and offending: Evidence, evaluation and evolution* (pp. 207–220). Chichester, UK: Wiley.

McMurran, M., Huband, N., & Duggan, C. (2008). A comparison of treatment completers and non-completers of an in-patient treatment programme for male personality-disordered offenders. *Psychology and Psychotherapy: Theory, Research and Practice, 81*, 193–198.

McNiel, D. E., & Binder, R. L. (2007). Effectiveness of a mental health court in reducing criminal recidivism and violence. *The American Journal of Psychiatry, 164*, 1395–1403.

McNeil, D. E., Binder, R. L., & Robinson, J. C. (2005). Incarceration associated with homelessness, mental disorder, and co-occurring substance abuse. *Psychiatric Services, 56*, 840–846.

Meares, T. L., & Fagan, J. (2008). Punishment, deterrence and social control: The paradox of punishment in minority communities. *Faculty Scholarship Series, 527*. Retrieved November 7, 2017, from http://digitalcommons.law.yale.edu/fss_papers/527

Meekins, T. (2006). Specialized justice: The over-emergence of specialty courts and the threat of a new criminal defense paradigm. *Suffolk University Law Review, 1*, 22–28.

Meekins, T. (2007). Risky business: Criminal specialty courts and ethical obligations of the zealous criminal defender. *Berkeley Journal of Criminal Law, 12*(1), 75–126.

Meierhofer, B., & Breen, P. D. (2013). *Process-descriptive study of judge-involved supervision programs in the federal system*. Washington, DC: Federal Judicial Center.

Meierhofer, B. S. (2011). Judge-involved supervision programs in the federal courts: Summary findings from the survey of chief United States probation officers. *Federal Probation, 75*, 37–46.

Messina, N., Burdon, W., Hagopian, G., & Prendergast, M. (2006). Predictors of prison-based treatment outcomes: A comparison of men and women participants. *The American Journal of Drug and Alcohol Abuse, 32*, 7–28.

Messina, N., Calhoun, S., & Warda, U. (2012). Gender-responsive drug court treatment: A randomized controlled trial. *Criminal Justice and Behavior, 39*, 1539–1558.

Meyer, W. G. (2011). Constitutional and legal issues in drug courts. In D. B. Marlowe & W. G. Meyer (Eds.), *The drug court judicial benchbook* (pp. 160–180). Alexandria, VA: National Drug Court Institute.

Meyer, W. G., & Tauber, J. (2011). The roles of the drug court judge. In D. B. Marlowe & W. G. Meyer (Eds.), *The drug court judicial benchbook* (pp. 45–61). Alexandria, VA: National Drug Court Institute.

Michigan Supreme Court State Court Administrative Office. (2008). *Michigan DUI courts outcome evaluation: Final report*. Retrieved on May 16, 2019, from https://council.legislature.mi.gov/Content/Files/sdtcac/mi_dui_outcome_eval_final_report_0308.pdf.

Milkman, H., & Wanberg, K. (2007). *Cognitive-behavioral treatment: A review and discussion for corrections professionals* (NIC# 021657). Washington, DC: US Department of Justice.

Miller, E. J. (2006). Role-based policing: Restraining police conduct "outside the legitimate investigative sphere." *California Law Review, 94*, 617–686.

Miller, E. J. (2007). The therapeutic effects of managerial reentry courts. *Federal Sentencing Reporter, 20*, 127–135.

Miller, H. A. (2006). A dynamic assessment of offender risk, needs, and strengths in a sample of pre-release general offenders. *Behavioral Sciences and the Law, 24*, 767–782.

Miller, J. M., & Khey, D. N. (2016). An implementation and process evaluation of the Louisiana 22nd judicial district's behavioral health court. *American Journal of Criminal Justice, 41*, 124–135.

Miller, L. A. (2008). *Trends in substance abuse intervention: The principles of self-authorship.* Paper presented at Stetson Law Conference. Retrieved November 6, 2017, from http://www.stetson.edu/law/conferences/highered/archive/2008/Trends_in_Substance_Abuse_Prevention.pdf

Miller, P. G., Curtis, A., Sonderlund, A., Day, A., & Droste, N. (2015). Effectiveness of interventions for convicted DUI offenders in reducing recidivism: A systematic review of the peer-reviewed scientific literature. *American Journal of Drug and Alcohol Abuse, 41*, 16–29.

Miller, R. B., & Hollist, C. S. (2007). Attrition bias. In N. Salkind (Ed.), *Encyclopedia of measurement and statistics* (pp. 57–60). Thousand Oaks, CA: Sage.

Mirchandani, R. (2008). Beyond therapy: Problem-solving courts and the deliberative democratic state. *Law and Social Inquiry, 33*, 853–893.

Mitchell, O., Wilson, D. B., Eggers, A., & MacKenzie, D. L. (2012). Assessing the effectiveness of drug courts on recidivism: A meta-analytic review of traditional and non-traditional drug courts. *Journal of Criminal Justice, 40*, 60–71.

Mitchell, O., Wilson, D. B., & MacKenzie, D. L. (2012). The effectiveness of incarceration-based drug treatment on criminal behavior: A systematic review. *Campbell Systematic Reviews, 18*, 1–75.

Monahan, J., Steadman, H. J., Silver, E., Appelbaum, P. S., Robbins, P. C., Mulvey, E. P., . . . Banks, S. (2001). *Rethinking risk assessment: The MacArthur study of mental disorder and violence.* New York: Oxford University Press.

Monchick, R., & Gehring, D. (2006, February). *Back on TRAC: Treatment, responsibility, and accountability on campus.* Paper presented at the 27th Annual National Conference on Law and Higher Education, Stetson University College of Law, Clearwater Beach, FL. Retrieved December 9, 2017, from http://www.stetson.edu/law/conferences/highered/archive/2006/BackonTRAC2.pdf

Moore, M., & Hiday, V. (2006). Mental health court outcomes: A comparison of re-arrest and re-arrest severity between mental health and traditional court participants. *Law and Human Behavior, 30*, 659–674.

Morgan, R. D., Fisher, W. H., Duan, N., Mandracchia, J. T., & Murray, D. (2010). Prevalence of criminal thinking among state prison inmates with serious mental illness. *Law and Human Behavior, 34*, 324–336.

Morrissey, J., Meyer, P., & Cuddeback, G. (2007). Extending assertive community treatment to criminal justice settings: Origins, current evidence, and future directions. *Community Mental Health Journal, 43*, 527–544.

Mulder, E., Brand, E., Bullens, R., & van Marle, H. (2011). Risk factors for overall recidivism and severity of recidivism in serious juvenile offenders. *International Journal of Offender Therapy and Comparative Criminology, 55*, 118–135.

Mumola, C. J., & Karberg, J. C. (2006). *Drug use and dependence, state and federal prisoners, 2004.* Washington, DC: US Department of Justice, Office of Justice Programs, Bureau of Justice Statistics.

Munetz, M., & Griffin, P. (2006). Use of the Sequential Intercept Model as an approach to decriminalization of people with serious mental illness. *Psychiatric Services, 57*, 544–549.

Munetz, M. R., Ritter, C., Teller, J. L. S., & Bonfine, N. (2014). Mental health court and assisted outpatient treatment: Perceived coercion, procedural justice, and program impact. *Psychiatric Services, 65*, 352–358.

Najavits, L. M. (n.d.). *Implementing seeking safety therapy for PTSD and substance abuse: Clinical guidelines*. Retrieved July 29, 2017, from http://www.bhrm.org/media/pdf/guidelines/PTSD.pdf

National Association of Drug Court Professionals. (1997). *Defining drug courts: The key components*. Washington, DC: US Department of Justice, Office of Justice Programs, Bureau of Justice Statistics. Retrieved April 15, 2018, from https://www.ncjrs.gov/pdffiles1/bja/205621.pdf

National Association of Drug Court Professionals. (2013). *Adult drug court best practice standards: Volume I*. Alexandria, VA: Author. Retrieved September 6, 2017, from http://www.allrise.org/sites/default/files/nadcp/AdultDrugCourtBestPracticeStandards.pdf

National Association of Drug Court Professionals. (2015). *Adult drug court best practice standards: Volume II*. Alexandria, VA: Author. Retrieved September 6, 2017, from http://www.nadcp.org/sites/default/files/2014/Best%20Practice%20Standards%20Vol.%20II._0.pdf

National Association of Drug Court Professionals. (2018a). *Adult drug court best practice standards: Volume I – Text revision*. Alexandria, VA: Author. Retrieved May 17, 2019, from https://www.nadcp.org/wp-content/uploads/2018/12/Adult-Drug-Court-Best-Practice-Standards-Volume-I-Text-Revision-December-2018-1.pdf

National Association of Drug Court Professionals. (2018b). *Adult drug court best practice standards: Volume II – Text revision*. Alexandria, VA: Author. Retrieved May 17, 2019, from https://www.nadcp.org/wp-content/uploads/2018/12/Adult-Drug-Court-Best-Practice-Standards-Volume-2-Text-Revision-December-2018-1.pdf

National Association of Drug Court Professionals. (2018c). *Treatment courts are justice reform*. Retrieved April 15, 2018 from http://www.nadcp.org/

National Center on Addiction & Substance Abuse. (2010). *Behind bars II: Substance abuse and America's prison population*. New York: Author.

National Drug Court Institute. (2001). *Ethical considerations for judges and attorneys in drug court*. Retrieved May 19, 2018, from https://www.ndci.org/wp-content/uploads/ethicalconsiderations.pdf

National Drug Court Institute. (2003). *Critical issues for defense attorneys in drug court*. Retrieved May 19, 2018, from http://www.ndci.org/sites/default/files/ndci/Mono4.CriticalIssues.pdf

National Drug Court Institute. (2007). *Timeline of drug courts and other problem solving courts in the United States*. Retrieved January 15, 2018, from http://www.nadcp.org/sites/default/files/nadcp/Timeline.pdf

National Drug Court Institute. (2013). *Critical issues for defense attorneys in drug court: Monograph series 4*. Washington, DC: Department of Justice, Bureau of Justice Assistance.

National Drug Court Institute & National Council of Juvenile and Family Court Judges. (2003). *Juvenile drug courts: Strategies in practice*. Washington, DC: Bureau of Justice Assistance, US Department of Justice. Retrieved September 6, 2017, from https://www.ncjrs.gov/pdffiles1/bja/197866.pdf

National Drug Court Resource Center. (2014). Problem solving courts today. Retrieved April 2, 2017, from http://www.ndcrc.org/content/how-many-problem-solving-courts-are-there.

National GAINS Center. (2002). *The Nathaniel Project: An alternative to incarceration program for people with serious mental illness who have committed felony offenses*. Delmar, NY: Author.

National Institute of Justice. (2000). *1999 annual report on drug use among adult and juvenile arrestees*. Retrieved from https://www.ncjrs.gov/pdffiles1/nij/181426.pdf

National Institute of Justice. (2015). *Number and types of drug courts*. Retrieved September 6, 2017, from https://www.nij.gov/topics/courts/drug-courts/Pages/welcome.aspx

National Legal Aid and Defender Association. (2001). *Performance guidelines for criminal defense representation*. Retrieved May 19, 2018, from http://www.nlada.org/defender-standards/performance-guidelines

National Reentry Resource Center. (2018). *NRRC facts and trends*. Retrieved January 20, 2018, from https://csgjusticecenter.org/nrrc/facts-and-trends/

Nezu, C. M., D'Zurilla, T. J., & Nezu, A. M. (2005). Problem solving therapy: Theory, practice, and application to sex offenders. In M. McMurran & J. McGuire (Eds.), *Social problem solving and offenders: Evidence, evaluation and evolution* (pp. 103–123). Chichester, UK: Wiley.

Nolan, J. L., Jr. (2003). Redefining criminal courts: Problem-solving and the meaning of justice. *American Criminal Law Review*, *40*, 1541–1563.

Norton, L., Johnson, J., & Woods, G. (2016). Burnout and compassion fatigue: What lawyers need to know. *University of Missouri at Kansas City Law Review*, *84*, 987–1002.

NPC Research. (2014). *Minnesota DWI courts: A summary of evaluation findings in nine DWI court programs*. Portland, OR: Author. Retrieved January 15, 2018, from https://dps.mn.gov/divisions/ots/reports-statistics/Documents/mn-dwi-summary.pdf

Nugent-Borakove, M. E. (2009). *Seattle Municipal Community Court: Outcome evaluation* (final report). Denver, CO: Justice Management Institute. Retrieved November 6, 2017, from https://www.seattle.gov/communitycourt/docs/JMI_study_10-09-09.pdf

Odegaard, A. M. (2007). Therapeutic jurisprudence: The impact of mental health courts on the criminal justice system. *North Dakota Law Review*, *83*, 225–259.

Office of National Drug Control Policy. (2010). *Veterans treatment courts*. Retrieved June 2, 2017, from https://obamawhitehouse.archives.gov/sites/default/files/ondcp/Fact_Sheets/veterans_treatment_courts_fact_sheet_12-13-10.pdf

Office of National Drug Control Policy. (2011). *Drug courts: A smart approach to criminal justice*. Retrieved June 2, 2017, from https://obamawhitehouse.archives.gov/sites/default/files/ondcp/Fact_Sheets/drug_courts_fact_sheet_5-31-11.pdf

Office of National Drug Control Policy. (2012). *2011 annual report: Arrestee drug abuse monitoring program II*. Washington, DC. Author.

Ogloff, J. R., & Davis, M. R. (2004). Advances in offender assessment and rehabilitation: Contributions of the risk-need-responsivity approach. *Psychology, Crime, and Law*, *10*, 229–242.

O'Keefe, C., Potenza, D. P., & Mueser, K. T. (1997). Treatment outcomes for severely mentally ill patients on conditional discharge to community-based treatment. *Journal of Nervous and Mental Disease*, *185*, 409–411.

O'Keefe, K. (2006). *The Brooklyn mental health court evaluation: Planning, implementation, courtroom dynamics, and participant outcomes*. New York: Center for Court Innovation.

Olson, D. A., & Lurigio, A. J. (2014). The long-term effects of prison-based drug treatment and aftercare services on recidivism. *Journal of Offender Rehabilitation*, *53*, 600–619.

Olver, M. E., Stockdale, K. C., & Wormith, J. S. (2011). A meta-analysis of predictors of offender treatment attrition and its relationship to recidivism. *Journal of Consulting and Clinical Psychology, 79*, 6–21.

Ong, G., Al-Attar, Z., Roberts, C., & Harsent, L. (2003). *Think First: An accredited community- based cognitive-behavioural programme in England and Wales. Findings from the prospective evaluation in three Probation Areas*. Oxford, UK: Probation Studies Unit, Centre for Criminological Research, University of Oxford. Retrieved July 29, 2017, from http://worldcat.org/identities/lccn-nr99015400/

Orr, C. H., Hall, J. W., Reimer, N. L., Mallett, E. A., O'Down, K., & Frazer, A. C. (2009). *America's problem-solving courts: The criminal costs of treatment and the case for reform*. Washington, DC: National Association of Criminal Defense Lawyers.

Ostrom, B. J. (2003). Domestic violence courts: Editorial introduction. *Criminology and Public Policy, 3*, 105–108.

Overall, J. E., & Gorham, D. R. (1962). The Brief Psychiatric Rating Scale. *Psychological Reports, 10*, 799–812.

Palermo, G. B. (2010). The Nevada mental health courts. *International Journal of Law and Psychiatry, 33*, 214–219.

Palmer, E. J., McGuire, J., Hatcher, R. M., Hounsome, J. C., Bilby, C. A. L., & Hollin, C. R. (2008). The importance of appropriate allocation to offending behavior programs. *International Journal of Offender Therapy and Comparative Criminology, 52*, 206–221.

Palmer, E. J., McGuire, J., Hatcher, R. M., Hounsome, J. C., Bilby, C. A. L., & Hollin, C. R. (2009). Allocation to offending behavior programs in the English and Welsh Probation Service. *Criminal Justice and Behavior, 36*, 909–922.

Pearson, F. S., Lipton, D. S., Cleland, C. M., & Yee, D. S. (2002). The effects of behavioural/cognitive–behavioural programmes on recidivism. *Crime and Delinquency, 48*, 476–496.

Perez, D. (2009). Applying evidence-based practices to community corrections supervision: An evaluation of residential substance abuse treatment for high-risk probationers. *Journal of Contemporary Criminal Justice, 25*, 442–458.

Peterson, J. K., Skeem, J., Kennealy, P., Bray, B., & Zvonkovic, A. (2014). How often and how consistently do symptoms directly precede criminal behavior among offenders with mental illness? *Law and Human Behavior, 38*, 439–449.

Petrila, J. (2005). Civil commitment: A therapeutic jurisprudence model. *Psychiatric Services, 58*, 572–573.

Petrila, J., & Fader-Towe, H. (2010). *Information sharing in criminal justice-mental health collaborations: Working with HIPAA and other privacy laws*. New York: Bureau of Justice Assistance Council of State Governments Justice Center.

Petrila, J., Poythress, N. G., McGaha, A., & Boothroyd, R. A. (2001). Preliminary observations from an evaluation of the Broward County mental health court. *Court Review, 37*, 14–22.

Petrosino, A., Turpin-Petrosino, C., & Finckenauer, J. O. (2000). Well-meaning programs can have harmful effects! Lessons from experiments of programs such as Scared Straight. *Crime and Delinquency, 46*, 354–379.

Petrosino, A., Turpin-Petrosino, C., Hollis-Peel, M. E., & Lavenberg, J. G. (2013). Scared Straight and other juvenile awareness programs for preventing juvenile delinquency: A systematic review. *Campbell Systematic Reviews, 5*, 1–55.

Petrucci, C. J. (2010). A descriptive study of a California domestic violence court: Program completion and recidivism. *Victims and Offenders, 5*, 130–160.

Pinard, M. (2006). An integrated perspective on the collateral consequences of criminal convictions and reentry issues faced by formerly incarcerated individuals. *Boston University Law Review, 86*, 623–690.

Pinard, M. (2010). Reflections and perspectives on reentry and collateral consequences. *Journal of Criminal Law and Criminology, 100*, 1213–1224.

Podgers, J. (2008). *ABA ethics opinion cautions judges of potential pitfalls in fundraising for problem-solving courts.* Retrieved June 24, 2018, from http://www.abajournal.com/magazine/article/aba_opinion_cautions_judges_to_avoid_ethics_pitfalls_of_social_media

Policy Research Associates, Inc. (2016). The Sequential Intercept Model. Retrieved June 1, 2017, from https://www.prainc.com/curesact-sim/.

Porporino, F. J., Fabiano, E. A., & Robinson, D. (1991). *Focusing on successful reintegration: Cognitive skills training for offenders* (Report No. R-19). Retrieved July 29, 2017, from http://publications.gc.ca/site/eng/9.568196/publication.html

Porter, R., Rempel, M., & Mansky, A. (2010). *What makes a court problem-solving?* Retrieved June 2, 2017, from http://www.courtinnovation.org/sites/default/files/What_Makes_A_Court_P_S.pdf

Poulin, F., Dishion, T. J., & Burraston, B. (2001). 3-year iatrogenic effects associated with aggregating high-risk adolescents in cognitive-behavioral preventive interventions. *Applied Developmental Science, 5*, 214–224.

Poythress, N. G., Petrila, J., McGaha, A., & Boothroyd, R. A. (2002). Perceived coercion and procedural justice in the Broward mental health court. *International Journal of Law and Psychiatry, 25*, 517–533.

Prendergast, M. L., Pearson, F. S., Podus, D., Hamilton, Z. K., & Greenwell, L. (2013). The Andrews' principles of risk, needs, and responsivity as applied in drug treatment programs: Meta-analysis of crime and drug use outcomes. *Journal of Experimental Criminology, 9*, 275–300.

Prins, S. J., Skeem, J. L., Mauro, C., & Link, B. G. (2015). Criminogenic factors, psychotic symptoms, and incident arrests among people with serious mental illnesses under intensive outpatient treatment. *Law and Human Behavior, 39*, 177–188.

Puzzanchera, C. (2013). Juvenile arrests 2011. Juvenile offenders and victims: National Report Series Bulletin. Retrieved September 6, 2017, from http://www.ojjdp.gov/pubs/244476.pdf

Quinn, M. (2000/2001). Whose team am I on anyway? Musings of a public defender about drug treatment court practice. *New York University Review of Law and Social Change, 26*(1-2), 37–75.

Raine, V. (2012, February). *Constitutional issues and problem solving courts in an instant.* Presented at the Community Justice Conference 2012, Washington, DC.

Ray, B., & Dollar, C. B. (2014). Exploring stigmatization and stigma management in mental health court: Assessing modified labeling theory in a new context. *Sociological Forum, 29*, 327–352.

Redlich, A. D. (2005). Voluntary, but knowing and intelligent? Comprehension in mental health courts. *Psychology, Public Policy, and Law, 11*, 605–619.

Redlich, A. D., & Han, W. (2014). Examining the links between therapeutic jurisprudence and mental health court completion. *Law and Human Behavior, 38*, 109–118.

Redlich, A. D., Hoover, S., Summers, A., & Steadman, H. J. (2010). Enrollment in mental health courts: Voluntariness, knowingness, and adjudicative competence. *Law and Human Behavior, 34*, 91–104.

Redlich, A., Liu, S., Steadman, H., Callahan, L., & Robbins, P. C. (2012). Is diversion swift? Comparing mental health court and traditional criminal justice processing. *Criminal Justice and Behavior, 39*, 420–433.

Redlich, A. D., Steadman, H. J., Monahan, J., Petrila, J., & Griffin, P. A. (2005). The second generation of mental health courts. *Psychology, Public Policy and Law, 11*, 527–538.

Redlich, A. D., Steadman, H. J., Monahan, J., Robbins, P. C., & Petrila, J. (2006). Patterns of practice in mental health courts: A national survey. *Law and Human Behavior, 30*, 347–362.

Reich, W. A., Picard-Fritsche, S., Cerniglia, L., & Hahn, J. W. (2014). *Predictors of program compliance and re-arrest in the Brooklyn mental health court.* New York: Center for Court Innovation.

Reif, S., Braude, L., Lyman, D. R., Dougherty, R. H., Daniels, A. S., Ghose, S. S., . . . Delphin-Rittmon, M. E. (2014). Peer recovery support for individuals with substance use disorders: Assessing the evidence. *Psychiatric Services, 65*, 853–861.

Rempel, M., Green, M., & Kralstein, D. (2012). The impact of adult drug courts on crime and incarceration: Findings from a multi-site quasi-experimental design. *Journal of Experimental Criminology, 8*, 165–192.

Reno, J. (2000). *Remarks of the Honorable Janet Reno, attorney general of the United States, on the Reentry Court Initiative at John Jay College of Criminal Justice.* Retrieved November 7, 2017, from https://www.justice.gov/archive/ag/speeches/2000/doc2.htm

Reuland, M. (2004). *A guide to implementing police-based diversion programs for people with mental illness.* Delmar, NY: Technical Assistance and Policy Analysis Center for Jail Diversion.

Reuland, M., Draper, L., & Norton, B. (2012). *Statewide law enforcement/mental health efforts: Strategies to support and sustain local initiatives.* New York: Council of State Governments Justice Center.

Reuland, M., Schwarzfeld, M., & Draper, L. (2009). *Law enforcement responses to people with mental illnesses: A guide to research-informed policy and practice.* New York: Council of State Governments Justice Center.

Reuland, M., & Yasuhara, K. (2015). Law enforcement and emergency services. In G. A. Griffin, K. Heilbrun, E. P. Mulvey, D. DeMatteo, & C. A. Schubert (Eds.), *The sequential intercept model and criminal justice* (pp. 40–56). New York: Oxford University Press.

Rhodes, W., Dyous, C., Kling, R., Hunt, D., & Luallen, J. (2012). Recidivism of offenders on federal community supervision. *Abt Associates, December, 21*, 110–126.

Ridgely, S., Engberg, J., Greenberg, M., Turner, S., DeMartini, C., & Dembosky, J. (2007). *Justice, treatment, and cost: An evaluation of the fiscal impact of the Allegheny County Mental Health Court.* Retrieved June 11, 2017, from http://www.rand.org/content/dam/rand/pubs/technical_reports/2007/RAND_TR439.pdf

Riger, S., Bennett, L. W., & Sigurvinsdottir, R. (2014). Barriers to addressing substance abuse in domestic violence court. *American Journal of Community Psychology, 53*, 208–217.

Robinson, D. (1995). *The impact of cognitive skills training on post-release recidivism among Canadian federal offenders* (Report No. R-41). Retrieved July 29, 2017, from http://publications.gc.ca/site/eng/379318/publication.html

Rochefort, D. A. (1984). Origins of the "third psychiatric revolution": The Community Mental Health Centers Act of 1963. *Journal of Health Politics, Policy and Law, 9*, 1–30.

Ronan, S. M., Collins, P. A., & Rosky, J. W. (2009). The effectiveness of Idaho DUI and misdemeanor/DUI courts: Outcome evaluation. *Journal of Offender Rehabilitation, 48*, 154–165.

Ropero-Miller, J. D., Stout, P. R., RTI International, & United States of America. (2009). Analysis of cocaine analytes in human hair: Evaluation of concentration ratios in different hair types, cocaine sources, drug-user populations, and surface-contaminated specimens. *NIJ Final Report Document* (22553).

Rosenbaum, P. R., & Rubin, D. B. (1983). The central role of the propensity score in observational studies for causal effects. *Biometrika, 70*, 41–55.

Rosich, K. J. (2007). *Race, ethnicity, and the criminal justice system*. Washington, DC: American Sociological Association.

Roskes, E. (1999). Offenders with mental disorders: A call to action. *Psychiatric Services, 50*, 1596.

Ross, R. R., Fabiano, E. A., & Ewles, C. D. (1988). Reasoning and rehabilitation. *International Journal of Offender Therapy and Comparative Criminology, 32*, 29–35.

Ross, R. R., Fabiano, E. A., & Ross, R. D. (1986). *Reasoning and rehabilitation: A handbook for teaching cognitive skills*. Ottawa, Ontario, Canada: T3 Associates.

Rossman, S. B., Rempel, M., Roman, J. K., Zweig, J. M., Lindquist, C. H., Green, M., . . . Farole, D. J., Jr. (2011). *The Multi-Site Adult Drug Court Evaluation: Vol. 4. The impact of drug courts*. Washington, DC: Urban Institute Justice Policy Center. Retrieved June 6, 2017, from https://www.ncjrs.gov/pdffiles1/nij/grants/237112.pdf

Rossman, S., Roman, J. K., & Zweig, J. (2011). *The multisite adult drug court evaluation: The impact of drug courts*. Retrieved June 6, 2017, from https://jpo.wrlc.org/bitstream/handle/11204/2050/3477.pdf? sequence=1

Rotter, M., & Barber-Rioja, V. (2015). Diversion programs and alternatives to incarceration. In R. L. Trestman, K. L. Appelbaum, & J. L. Metzner (Eds.), *Oxford textbook of correctional psychiatry* (pp. 107–111). New York: Oxford University Press.

Rottman, D., & Casey, P. (1999, July). *Therapeutic jurisprudence and the emergence of problem-solving courts*. Retrieved May 16, 2019, from https://www.academia.edu/5973770/Therapeutic_Jurisprudence_and_the_Emergence_of_Problem-Solving_Courts

Rowland, M. G. (2016, December). Assessing the case for the formal recognition and expansion of federal problem-solving courts. *Federal Probation, 80*(3), 2–14.

Rubin, A. (2008). *Practitioner's guide to using research for evidence-based practice*. Hoboken, NJ: Wiley.

Russell, R. T. (2009). Veteran treatment court: A proactive approach. *New England Journal of Crime and Civil Confinement, 35*, 357–372.

Sabol, W. J., & Minton, T. D. (2008). *Jail inmates at midyear 2007*. Washington, DC: Bureau of Justice Statistics, United States Department of Justice.

Sacks, S., McKendrick, K., Sacks, J. Y., & Cleland, C. M. (2010). Modified therapeutic community for co-occurring disorders: Single investigator meta-analysis. *Substance Abuse, 31*, 146–161.

Sacks, S., Sacks, J. Y., McKendrick, K., Banks, S., & Stommel, J. (2004). Modified TC for MICA offenders: Crime outcomes. *Behavioral Sciences and the Law, 22*, 477–501.

SAMHSA's GAIN Center. (2013). *Developing a comprehensive plan for behavioral health and criminal justice collaboration: The Sequential Intercept Model* (3rd ed.). Delmar, NY: Policy Research Associates.

Sarteschi, C. M., Vaughn, M. G., & Kim, K. (2011). Assessing the effectiveness of mental health courts: A quantitative review. *Journal of Criminal Justice, 39*, 12–20.

Second Chance Act of 2007. Pub. L. 110-199, 122 Stat. 657 (2008).

Severson, M. E., Bruns, K., Veeh, C., & Lee, J. (2011). Prisoner reentry programming: Who recidivates and when? *Journal of Offender Rehabilitation, 50*, 327–348.

Severson, M. E., Veeh, C., Bruns, K., & Lee, J. (2012). Who goes back to prison; Who does not: A multiyear review of reentry program participants. *Journal of Offender Rehabilitation, 51*, 295–315.

Sevigny, E. L., Fuleihan, B. K., & Ferdik, F. V. (2013). Do drug courts reduce the use of incarceration?: A meta-analysis. *Journal of Criminal Justice, 41*, 416–425.

Shafer, M., Arthur, B., & Franczak, M. (2004). An analysis of post-booking jail diversion programming for persons with co-occurring disorders. *Behavioral Sciences and the Law, 22*, 771–785.

Shaffer, D. K. (2011). Looking inside the black box of drug courts: A meta-analytic review. *Justice Quarterly, 28*, 493–521.

Shaffer, H. J., Nelson, S. E., LaPlante, D. A., LaBrie, R. A., Albanese, M., & Caro, G. (2007). The epidemiology of psychiatric disorders among repeat DUI offenders accepting a treatment-sentencing option. *Journal of Consulting and Clinical Psychology, 75*, 795–804.

Shern, D. L., Wilson, N. Z., Coen, A. S., Patrick, D. C., Foster, M., Bartsch, D. A., & Demmler, J. (1994). Client outcomes II: Longitudinal client data from the Colorado Treatment Outcome Study. *The Milbank Quarterly, 72*, 123–148.

Simon, W. H. (2000). *The practice of justice: A theory of lawyers' ethics*. Cambridge, MA: Harvard University Press.

Skeem, J., & Bibeau, L. (2008). How does violence potential relate to crisis intervention team responses to emergencies? *Psychiatric Services, 59*, 201–204.

Skeem, J., & Eno Louden, J. (2006). Toward evidence-based practice for probationers and parolees mandated to mental health treatment. *Psychiatric Services, 57*, 333–342.

Skeem, J. L., Manchak, S., & Peterson, J. K. (2011). Correctional policy for offenders with mental illness: Creating a new paradigm for recidivism reduction. *Law and Human Behavior, 35*, 110–126.

Skeem, J., & Monahan, J. (2011). Current directions in violence risk assessment. *Current Directions in Psychological Science, 20*, 38–42.

Skeem, J. L., Steadman, H. J., & Manchak, S. M. (2015). Applicability of the Risk-Needs-Responsivity Model to persons with mental illness involved in the criminal justice system. *Psychiatric Services, 66*, 916–922.

Skeem, J. L., Winter, E., Kennealy, P. J., Louden, J. E., & Tatar, J. R. (2014). Offenders with mental illness have criminogenic needs, too: Toward recidivism reduction. *Law and Human Behavior, 38*, 212–224.

Slattery M., Dugger M. T., Lamb T. A., & Williams L. (2013). Catch, treat, and release: Veteran treatment courts address the challenges of returning home. *Substance Use and Misuse, 48*, 922–932.

Sloan, F. A., Chepke, L. M., Davis, D. V., Acquah, K., & Zold-Kilbourn, P. (2013). Effects of admission and treatment strategies of DWI courts on offender outcomes. *Accident Analysis and Prevention, 53*, 112–120.

Smee, D. E., McGuire, J., Garrick, T., Sreenivasan, S., Dow, D., & Woehl, D. (2013). Critical concerns in Iraq/Afghanistan war veteran-forensic interface: Veterans treatment court as diversion in rural communities. *Journal of the American Academy of Psychiatry and the Law, 41*, 256–262.

Smith, A. (2003). The difference in criminal defense and the difference it makes. *Washington University Journal of Law and Policy, 11*, 83–138.

Snedeker, K. A., Beach, L. R., & Corcoran, K. E. (2017). Beyond the "revolving door?": Incentives and criminal recidivism in a mental health court. *Criminal Justice and Behavior, 44*, 1141–1162.

Sneed, Z., Koch, D. S., Estes, H., & Quinn, J. (2006). Employment and psychosocial outcomes for offenders with mental illness. *The International Journal of Psychosocial Rehabilitation, 10*, 103–112.

Soderstrom, I. R. (2007). Mental illness in offender populations: Prevalence, duty and implications. *Journal of Offender Rehabilitation, 45*, 1–17.

Solop, F. I., Wonders, N. A., Hagen, K. K., McCarrier, K., Ross, K., Thompson, I., . . . Rector, P. (2003). *Coconino County DUI/Drug Court evaluation*. Flagstaff, AZ: Northern Arizona University, Social Research Laboratory. Retrieved November 6, 2017, from https://pdfs.semanticscholar.org/c85f/f5c84649d3db156c4e0f3d7d0e0dad992507.pdf

Spelman, J. (2003). An initial comparison of graduates and terminated clients in America's largest re-entry court. *Corrections Today, 65*, 74–77, 83.

Spinak, J. M. (2003). Why defenders feel defensive: The defender's role in problem-solving courts. *American Criminal Law Review, 40*, 1617.

Spivack, G., Platt, J. J., & Shure, M. B. (1976). *The problem solving approach to adjustment*. San Francisco, CA: Jossey-Bass.

Stansfield, R., Mowen, T. J., O'Connor, T., & Boman, J. H. (2017). The role of religious support in reentry: Evidence from the SVORI data. *Journal of Research in Crime and Delinquency, 54*, 111–145.

Steadman, H. J., Davidson, S., & Brown, C. (2001). Mental health courts: Their promise and unanswered questions. *Psychiatric Services, 52*, 457–458.

Steadman, H. J., Deane, M., Borum, R., & Morrissey, J. (2000). Comparing outcomes of major models of police responses to mental health emergencies. *Psychiatric Services, 51*, 645–649.

Steadman, H. J., Mulvey, E. P., Monahan, J., Robbins, P. C., Appelbaum, P. S., Grisso, T., . . . Silver, E. (1998). Violence by people discharged from acute psychiatric inpatient facilities and by others in the same neighborhoods. *Archives of General Psychiatry, 55*, 393–401.

Steadman, H. J., & Naples, M. (2005). Assessing the effectiveness of jail diversion programs for persons with serious mental illness and co-occurring substance use disorders. *Behavioral Sciences and the Law, 23*, 163–170.

Steadman, H. J., Osher, F. C., Robbins, P. C., Case, B., & Samuels, S. (2009). Prevalence of serious mental illness among jail inmates. *Psychiatric Services, 60*, 761–765.

Steadman, H. J., Redlich, A., Callahan, L., Robbins, P. C., & Vesselinov, R. (2011). Effect of mental health courts on arrests and jail days: A multisite study. *Archives of General Psychiatry, 68*, 167–172.

Steadman, H. J., Redlich, A. D., Griffin, P., Petrila, J., & Monahan, J. (2005). From referral to disposition: Case processing in seven mental health courts. *Behavioral Sciences and the Law, 23*, 215–226.

Stein, D. M., Deberard, S., & Homan, K. (2013). Predicting success and failure in juvenile drug treatment court: A meta-analytic review. *Journal of Substance Abuse Treatment, 44*, 159–168.

Stein, D. M., Deberard, S., & Homan, K. (2015). The effectiveness of juvenile drug treatment courts: A meta-analytic review of literature. *Journal of Child and Adolescent Substance Abuse, 24*, 80–93.

Sterns, A. A., Lax, G., Sed, C., Keohane, P., &. Sterns, R. S. (2008). The growing wave of older prisoners: A national survey of older prisoner health, mental health and programming. *Corrections Today, 70*, 70–76.

Stohr, M. K., Hemmens, C., Buane, D., Dayley, J., Gornik, M., Kjaer, K., & Noon, C. (2001). *Residential substance abuse treatment for state prisoners (RSAT) partnership process evaluation, final report* (NCJ publication No. 187352). Retrieved July 29, 2017, from https://www.ncjrs.gov/pdffiles1/nij/grants/187352.pdf

Strauss, G., Glenn, M., Reddi, T., Afaq, I., Podolskava, A., Rybakova, T., & El-Mallakh, R. (2005). Psychiatric disposition of patients brought in by crisis intervention team police officers. *Community Mental Health Journal, 41*, 223–230.

Strong, S. M., Rantala, R. R., & Kyckelhahn, T. (2016). *Census of problem-solving courts, 2012*. US Department of Justice, Office of Justice Programs, Bureau of Justice Statistics. Retrieved November 6, 2017, from https://www.bjs.gov/content/pub/pdf/cpsc12.pdf

Sviridoff, M., Rottman, D. B., Ostrom, B., & Curtis, R. (2000). *Dispensing justice locally: The implementation and effects of the Midtown Community Court*. New York: Routledge. Retrieved on November 6, 2017, from www.courtinnovation.org/pdf/disp_just_loc.pdf

Sviridoff, M., Rottman D. B., Weidner R., Cheesman F., Curtis R., Hansen R., & Ostrom B. (2002). *Dispensing justice locally: The impacts, costs and benefits of the Midtown Community Court*. Washington, DC: US Department of Justice, Office of Justice Programs, National Institute of Justice. Retrieved November 6, 2017, from https://www.ncjrs.gov/pdffiles1/nij/grants/196397.pdf

Swanson, J. W., Swartz, M. S., Wagner, H. R., Burns, B. J., Borum, R., & Hiday, V. A. (2000). Involuntary out-patient commitment and reduction of violent behaviour in persons with severe mental illness. *British Journal of Psychiatry, 176*, 324–331.

Tauber, J. (2011). Drug courts: Back to the future. In D. B. Marlowe & W. G. Meyer (Eds.), *The drug court judicial benchbook* (pp. 7–17). Alexandria, VA: National Drug Court Institute.

Taxman, F. S., & Marlowe, D. (2006). Risk, needs, responsivity: In action or inaction? *Crime and Delinquency, 52*, 3–6.

Taylor, C. J. (2013). Tolerance of minor setbacks in a challenging reentry experience: An evaluation of a federal reentry court. *Criminal Justice Policy Review, 24*, 49–70.

Taylor, P. (2014). Building recovery-oriented systems of care for drug court participants. *National Drug Court Institute: Drug court practitioner fact sheet, IX*(1), 1–8. Retrieved September 6, 2017, from https://www.ndci.org/wp-content/uploads/Recovery-Oriented%20Systems%20of%20Care.pdf

Teller, J., Munetz, M., Gil, K., & Ritter, C. (2006). Crisis intervention team training for police officers responding to mental disturbance calls. *Psychiatric Services, 57*, 232–237.

Thanner, M. H., & Taxman, F. S. (2003). Responsivity: The value of providing intensive services to high-risk offenders. *Journal of Substance Abuse Treatment, 24*, 137–147.

Thompson, A. C. (2004). Navigating the hidden obstacles to ex-offender reentry. *Boston College Law Review, 45*, 255–306.

Thompson, M., Osher, F., & Tomasini-Joshi, D. (2007). *Improving responses to people with mental illnesses: The essential elements of a mental health court*. New York: Council of State Governments Justice Center.

Tong, L. S. J., & Farrington, D. P. (2006). How effective is the "Reasoning and Rehabilitation" programme in reducing reoffending? A meta-analysis of evaluations in four countries. *Psychology, Crime and Law, 12*, 3–24.

Torrey, E. F., Kennard, A. D., Eslinger, D., Lamb, R., & Pavle, J. (2010). *More mentally ill persons are in jails and prisons than in hospitals: A survey of the states.* Retrieved June 3, 2017, from http://www.treatmentadvocacycenter.org/storage/documents/final_jails_v_hospitals_study.pdf

Torrey, E. F., Stanley, J., Monahan, J., & Steadman, H. J. (2008). The MacArthur Violence Risk Assessment Study revisited: Two views ten years after its initial publication. *Psychiatric Services, 59*, 147–152.

Travis, J. (2000). *But they all come back: Rethinking prisoner reentry.* Washington, DC: US Department of Justice, Office of Justice Programs, National Institute of Justice.

Travis, J. (2005). *But they all come back: Facing the challenges of prisoner reentry.* Washington, DC: Urban Institute Press.

Trawver, K. R. (2013, January). *Who succeeds in mental health courts? Identifying predictors of program retention and legal recidivism.* Poster session presented at the 2013 Annual Conference of the Society for Social Work and Research Conference, San Diego, CA.

Tribal Law and Policy Institute. (2014a). *Overview of tribal healing to wellness courts* (2nd ed.). Washington, DC: Bureau of Justice Assistance, US Department. of Justice. Retrieved December 9, 2017, from http://www.wellnesscourts.org/files/THWC Overview Final - Sept 2014.pdf

Tribal Law and Policy Institute. (2014b). *Tribal healing to wellness courts: The key components.* Washington, DC: Bureau of Justice Assistance, US Department of Justice. Retrieved December 9, 2017, from http://www.wellnesscourts.org/files/Tribal%20Healing%20to%20Wellness%20Courts%20The%20Key%20Components.pdf

Trupin, E., & Richards, H. (2003). Seattle's mental health courts: Early indicators of effectiveness. *International Journal of Law and Psychiatry, 26*, 33–53.

Turner, S., Greenwood, P. Fain, T., & Deschenes, E. (1999). Perceptions of drug court: How offenders view ease of program completion, strengths and weaknesses, and the impact on their lives. *National Drug Court Institute Review, 2*, 61–85.

Tutty, L., Wyllie, K., Abbott, P., Mackenzie, J., Ursel., E. J., & Koshan, J. M. (2008). *The justice response to domestic violence: A literature review.* Retrieved November 6, 2017, from https://www.ucalgary.ca/resolve/reports/ 2008/2008-01.pdf

Tyler, T. (1998). *The social psychology of procedural justice.* New York: Plenum.

Tyler, T. R. (2006). *Why people obey the law.* Princeton, NJ: Princeton University Press

US Const. amend. IV. Retrieved May 16, 2019, from https://usconstitution.net/const.html

US Const. amend. VIX. Retrieved May 16, 2019, from https://usconstitution.net/const.html

US Department of Health and Human Services. (1999). *Mental health: A report of the surgeon general.* Rockville, MD: US Department of Health and Human Services, Substance Abuse and Mental Health Services Administration, Center for Mental Health Services, National Institutes of Health, National Institute of Mental Health.

US Department of Justice. (2010). Office of Justice Programs' management of its Offender Reentry Initiatives. Retrieved November 7, 2017, from http://www.justice.gov/oig/reports/OJP/a1034.pdf

US Department of Justice, The United States Attorney's Office, Central District of California. (2017, January 12). *Conviction and sentence alternatives program (CASA).* Retrieved November 5, 2017, from https://www.justice.gov/usao-cdca/conviction-and-sentence-alternatives-program-casa

Vance, S. E. (2011). Federal reentry court programs: A summary of recent evaluations. *Federal Probation, 75*, 64–73.

Van Dorn, R. A., Andel, R., Boaz, T. L., Desmarais, S. L., Chandler, K., Becker, M. A., & Howe, A. (2011). Risk of arrest in persons with schizophrenia and bipolar disorder in a Florida Medicaid program: The role of atypical antipsychotics, conventional neuroleptics, and routine outpatient behavioral health services. *Journal of Clinical Psychiatry, 72*, 502–508.

Van Dorn, R. A., Desmarais, S. L., Petrila, J., Haynes, D., & Singh, J. P. (2013). Effects of outpatient treatment on risk of arrest of adults with serious mental illness and associated costs. *Psychiatric Services, 64*, 856–862.

Van Vleet, R. K., Hickert, A. O., Becker, E. E., & Kunz, C. (2008). *Evaluation of the Salt Lake County mental health court* (final report). Salt Lake City: Utah Criminal Justice Center, University of Utah.

Vaughan, T. J., Holleran, L. B., & Brooks, R. (2019). Exploring therapeutic and militaristic contexts in a veteran treatment court. *Criminal Justice Policy Review, 30*, 79–101.

Veeh, C. A., Severson, M. E., & Lee, J. (2017). Evaluation of a Serious and Violent Offender Reentry Initiative (SVORI) program in a midwest state. *Criminal Justice Policy Review, 28*, 238–254.

Vermont Recovery Network. (2013). *Helping people take responsibility for recovery.* Retrieved September 6, 2017, from https://vtrecoverynetwork.org/PDF/Take_Responsibility_for_Recovery.pdf

Viglione, J., Rudes, D., & Taxman, F. S. (2015). Misalignment in supervision: Implementing risk/needs assessment instruments in probation. *Criminal Justice and Behavior, 42*, 263–285.

Wagner, P., & Rabuy, B. (2017). *Mass incarceration: The whole pie 2017.* North Hampton, MA: Prison Policy Initiative.

Wakeling, H. C. (2007). The psychometric validation of the Social Problem Solving Inventory-Revised with UK incarcerated sexual offenders. *Sexual Abuse, 19*, 217–236.

Wales, H., Hiday, V., & Ray, B. (2010). Procedural justice and the mental health court judge's role in reducing recidivism. *International Journal of Law and Psychiatry, 33*, 265–271.

Wallace, S., & Carroll, D. (2004). The implementation and impact of indigent defense standards. *Southern University Law Review, 30*, 245–328.

Walters, G. D. (2015). Recidivism and the "worst of both worlds" hypothesis: Do substance misuse and crime interact or accumulate? *Criminal Justice and Behavior, 42*, 435–451.

Warren-Kigenyi, N., & Coleman, H. (2014). DWI recidivism in the United States: An examination of state-level driver data and the effect of look-back periods on recidivism prevalence (DOT HS 811 991). Washington, DC: National Highway Traffic Safety Administration, US Department of Transportation. Retrieved November 6, 2017, from http://www.nhtsa.gov/staticfiles/nti/pdf/811991-DWI_Recidivism_in_USA-tsf-rn.pdf

Watson, A., Hanrahan, P., Luchins, D., & Lurigio, A. (2001). Mental health courts and the complex issue of mentally ill offenders. *Psychiatric Services, 52*, 477–481.

Watson, A., Ottati, V., Morabito, M., Draine, J., Kerr, A., & Angell, B. (2010). Outcomes of police contacts with persons with mental illness: The impact of CIT. *Administration and Policy in Mental Health and Mental Health Services Research, 37*, 302–317.

Webster, C. D., Martin, M. L., Brink, J., Nicholls, T. L., & Middleton, C. (2004). *Manual for the Short-Term Assessment of Risk and Treatability (START)* (Version 1.0, Consultation ed.). Hamilton, ON, Canada: St. Joseph's Healthcare.

Weidner, R., & Davis, C. (2000). *Benefits and costs of the Hennepin County Community Court—A preliminary analysis.* Minneapolis, MN: Institute on Criminal Justice, University of Minnesota Law School.

Werkmeister, W. (2015, June). *Drug courts: Are they all they are cracked up to be?* Retrieved April 15, 2018 from http://ksr.hkspublications.org/2015/06/26/drug-courts-are-they-all-they-are-cracked-up-to-be/

Wexler, D. B. (2001). Robes and rehabilitation: How judges can help offenders "make good." *Court Review, 38*, 18–23.

Wexler, D. B. (2006). Therapeutic jurisprudence and changing concepts of legal scholarship. *Behavioral Sciences and the Law, 11*, 17–29.

Wexler, D. B., & Winick, B. J. (1991). *Essays in therapeutic jurisprudence.* Durham, NC: Carolina Academic Press.

Wexler, D. B., & Winick, B. J. (1996). *Law in a therapeutic key: Developments in therapeutic jurisprudence.* Durham, NC: Carolina Academic Press.

Wiener, R. L., Winick, B. J., Georges, L. S., & Castro, A. (2010). A testable theory of problem solving courts: Avoiding past empirical and legal failures. *International Journal of Law and Psychiatry, 33*, 417–427.

Wilper, A. P., Woolhandler, S., Boyd, J. W., Lasser, K. E., McCormick, D., Bor, D. H., & Himmelstein, D. U. (2009). The health and health care of US prisoners: Results of a nationwide survey. *American Journal of Public Health 99*, 668–672.

Wilson, A. B., Draine, J., Hadley, T., Metraux, S., & Evans, A. (2011). Examining the impact of mental illness and substance use on recidivism in a county jail. *International Journal of Law and Psychiatry, 34*, 264–268.

Wilson, D. B., Bouffard, L. A., & MacKenzie, D. L. (2005). A quantitative review of structured, group-oriented, cognitive-behavioral programs for offenders. *Criminal Justice and Behavior, 32*, 172–204.

Wilson, D. B., Mitchell, O., & Mackenzie, D. (2006). A systematic review of drug court effects on recidivism. *Journal of Experimental Criminology, 2*, 459–487.

Wilson, J. (2011). What did we learn from the evaluation of Project Greenlight? *Federal Sentencing Reporter, 24*, 76–79.

Wilson, J., & Davis, R. (2006). Good intentions meet hard realities: An evaluation of the Project Greenlight reentry program. *Criminology and Public Policy, 5*, 303–308.

Wilson, J., & Zozula, C. (2012). Risk, recidivism, and (re)habilitation: Another look at Project Greenlight. *The Prison Journal, 92*, 203–230.

Wilson, J. L., Bandyopadhyay, S., Yang, H., Cerulli, C., & Morse, D. S. (2018). Identifying predictors of substance use and recidivism outcome trajectories among drug treatment court clients. *Criminal Justice and Behavior, 45*, 447–467.

Winick, B. J. (2000). Applying the law therapeutically in domestic violence cases. *University of Missouri—Kansas City Law Review, 69*, 33–91.

Winick, B. J. (2003). Therapeutic jurisprudence and problem solving courts. *Fordham Urban Law Journal, 30*, 1055–1103.

Winick, B. J. (2005). *Civil commitment: A therapeutic jurisprudence model.* Durham, NC: Carolina Academic Press.

Winick, B. J., & Wexler, D. B. (Eds.). (2003). *Judging in a therapeutic key: Therapeutic jurisprudence and the courts*. Durham, NC: Carolina Academic Press.

Wolf, R. V. (2007). *Principles of problem-solving justice*. Retrieved April 10, 2017, from http://www.courtinnovation.org/sites/default/files/Principles.pdf

Wolf, R. V. (2011). *Reentry courts: Looking ahead: A conversation about strategies for offender reintegration*. New York: Center for Court Innovation.

Wolff, N. (2000). Using randomized controlled trials to evaluate socially complex services: Problems, challenges and recommendations. *Journal of Mental Health Policy and Economics, 3*, 97–109.

Wolff, N., Fabrikant, N., & Belenko, S. (2011). Mental health courts and their selection processes: Modeling variation for consistency. *Law and Human Behavior, 35*, 402–412.

Wolff, N., & Pogorzelski, W. (2005). Measuring the effectiveness of mental health courts: Challenges and recommendations. *Psychology, Public Policy, and Law, 11*, 539–569.

Worcel, S. D., Furrer, C. J., Green, B. L., Burrus, S. W., & Finigan, M. W. (2008). Effects of family treatment drug courts on substance abuse and child welfare outcomes. *Child Abuse Review, 17*, 427–443.

Wright, D. (1997). Getting out of the asylum: Understanding the confinement of the insane in the nineteenth century. *Social History of Medicine, 10*, 137–155.

Yelderman, L. A. (2016). An assessment of juvenile drug courts' knowledge of evidence-based practices, data collection, and the use of AA/NA. *Juvenile and Family Court Journal, 67*, 33–48.

Young, D., & Belenko, S. (2002). Program retention and perceived coercion in three models of mandatory drug treatment. *Journal of Drug Issues, 32*, 297–328.

Zamble, E., & Quinsey, V. L. (1997). *The criminal recidivism process*. Cambridge, UK: Cambridge University Press.

Zlotnick, C., Johnson, J., & Najavits, L. M. (2009). Randomized controlled pilot study of cognitive-behavioral therapy in a sample of incarcerated women with substance use disorder and PTSD. *Behavior Therapy, 40*, 325–336.

Zlotnick, C., Najavits, L, M., Rohsenow, D. J., & Johnson, D. M. (2003). A cognitive-behavioral treatment for incarcerated women with substance abuse disorder and posttraumatic stress disorder: Findings from a pilot study. *Journal of Substance Abuse Treatment, 25*, 99–105.

Index

Page numbers followed by *t*, *f*, or *n* denote tables, figures, and footnotes respectively.

For the benefit of digital users, indexed terms that span two pages (e.g., 52–53) may, on occasion, appear on only one of those pages.

www.ingramcontent.com/pod-product-compliance
Lightning Source LLC
Chambersburg PA
CBHW050014250725
30135CB00003B/46